THIRD EDITION

iOS Swift Game Development
Cookbook

Jonathon Manning and Paris Buttfield-Addison

Beijing · Boston · Farnham · Sebastopol · Tokyo

iOS Swift Game Development Cookbook

by Jonathon Manning and Paris Buttfield-Addison

Published by O'Reilly Media, Inc., 1005 Gravenstein Highway North, Sebastopol, CA 95472.

O'Reilly books may be purchased for educational, business, or sales promotional use. Online editions are also available for most titles (*http://oreilly.com/safari*). For more information, contact our corporate/institutional sales department: 800-998-9938 or *corporate@oreilly.com*.

Acquisitions Editor: Rachel Roumeliotis	**Indexer:** WordCo Indexing Services, Inc.
Development Editor: Jeff Bleiel	**Interior Designer:** David Futato
Production Editor: Justin Billing	**Cover Designer:** Karen Montgomery
Copyeditor: Kim Cofer	**Illustrator:** Rebecca Demarest
Proofreader: Christina Edwards	

April 2014:	First Edition
May 2015:	Second Edition
September 2018:	Third Edition

Revision History for the Third Edition

2018-09-27:   First Release

See *http://oreilly.com/catalog/errata.csp?isbn=9781491999080* for release details.

978-1-491-99908-0

[LSI]

Table of Contents

Preface... ix

1. Laying Out a Game.. 1
    1.1 Laying Out Your Engine   1
    1.2 Creating an Inheritance-Based Game Layout   2
    1.3 Creating a Component-Based Game Layout   4
    1.4 Creating a Component-Based Game Layout Using GameplayKit   7
    1.5 Calculating Delta Times   9
    1.6 Detecting When the User Enters and Exits Your Game   11
    1.7 Updating Based on a Timer   13
    1.8 Updating Based on When the Screen Updates   14
    1.9 Pausing a Game   15
    1.10 Calculating Time Elapsed Since the Game Start   16
    1.11 Working with Closures   17
    1.12 Writing a Method That Calls a Closure   19
    1.13 Working with Operation Queues   20
    1.14 Performing a Task in the Future   22
    1.15 Making Operations Depend on Each Other   23
    1.16 Filtering an Array with Closures   24
    1.17 Loading New Assets During Gameplay   24
    1.18 Adding Unit Tests to Your Game   26
    1.19 2D Grids   28
    1.20 Using Randomization   30
    1.21 Building a State Machine   31

2. Views and Menus.. 35
    2.1 Working with Storyboards   36
    2.2 Creating View Controllers   42

2.3 Using Segues to Move Between Screens   49
2.4 Using Constraints to Lay Out Views   53
2.5 Adding Images to Your Project   56
2.6 Slicing Images for Use in Buttons   58
2.7 Using UI Dynamics to Make Animated Views   59
2.8 Moving an Image with Core Animation   61
2.9 Rotating an Image View   63
2.10 Animating a Popping Effect on a View   64
2.11 Theming UI Elements with UIAppearance   66
2.12 Rotating a UIView in 3D   68
2.13 Overlaying Menus on Top of Game Content   70
2.14 Designing Effective Game Menus   71

3. Input. 73
3.1 Detecting When a View Is Touched   74
3.2 Responding to Tap Gestures   75
3.3 Dragging an Image Around the Screen   76
3.4 Detecting Rotation Gestures   78
3.5 Detecting Pinching Gestures   81
3.6 Creating Custom Gestures   82
3.7 Receiving Touches in Custom Areas of a View   86
3.8 Detecting Shakes   87
3.9 Detecting Device Tilt   88
3.10 Getting the Compass Heading   92
3.11 Accessing the User's Location   93
3.12 Calculating the User's Speed   97
3.13 Pinpointing the User's Proximity to Landmarks   98
3.14 Receiving Notifications When the User Changes Location   99
3.15 Looking Up GPS Coordinates for a Street Address   103
3.16 Looking Up Street Addresses from the User's Location   104
3.17 Using the Device as a Steering Wheel   105
3.18 Detecting Magnets   107
3.19 Utilizing Inputs to Improve Game Design   109

4. Sound. 111
4.1 Playing Sound with AVAudioPlayer   111
4.2 Recording Sound with AVAudioRecorder   114
4.3 Working with Multiple Audio Players   115
4.4 Cross-Fading Between Tracks   117
4.5 Synthesizing Speech   119
4.6 Getting Information About What the Music App Is Playing   121
4.7 Detecting When the Currently Playing Track Changes   123

4.8 Controlling Music Playback   124
4.9 Allowing the User to Select Music   125
4.10 Cooperating with Other Applications' Audio   127
4.11 Determining How to Best Use Sound in Your Game Design   129

5. Data Storage.. 131
5.1 Storing Structured Information   131
5.2 Storing Data Locally   133
5.3 Using iCloud to Save Games   134
5.4 Using the iCloud Key-Value Store   139
5.5 Deciding When to Use Files or a Database   142
5.6 Managing a Collection of Assets   143
5.7 Storing Information in UserDefaults   145
5.8 Implementing the Best Data Storage Strategy   147
5.9 In-Game Currency   147
5.10 Setting Up CloudKit   149
5.11 Adding Records to a CloudKit Database   150
5.12 Querying Records to a CloudKit Database   151
5.13 Deleting Records from a CloudKit Database   155

6. 2D Graphics and SpriteKit...................................... 157
6.1 Getting Familiar with 2D Math   158
6.2 Creating a SpriteKit View   164
6.3 Creating a Scene   165
6.4 Adding a Sprite   168
6.5 Adding a Text Sprite   169
6.6 Determining Available Fonts   170
6.7 Including Custom Fonts   171
6.8 Transitioning Between Scenes   172
6.9 Moving Sprites and Labels Around   174
6.10 Adding a Texture Sprite   176
6.11 Creating Texture Atlases   177
6.12 Using Shape Nodes   178
6.13 Using Blending Modes   179
6.14 Using Image Effects to Change the Way That Sprites Are Drawn 180
6.15 Using Bézier Paths   181
6.16 Creating Smoke, Fire, and Other Particle Effects   183
6.17 Shaking the Screen   184
6.18 Animating a Sprite   185
6.19 Parallax Scrolling   187
6.20 Creating Images Using Noise   194

7. Physics... **197**

7.1 Reviewing Physics Terms and Definitions   197
7.2 Adding Physics to Sprites   199
7.3 Creating Static and Dynamic Objects   200
7.4 Defining Collider Shapes   201
7.5 Setting Velocities   203
7.6 Working with Mass, Size, and Density   204
7.7 Creating Walls in Your Scene   205
7.8 Controlling Gravity   207
7.9 Keeping Objects from Falling Over   208
7.10 Controlling Time in Your Physics Simulation   208
7.11 Detecting Collisions   209
7.12 Finding Objects   210
7.13 Working with Joints   212
7.14 Working with Forces   213
7.15 Adding Thrusters to Objects   214
7.16 Creating Explosions   215
7.17 Using Device Orientation to Control Gravity   217
7.18 Dragging Objects Around   218
7.19 Creating a Car   221

8. SceneKit... **225**

8.1 Setting Up for SceneKit   225
8.2 Creating a SceneKit Scene   226
8.3 Showing a 3D Object   226
8.4 Working with SceneKit Cameras   227
8.5 Creating Lights   228
8.6 Animating Objects   229
8.7 Working with Text Nodes   230
8.8 Customizing Materials   231
8.9 Texturing Objects   232
8.10 Normal Mapping   232
8.11 Constraining Objects   233
8.12 Loading COLLADA Files   234
8.13 Using 3D Physics   235
8.14 Adding Reflections   236
8.15 Hit-Testing the Scene   236
8.16 Loading a Scene File   237
8.17 Particle Systems   238
8.18 Using Metal   239

9. Artificial Intelligence and Behavior. 241
9.1 Making Vector Math Nicer in Swift   241
9.2 Making an Object Move Toward a Position   243
9.3 Making Things Follow a Path   245
9.4 Making an Object Intercept a Moving Target   246
9.5 Making an Object Flee When It's in Trouble   247
9.6 Making an Object Decide on a Target   248
9.7 Making an Object Steer Toward a Point   249
9.8 Making an Object Know Where to Take Cover   250
9.9 Calculating a Path for an Object to Take   251
9.10 Pathfinding on a Grid   256
9.11 Finding the Next Best Move for a Puzzle Game   257
9.12 Determining If an Object Can See Another Object   258
9.13 Tagging Parts of Speech with NSLinguisticTagger   260
9.14 Using AVFoundation to Access the Camera   262
9.15 Importing a Core ML Model   265
9.16 Identifying Objects in Images   265
9.17 Using AI to Enhance Your Game Design   270

10. Working with the Outside World. 271
10.1 Detecting Controllers   273
10.2 Getting Input from a Game Controller   275
10.3 Showing Content via AirPlay   277
10.4 Using External Screens   278
10.5 Designing Effective Graphics for Different Screens   281
10.6 Dragging and Dropping   283
10.7 Providing Haptic Feedback with UIFeedbackGenerator   290
10.8 Recording the Screen with ReplayKit   292
10.9 Displaying Augmented Reality with ARKit   295
10.10 Hit-Testing the AR Scene   300
10.11 Using TestFlight to Test Your App   303
10.12 Using Fastlane to Build and Release Your App   303

11. Performance and Debugging. 305
11.1 Improving Your Frame Rate   305
11.2 Making Levels Load Quickly   308
11.3 Dealing with Low-Memory Issues   309
11.4 Tracking Down a Crash   311
11.5 Working with Compressed Textures   312
11.6 Working with Watchpoints   316
11.7 Logging Effectively   317
11.8 Creating Breakpoints That Use Speech   318

Index. 321

Preface

Games rule mobile devices. The iPhone, iPad, and iPod touch are all phenomenally powerful gaming platforms, and making amazing games that your players can access at a moment's notice has never been easier. The iTunes App Store category with the most apps is Games; it includes games ranging from simple one-minute puzzle games to in-depth, long-form adventures. The time to jump in and make your own games has never been better. We say this having been in iOS game development since the App Store opened. Our first iOS game, in 2008, a little strategy puzzler named *Culture*, led us to working on hundreds of other awesome projects, ranging from a digital board game for museums to educational children's games, and everything in between! The possibilities for games on this platform are only becoming wider and wider.

This book provides you with simple, direct solutions to common problems found in iOS game programming using Swift. Whether you're stuck figuring out how to give objects physical motion, or just want a refresher on common gaming-related math problems, you'll find simple, straightforward answers, explanations, and sample projects. This book is part tutorial and part reference. It's something you'll want to keep handy to get new ideas about what's possible through a series of recipes, as well as for a quick guide to find answers on a number of topics.

Audience

We assume that you're a reasonably capable programmer, and that you know at least a little bit about developing for iOS: what Xcode is and how to get around in it, how to use the iOS Simulator, and the basics of the Swift programming language. We also assume you know how to use an iOS device. We don't assume any existing knowledge of game development on any platform, but we're guessing that you're reading this book with a vague idea about the kind of game you'd like to make.

This book isn't based on any particular genre of games—you'll find the recipes in it applicable to all kinds of games, though some will suit some genres more than others.

Organization of This Book

Each chapter of this book contains *recipes*: short solutions to common problems found in game development. The book is designed to be read in any order; you don't need to read it cover-to-cover, and you don't need to read any chapter from start to finish. (Of course, we encourage doing that, because you'll probably pick up on stuff you didn't realize you wanted to know.)

Each recipe is structured like this: the *problem* being addressed is presented, followed by the *solution*, which explains the technique of solving the problem (or implementing the feature, and so on). Following the solution, the recipe contains a *discussion* that goes into more detail on the solution, which gives you more information about what the solution does, other things to watch out for, and other useful knowledge.

Here is a concise breakdown of the material each chapter covers:

Chapter 1, Laying Out a Game

> This chapter discusses different ways to design the architecture and code layout of your game, how to work with timers in a variety of ways, and how blocks work in iOS. You'll also learn how to schedule work to be performed in the future using blocks and operation queues, and how to add unit tests to your project.

Chapter 2, Views and Menus

> This chapter focuses on interface design and working with UIKit, the built-in system for displaying user interface graphics. In addition to providing common objects like buttons and text fields, UIKit can be customized to suit your needs— for some kinds of games, UIKit might be the only graphical tool you'll need.

Chapter 3, Input

> In this chapter, you'll learn how to get input from the user so that you can apply it to your game. This includes touching the screen, detecting different types of gestures (such as tapping, swiping, and pinching), as well as other kinds of input like the user's current position on the planet, or motion information from the variety of built-in sensors in the device.

Chapter 4, Sound

> This chapter discusses how to work with sound effects and music. You'll learn how to load and play audio files, how to work with the user's built-in music library, and how to make your game's sound work well when the user wants to listen to his or her music while playing your game.

Chapter 5, Data Storage

> This chapter is all about storing information for later use. The information that games need to save ranges from the very small (such as high scores), to medium (saved games), all the way up to very large (collections of game assets). In this chapter, you'll learn about the many different ways that information can be

stored and accessed, and which of these is best suited for what you want to do, as well as how to make use of iCloud features.

Chapter 6, 2D Graphics and SpriteKit

This chapter discusses SpriteKit, the 2D graphics system built into iOS. SpriteKit is both powerful and very easy to use; in this chapter, you'll learn how to create a scene, how to animate sprites, and how to work with textures and images. This chapter also provides you with info you can use to brush up on your 2D math skills.

Chapter 7, Physics

In this chapter, you'll learn how to use the 2D physics simulation that's provided as part of SpriteKit. Physics simulation is a great way to make your game's movements feel more realistic, and you can use it to get a lot of great-feeling game for very little programmer effort. You'll learn how to work with physics bodies, joints, and forces, as well as how to take user input and make it control your game's physical simulation.

Chapter 8, SceneKit

This chapter covers Scene Kit, Apple's new 3D framework. It has recipes for showing 3D objects with Scene Kit; working with cameras, lights, and textures; and using physics in 3D.

Chapter 9, Artificial Intelligence and Behavior

This chapter discusses how to make objects in your game behave on their own, and react to the player. You'll learn how to make one object chase another, how to make objects flee from something, and how to work out a path from one point to another while avoiding obstacles. You'll also learn how to use Core ML and Vision to detect objects seen by the camera.

Chapter 10, Working with the Outside World

This chapter discusses the ways that your game can interact with the outside world: external displays, like televisions and monitors; game controllers that provide additional input methods, like thumbsticks and physical buttons; and cameras. You'll learn how to detect, use, and design your game to take advantage of additional hardware where it's present. You'll also learn how to make use of ARKit for augmented reality.

Chapter 11, Performance and Debugging

The last chapter of the book looks at improving your game's performance and stability. You'll learn how to take advantage of advanced Xcode debugging features, how to use compressed textures to save memory, and how to make your game load faster.

Additional Resources

You can download the code samples from this book (or fork using GitHub) at *http://www.secretlab.com.au/books/ios-game-dev-cookbook-swift*.

O'Reilly has a number of other excellent books on game development and software development (both generally and related to iOS) that can help you on your iOS game development journey, including:

- *Physics for Game Developers*
- *Learning Cocoa with Objective-C* (by us!)
- *Swift Development with Cocoa* (also by us!)
- *Programming iOS 8*

We strongly recommend that you add Gamasutra (*http://gamasutra.com*) to your regular reading list, due to its high-quality coverage of game industry news.

Game designer Marc LeBlanc's website (*http://8kindsoffun.com*) is where he collects various presentations, notes, and essays. We've found him to be a tremendous inspiration.

Finally, we'd be remiss if we didn't link to our own blog (*http://secretlab.com.au*).

Conventions Used in This Book

The following typographical conventions are used in this book:

Italic
: Indicates new terms, URLs, email addresses, filenames, and file extensions.

`Constant width`
: Used for program listings, as well as within paragraphs to refer to program elements such as variable or function names, databases, data types, environment variables, statements, and keywords.

`Constant width bold`
: Shows commands or other text that should be typed literally by the user.

`Constant width italic`
: Shows text that should be replaced with user-supplied values or by values determined by context.

This element signifies a tip or suggestion.

 This element signifies a general note.

 This element indicates a warning or caution.

Using Code Examples

Supplemental material (code examples, exercises, etc.) is available for download at *http://www.secretlab.com.au/books/ios-game-dev-cookbook-swift*.

This book is here to help you get your job done. In general, if example code is offered with this book, you may use it in your programs and documentation. You do not need to contact us for permission unless you're reproducing a significant portion of the code. For example, writing a program that uses several chunks of code from this book does not require permission. Selling or distributing a CD-ROM of examples from O'Reilly books does require permission. Answering a question by citing this book and quoting example code does not require permission. Incorporating a significant amount of example code from this book into your product's documentation does require permission.

We appreciate, but do not require, attribution. An attribution usually includes the title, author, publisher, and ISBN. For example: "*iOS Swift Game Development Cookbook*, Third Edition, by Jonathan Manning and Paris Buttfield-Addison (O'Reilly). Copyright 2018 Secret Lab, 978-1-491-99908-0."

If you feel your use of code examples falls outside fair use or the permission given above, feel free to contact us at *permissions@oreilly.com*.

O'Reilly Safari

 *Safari* (formerly Safari Books Online) is a membership-based training and reference platform for enterprise, government, educators, and individuals.

Members have access to thousands of books, training videos, Learning Paths, interactive tutorials, and curated playlists from over 250 publishers, including O'Reilly Media, Harvard Business Review, Prentice Hall Professional, Addison-Wesley Professional, Microsoft Press, Sams, Que, Peachpit Press, Adobe, Focal Press, Cisco Press, John Wiley & Sons, Syngress, Morgan Kaufmann, IBM Redbooks, Packt, Adobe Press, FT Press, Apress, Manning, New Riders, McGraw-Hill, Jones & Bartlett, and Course Technology, among others.

For more information, please visit *http://oreilly.com/safari*.

How to Contact Us

Please address comments and questions concerning this book to the publisher:

O'Reilly Media, Inc.
1005 Gravenstein Highway North
Sebastopol, CA 95472
800-998-9938 (in the United States or Canada)
707-829-0515 (international or local)
707-829-0104 (fax)

We have a web page for this book, where we list errata, examples, and any additional information. You can access this page at *http://bit.ly/ios-swift-game-dev-errata*.

To comment or ask technical questions about this book, send email to *bookquestions@oreilly.com*.

For more information about our books, courses, conferences, and news, see our website at *http://www.oreilly.com*.

Find us on Facebook: *http://facebook.com/oreilly*

Follow us on Twitter: *http://twitter.com/oreillymedia*

Watch us on YouTube: *http://www.youtube.com/oreillymedia*

Acknowledgments

Jon thanks his mother, father, and the rest of his crazily extended family for their tremendous support.

Paris thanks his mother, without whom he wouldn't be doing anything nearly as interesting, let alone writing books.

We'd all like to thank Rachel Roumeliotis, whose skill and advice were invaluable to completing the book. Likewise, all the O'Reilly Media staff we've interacted with over the course of writing the book have been the absolute gurus of their fields.

A huge thank you to Tony Gray and the Apple University Consortium (AUC) (*http://www.auc.edu.au*) for the monumental boost they gave us and others listed on this page. We wouldn't be writing this book if it weren't for them. And now you're writing books, too, Tony—sorry about that!

Thanks also to Neal Goldstein, who deserves full credit and/or blame for getting us into the whole book-writing racket.

We're thankful for the support of the goons at MacLab (who know who they are and continue to stand watch for Admiral Dolphin's inevitable apotheosis), as well as Professor Christopher Lueg, Dr. Leonie Ellis, and the rest of the staff at the University of Tasmania for putting up with us. "Apologies" to Mark Pesce. He knows why.

Additional thanks to Mars G., Tim N., Dave J., Rex S., Nic W., Andrew B., Jess L., Alec H., Scott B., Bethany H., Adam S., and Rebekah S., for a wide variety of reasons. And very special thanks to the team of hard-working engineers, writers, artists, and other workers at Apple, without whom this book (and many others like it) would not have reason to exist.

Finally, thank *you* very much for buying our book—we appreciate it! And if you have any feedback, please let us know. You can email us at *lab@secretlab.com.au* and find us on Twitter at @thesecretlab (*http://twitter.com/thesecretlab*).

CHAPTER 1

Laying Out a Game

Games are software, and the best software has had some thought put into it regarding how it's going to work. When you're writing a game, you need to keep in mind how you're going to handle the individual tasks that the game needs to perform, such as rendering graphics, updating artificial intelligence (AI), handling input, and the hundreds of other small tasks that your game will need to deal with.

In this chapter, you'll learn about ways you can lay out the structure of your game that will make development easier. You'll also learn how to organize the contents of your game so that adding more content and gameplay elements is easier, and find out how to make your game do multiple things at once.

1.1 Laying Out Your Engine

Problem

You want to determine the best way to lay out the architecture of your game.

Solution

The biggest thing to consider when you're thinking about how to best lay out your game is how the game state will be updated. There are three main things that can cause the state of the game to change:

Input from the user
> The game may change state when the user provides some input, such as tapping a button or typing some text. Turn-based games are often driven by user input (e.g., in a game of chess, the game state might only be updated when the user finishes moving a piece).

Timers

The game state may change every time a timer goes off. The delay between timer updates might be very long (some web-based strategy games have turns that update only once a day), or very short (such as going off every time the screen finishes drawing). Most real-time games, like shooters or real-time strategy games, use very short-duration timers.

Input from outside

The game state may change when information from outside the game arrives. The most common example of this is some information arriving from the network, but it can also include data arriving from built-in sensors, such as the accelerometer.

Sometimes, this kind of updating is actually a specific type of timer-based update, because some networks or sensors need to be periodically checked to see if new information has arrived.

Discussion

None of these methods are mutually exclusive. You can, for example, run your game on a timer to animate content, and await user input to move from one state to the next.

Updating every frame is the least efficient option, but it lets you change state often, which makes the game look smooth.

1.2 Creating an Inheritance-Based Game Layout

Problem

You want to use an inheritance-based (i.e., a hierarchy-based) architecture for your game, which is simpler to implement.

Solution

First, define a class called GameObject:

```
class GameObject {
    func update(deltaTime : Float) {

        // 'deltaTime' is the number of seconds since
        // this was last called.

        // This method is overriden by subclasses to update
        // the object's state - position, direction, and so on.
    }
}
```

When you want to create a new *kind* of game object, you create a subclass of the Game Object class, which inherits all of the behavior of its parent class and can be customized:

```
class Monster: GameObject {

    var hitPoints : Int = 10 // how much health we have
    var target : GameObject? // the game object we're attacking

    override func update(deltaTime: Float) {

        super.update(deltaTime: deltaTime)

        // Do some monster-specific updating

    }

}
```

Discussion

In an inheritance-based layout, as shown in Figure 1-1, you define a single base class for your game object (often called GameObject), which knows about general tasks like being updated, and then create subclasses for each specific type of game object. This hierarchy of subclasses can be multiple levels deep (e.g., you might subclass the Game Object class to make the Monster subclass, and then subclass *that* to create the Goblin and Dragon classes, each of which has its own different kinds of monster-like behavior).

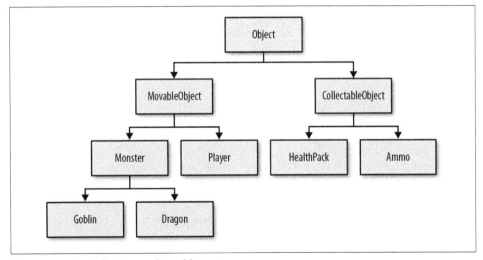

Figure 1-1. An inheritance-based layout

The advantage of a hierarchy-based layout is that each object is able to stand alone: if you have a Dragon object, you know that all of its behavior is contained inside that single object, and it doesn't rely on other objects to work. The downside is that you can often end up with a very deep hierarchy of different game object types, which can be tricky to keep in your head as you program.

1.3 Creating a Component-Based Game Layout

Problem

You want to use a component-based architecture for your game, which allows for greater flexibility.

Solution

 This recipe walks you through how you'd construct your own entity-component system, which is something worth knowing. However, Apple's GameplayKit framework provides a set of classes for you that do the same work. To get the most out of this particular recipe, read it for your own education, and then use the next recipe's solution in your own projects.

First, define a Component class. This class represents components that are attached to game objects—it is a very simple class that, at least initially, only has a single method and a single property:

```
class Component {

    // The game object this component is attached to
    var gameObject : GameObject?

    func update(deltaTime : Float) {
        // Update this component
    }

}
```

Next, define a GameObject class. This class represents game objects:

```
class GameObject {

    // The collection of Component objects attached to us
    var components : [Component] = []

    // Add a component to this gameobject
    func add(component : Component) {
        components.append(component)
```

```swift
        component.gameObject = self
}

// Remove a component from this game object, if we have it
func remove(component : Component) {

    // Figure out the index at which this component exists

    // Note the use of the === (three equals) operator,
    // which checks to see if two variables refer to the same object
    // (as opposed to "==", which checks to see if two variables
    // have the same value, which means different things for
    // different types of data)

    if let index = components.index(where: { $0 === component}) {
        component.gameObject = nil
        components.remove(at: index)
    }
}

// Update this object by updating all components
func update(deltaTime : Float) {

    for component in self.components {
        component.update(deltaTime: deltaTime)
    }

}

// Returns the first component of type T attached to this
// game object
func findComponent<T: Component>() -> T?{

    for component in self.components {
        if let theComponent = component as? T {
            return theComponent
        }
    }

    return nil;
}

// Returns an array of all components of type T
// (this returned array might be empty)
func findComponents<T: Component>() -> [T] {

    var foundComponents : [T] = []

    for component in self.components {
        if let theComponent = component as? T {
            foundComponents.append(theComponent)
        }
```

```
        }

        return foundComponents
    }

}
```

Using these objects looks like this:

```
// Define a type of component
class DamageTaking : Component {
    var hitpoints : Int = 10

    func takeDamage(amount : Int) {
        hitpoints -= amount
    }
}

// Make an object - no need to subclass GameObject,
// because its behavior is determined by which
// components it has
let monster = GameObject()

// Add a new Damageable component
monster.add(component: DamageTaking())

// Get a reference to the first Damageable component
let damage : DamageTaking? = monster.findComponent()
damage?.takeDamage(amount: 5)

// When the game needs to update, send all game
// objects the "update" message.
// This makes all components run their update logic.
monster.update(deltaTime: 0.33)
```

Discussion

In a component-based architecture, as shown in Figure 1-2, each game object is made up of multiple components. Compare this to an inheritance-based architecture, where each game object is a subclass of some more general class (see Recipe 1.2).

A component-based layout means you can be more flexible with your design and not worry about inheritance issues. For example, if you've got a bunch of monsters, and you want one specific monster to have some new behavior (such as, say, exploding every five seconds), you just write a new component and add it to that monster. If you later decide that you want other monsters to also have that behavior, you can add that behavior to them, too.

In a component-based architecture, each game object has a list of components. When something happens to an object—for example, the game updates, or the object is added to or removed from the game—the object goes through all of its components and notifies them. This gives them the opportunity to respond in their own way.

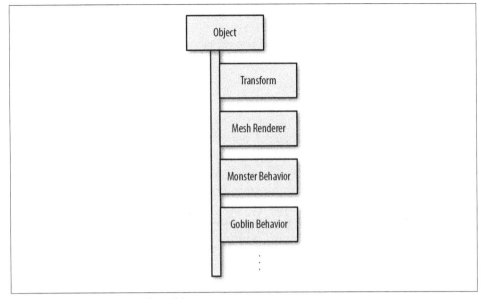

Figure 1-2. A component-based layout

The main problem with component-based architectures is that it's more laborious to create multiple copies of an object, because you have to create and add the same set of components every time you want a new copy.

 The findComponent and findComponents methods are worth a little explanation. These functions are designed to let you get a reference to a component, or an array of components, attached to the game object. The functions use *generics* to make them return an array of the type of component you expect. This means that you don't need to do any type casting in your code—you're guaranteed to receive objects that are the right type.

1.4 Creating a Component-Based Game Layout Using GameplayKit

Problem

You want to use a component-based layout in your game (see Recipe 1.3), but you don't want to have to write your own component system.

Solution

You can use the GameplayKit framework's GKEntity and GKComponent classes to implement an entity-component based layout to your game.

To begin using these classes, you import the GameplayKit framework in your code:

```
import GameplayKit
```

Next, you subclass the GKComponent class, and implement the behavior needed for each type of component, such as its visual representation:

```
// Two example components
class GraphicsComponent : GKComponent {
    override func update(deltaTime seconds: TimeInterval) {
        print("Drawing graphics!")
    }
}

class PhysicsComponent : GKComponent {
    override func update(deltaTime seconds: TimeInterval) {
        print("Simulating physics!")
    }
}
```

When you've defined your component types, you can construct entities and attach components to them. You typically don't subclass GKEntity; instead, they just act as containers for your GKComponent subclasses:

```
// Create an entity, and attach some components
let entity = GKEntity()

entity.addComponent(GraphicsComponent())
entity.addComponent(PhysicsComponent())
```

To update all of the components on an entity, call the entity's update method, and provide the delta time—that is, the number of seconds since the last update was run:

```
// Update all components in each object
for entity in entities {
    entity.update(deltaTime: 0.033)
}
```

Discussion

Using the built-in GameplayKit classes for entities and components can save you having to write and debug your own systems.

In addition to calling update on your GKEntity objects, you can also group components together, and update them all at once. This can be useful when you want to ensure that, for example, all physics calculations for all objects have been performed before any rendering is done.

To do this, use the `GKComponentSystem` class. For each type of component you're working with, define a `GKComponentSystem` and specify the type of component it should handle:

```
let graphicsComponentSystem =
    GKComponentSystem(componentClass: GraphicsComponent.self)
let physicsComponentSystem =
    GKComponentSystem(componentClass: PhysicsComponent.self)
```

After you've created an instance of a `GKEntity`, you can add any components present on it by passing that entity to the system's `addComponent(foundIn:)` method. Because component systems are configured to use a single class of component, they can be given an entity with multiple different kinds of components on them, and they'll add only the type they're looking for:

```
for entity in entities {
    graphicsComponentSystem.addComponent(foundIn: entity)
    physicsComponentSystem.addComponent(foundIn: entity)
}
```

A component system, much like an entity, can be updated, using the `update(delta Time:)` method:

```
// Update all of the graphics components
graphicsComponentSystem.update(deltaTime: 0.033)

// And then all of the physics components
physicsComponentSystem.update(deltaTime: 0.033)
```

1.5 Calculating Delta Times

Problem

You want to know how many seconds have elapsed since the last time the game updated.

Solution

First, decide which object should be used to keep track of time. This may be a view controller, an `SKScene`, a `GLKViewController`, or something entirely custom.

Create an instance variable inside that object:

```
class TimeKeeper {

    var lastFrameTime : Double = 0.0

}
```

Then, each time your game is updated, get the current time in milliseconds, and subtract `lastFrameTime` from that. This gives you the amount of time that has elapsed since the last update.

When you want to make something happen at a certain rate—for example, moving at 3 meters per second—multiply the rate by the delta time:

```
func update(currentTime : Double) {

    // Calculate the time since this method was last called
    let deltaTime = currentTime - lastFrameTime

    // Move at 3 units per second
    let movementSpeed = 3.0

    // Multiply by deltaTime to work out how far
    // an object needs to move this frame
    someMovingObject.move(distance: movementSpeed * deltaTime)

    // Set last frame time to current time, so that
    // we can calculate the delta time when we're next
    // called
    lastFrameTime = currentTime
}
```

Discussion

"Delta time" means "change in time." Delta times are useful for keeping track of how much time has elapsed from one point in time to another—in games, this means the time from one frame to the next. Because the game content changes frame by frame, the amount of time between frames becomes important.

Additionally, the amount of time between frames might change a little. You should always be aiming for a constant frame rate of 60 frames per second (i.e., a delta time of 16 milliseconds: $1 \div 60 \approx 0.0166...$); however, this may not always be achievable, depending on how much work needs to be done in each frame. This means that delta time might vary slightly, so calculating the delta time between each frame becomes necessary if you want rates of change to appear constant.

Some engines give you the delta time directly. For example, `CADisplayLink` gives you a `duration` property (see Recipe 1.8).

Some engines give you just the current time, from which you can calculate the delta time. For example, the `SKScene` class passes the `currentTime` parameter to the `update:` method (discussed further in Recipe 7.15).

In other cases (e.g., if you're doing the main loop yourself), you won't have easy access to either. In these cases, you need to get the current time yourself:

```
let currentTime = Date.timeIntervalSinceReferenceDate as Double
```

1.6 Detecting When the User Enters and Exits Your Game

Problem

You want to detect when the user leaves your game, so that you can pause the game. You also want to know when the user comes back.

Solution

To get notified when the user enters and exits your game, you register to receive notifications from a `NotificationCenter`. The specific notifications that you want to receive are `UIApplicationDidBecomeActive`, `UIApplicationWillEnterForeground`, `UIApplicationWillResignActive`, and `UIApplicationDidEnterBackground`:

```swift
override func viewDidLoad() {
    super.viewDidLoad()

    let center = NotificationCenter.default

    let didBecomeActive = #selector(
        ViewController.applicationDidBecomeActive(notification:)
    )

    let willEnterForeground = #selector(
        ViewController.applicationWillEnterForeground(notification:)
    )

    let willResignActive = #selector(
        ViewController.applicationWillResignActive(notification:)
    )

    let didEnterBackground = #selector(
        ViewController.applicationDidEnterBackground(notification:)
    )

    center.addObserver(self,
                       selector: didBecomeActive,
                       name: UIApplication.didBecomeActiveNotification,
                       object: nil)

    center.addObserver(self,
                       selector: willEnterForeground,
                       name: UIApplication.willEnterForegroundNotification,
                       object: nil)

    center.addObserver(self,
                       selector: willResignActive,
                       name: UIApplication.willResignActiveNotification,
                       object: nil)
```

```
            center.addObserver(self,
                        selector: didEnterBackground,
                        name: UIApplication.didEnterBackgroundNotification,
                        object: nil)
    }

    @objc func applicationDidBecomeActive(notification : Notification) {
        print("Application became active")
    }

    @objc func applicationDidEnterBackground(notification : Notification) {
        print("Application entered background - unload textures!")
    }

    @objc func applicationWillEnterForeground(notification : Notification) {
        print("Application will enter foreground - reload " +
            "any textures that were unloaded")
    }

    @objc func applicationWillResignActive(notification : Notification) {
        print("Application will resign active - pause the game now!")
    }

    deinit {
        // Remove this object from the notification center
        NotificationCenter.default.removeObserver(self)
    }
}
```

Discussion

On iOS, only one app can be the "active" application (i.e., the app that is taking up the screen and that the user is interacting with). This means that apps need to know when they become the active one, and when they stop being active.

When your game is no longer the active application, the player can't interact with it. This means that the game should pause (see Recipe 1.9). When the game resumes being the active application, the player should see a pause screen.

 Pausing, of course, only makes sense in real-time games, such as shooters, driving games, arcade games, and so on. In a turn-based game, like a strategy or puzzle game, you don't really need to worry about the game being paused.

In addition to being the active application, an application can be in the *foreground* or the *background*. When an application is in the foreground, it's being shown on the screen. When it's in the background, it isn't visible at all. Apps that are in the background become *suspended* after a short period of time to save battery power. Apps that enter the background should reduce their memory consumption as much as possible; if your app consumes a large amount of memory while it is in the background, it is more likely to be terminated by iOS.

1.7 Updating Based on a Timer

Problem

You want to update your game after a fixed amount of time.

Solution

Use a Timer to receive a message after a certain amount of time, or to receive an update on a fixed schedule.

First, add an instance variable to your view controller:

```
var timer : Timer?
```

Next, add a method that takes a Timer parameter:

```
@objc
func updateWithTimer(timer: Timer) {
    // Timer went off; update the game
    print("Timer went off!")
}
```

Finally, when you want to start the timer:

```
// Start a timer
self.timer = Timer.scheduledTimer(timeInterval: 0.5,
                target: self,
                selector: #selector(ViewController.updateWithTimer(timer:)),
                          userInfo: nil,
                          repeats: true)
```

To stop the timer:

```
// Stop a timer
self.timer?.invalidate()
self.timer = nil
```

Discussion

A Timer waits for a specified number of seconds, and then calls a method on an object that you specify. You can change the number of seconds by changing the time Interval parameter.

You can also make a timer either fire only once or repeat forever, by changing the `repeats` parameter to `false` or `true`, respectively.

1.8 Updating Based on When the Screen Updates

Problem

You want to update your game every time the screen redraws.

Solution

Use a `CADisplayLink`, which sends a message every time the screen is redrawn.

First, `import` the `QuartzCore` framework:

```
import QuartzCore
```

Next, add an instance variable to your view controller:

```
var displayLink : CADisplayLink?
```

Next, add a method that takes a single parameter (a `CADisplayLink`):

```
@objc func screenUpdated(displayLink : CADisplayLink) {
    // Update the game.
}
```

Finally, add this code when you want to begin receiving updates:

```
// Get a reference to the method we want to run when the
// display updates
let screenUpdated = #selector(screenUpdated(displayLink:))

// Create and schedule the display link
displayLink = CADisplayLink(target: self, selector: screenUpdated)
displayLink?.add(to: RunLoop.main, forMode: RunLoop.Mode.common)
```

When you want to pause receiving updates, set the `paused` property of the `CADisplayLink` to `true`:

```
// Pause the display link
displayLink?.isPaused = true
```

When you want to stop receiving updates, call `invalidate` on the `CADisplayLink`:

```
// Remove the display link; once done, you need to
// remove it from memory by setting all references to it to nil
displayLink?.invalidate()
displayLink = nil
```

Discussion

When we talk about "real-time" games, what comes to mind are objects like the player, vehicles, and other things moving around the screen, looking like they're in continuous motion. This isn't actually what happens, however—what's really going on is that the screen is redrawing itself every 1/60 of a second, and every time it does this, the locations of some or all of the objects on the screen change slightly. If this is done fast enough, the human eye is fooled into thinking that everything's moving continuously.

 In fact, you don't technically *need* to update as quickly as every 1/60 of a second—anything moving faster than 25 frames per second (in other words, one update every 1/25 of a second) will look like motion. However, faster updates yield smoother-looking movement, and you should always aim for 60 frames per second. In games where that's not possible, 30 frames per second is generally acceptable.

You'll get the best results if you update your game at the same rate as the screen. You can achieve this with a `CADisplayLink`, which uses the Core Animation system to figure out when the screen has updated. Every time this happens, the `CADisplayLink` sends its target a message, which you specify.

It's worth mentioning that you can have as many `CADisplayLink` objects as you like, though they'll all update at the same time.

1.9 Pausing a Game

Problem

You want to be able to pause parts of your game, but still have other parts continue to run.

Solution

Keep track of the game's "paused" state in a `Bool` variable. Then, divide your game objects into two categories—ones that run while paused, and ones that don't run while paused:

```
for gameObject in gameObjects {

    // Update it if we're not paused, or if this game object
    // ignores the paused state
    if paused == false || gameObject.canPause == false {
        gameObject.update(deltaTime: deltaTime)
```

```
        }

    }
```

Discussion

The simplest possible way to pause the game is to keep track of a pause state; every time the game updates, you check to see if the pause state is set to `true`, and if it is, you don't update any game objects.

However, you often don't want every single thing in the game to freeze. For example:

- The user interface may need to continue to animate.
- The network may need to keep communicating with other computers, rather than stopping entirely.

In these cases, having special objects that never get paused makes more sense.

1.10 Calculating Time Elapsed Since the Game Start

Problem

You want to find out how much time has elapsed since the game started.

Solution

When the game starts, create a `Date` object and store it:

```
// Store the time when the game started as a property
var gameStartDate : Date?

// When the game actually begins, store the current date
self.gameStartDate = Date()
```

When you want to find out how much time has elapsed since the game started, create a second `Date` and use the `timeIntervalSince` method to calculate the time:

```
let now = Date()
let timeSinceGameStart = now
    .timeIntervalSince(self.gameStartDate!)
NSLog("The game started \(timeSinceGameStart) seconds ago")
```

Discussion

`Date` objects represent moments in time. They're the go-to object for representing any instant of time that you want to be able to refer to again later, such as when your game starts. `Date` objects can refer to practically any date in the past or future and are very precise.

When you create a `Date` with the `Date()` initializer, you get back a `Date` object that refers to the current time (i.e., the instant when the `Date` object was created).

To determine the interval between two dates, you use `timeIntervalSince`. This method returns a `TimeInterval`, which is actually another term for a floating-point number. These values are represented in seconds, so it's up to your code to do things like determine the number of hours and minutes:

```
let formatter = DateComponentsFormatter()
formatter.allowedUnits = [.hour, .minute, .second]
formatter.unitsStyle = .positional

let formattedString = formatter.string(from: timeSinceGameStart) ?? ""
print("Time elapsed: \(formattedString)")
```

1.11 Working with Closures

Problem

You want to store some code in a variable for later execution.

Solution

Closures are ideal for this:

```
class GameObject {
    // define a type of closure that takes a single GameObject
    // as a parameter and returns nothing
    var onCollision : ((GameObject) -> Void)?
}

// Create two objects for this example
let car = GameObject()
let brickWall = GameObject()

// Provide code to run when the car hits any another object
car.onCollision = { (objectWeHit) in
    print("Car collided with \(objectWeHit)")
}

// later, when a character collides:
car.onCollision?(brickWall) // note the ? - this means that
// the code will only run if onCollision
// is not nil
```

Discussion

Closures are a language feature in Swift that allow you to store chunks of code in variables, which can then be worked with like any other variable.

Here's an example of a simple closure:

```
var multiplyNumber : (Int) -> Int ❶

multiplyNumber = { (number) -> Int in ❷

    return number * 2

}

multiplyNumber(2) ❸
```

❶ This is how you define a variable that stores a closure. In this case, the closure returns an `Int`, is named `multiplyNumber`, and accepts a single `Int` parameter.

❷ This is how you declare a closure. Just like any other variable, once a closure is defined, it needs to be given a value. In this case, we're providing a closure that takes an `Int` and returns an `Int`, just like the variable's definition.

❸ Calling a closure works just like calling any other function.

How closures work

So far, this just seems like a very roundabout way to call a function. However, the real power of closures comes from two facts:

- Closures *capture the state* of any other variables their code references.
- Closures are objects, just like everything else. They stay around until you need them. If you store a closure, you can call it however often you like.

This is extremely powerful, because it means that your game doesn't need to carefully store values for later use; if a closure needs a value, it automatically keeps it.

You define a closure by describing the parameters it receives and the type of information it returns. To help protect against mistakes, you can also create a *type alias* for closures, which defines a specific type of closure. This allows you to declare variables with more easily understandable semantics:

```
typealias ErrorHandler = (Error) -> Void

var myErrorHandler : ErrorHandler

myErrorHandler = { (theError) in
    // do work with theError
    print("i SPILL my DRINK! \(theError)")
}
```

Closures and other objects

When a closure is created, the compiler looks at all of the variables that the closure is referencing. If a variable is a value type, like an `int` or a `float`, that value is simply copied. However, if the variable is a reference type, like an instance of a class, it can't be copied because it could potentially be very large. Instead, the object is *retained* by the closure. When a closure is freed, any objects retained by the closure are released.

This means that if you have a closure that references another object, that closure will keep the other object around. This is usually what you want, because it would be annoying to have to remember to keep the variables referenced by closures in memory. However, sometimes that's not what you want.

One example is when you want a closure to run in two seconds' time that causes an enemy object to run an attack animation. However, between the time you schedule the closure and the time the closure runs, the enemy is removed from the game. If the closure has a strong reference to the enemy, the enemy isn't actually removed from memory until the closure is scheduled to run, which could have unintended side effects.

To get around this problem, you use *weak references*. A weak reference is a reference that does not keep an object in memory; additionally, if the object that is being referred to is removed (because all owning references to it have gone away), the weak reference will automatically be set to `nil`. For more information on weak references, see *The Swift Programming Language*'s chapter on Automatic Reference Counting (*http://bit.ly/auto_ref_counting*).

1.12 Writing a Method That Calls a Closure

Problem

You want to write a method that, after performing its work, calls a closure to indicate that the work is complete.

For example, you want to tell a character to start moving to a destination, and then run a closure when the character finishes moving.

Solution

To create a method that takes a closure as a parameter, you just do this:

```
func move(to position : CGPoint, completion: (()->Void)?) {

    // Do the actual work of moving to the location, which
    // might take place over several frames

    // Call the completion handler, if it exists
```

```
    completion?()
}

let destination = CGPoint(x: 5, y: 3)

// Call the function and provide the closure as a parameter
move(to: destination) {
    print("Arrived!")
}
```

Discussion

Methods that take a closure as a parameter are useful for when you're writing code that starts off a long-running process, and you want to run some code at the conclusion of that process but want to keep that conclusion code close to the original call itself.

Before closures were added to the Swift language, the usual technique was to write two methods: one where you started the long-running process, and one that would be called when the process completed. This separates the various parts of the code, which decreases the readability of your code; additionally, passing around variables between these two methods is more complicated (because you need to manually store them in a temporary variable at the start, and retrieve them at the end; with closures, you just use the variables without any additional work).

 If the last parameter that you pass to a function or method is a closure, you can place the closure outside the function call's parentheses. It can look a little cleaner.

1.13 Working with Operation Queues

Problem

You want to put chunks of work in a queue, so that they're run when the operating system has a moment to do them.

Solution

Use an `OperationQueue` to schedule closures to be run in the background without interfering with more time-critical tasks like rendering or accepting user input:

```
// Create a work queue to put tasks on
let concurrentQueue = OperationQueue()

// This queue can run 10 operations at the same time, at most
```

```
concurrentQueue.maxConcurrentOperationCount = 10

// Add some tasks
concurrentQueue.addOperation {
    UploadHighScores()
}

concurrentQueue.addOperation {
    SaveGame()
}

concurrentQueue.addOperation {
    DownloadMaps()
}
```

Discussion

An operation queue is a tool for running chunks of work. Every application has an operation queue called the *main queue*. The main queue is the queue that normal application tasks (e.g., handling touches, redrawing the screen, etc.) are run on.

Running Operations on the Main Queue

Many tasks can only be run on the main queue, including updating anything run by UIKit. It's also a good idea to only have a single operation queue that's in charge of sending OpenGL instructions - don't try to use it from multiple queues at once.

The main queue is a specific OperationQueue, which you can access using the main method:

```
let mainQueue = OperationQueue.main

mainQueue.addOperation { () -> Void in
    ProcessPlayerInput()
}
```

It's often the case that you want to do something in the background (i.e., on another operation queue), and then alert the user when it's finished. However, as we've already mentioned, you can only do UIKit tasks (e.g., displaying an alert box) on the main queue.

To address this, you can put tasks on the main queue from inside a background queue:

```
let backgroundQueue = OperationQueue()

backgroundQueue.addOperation { () -> Void in

    // Do work in the background

    OperationQueue.main.addOperation {
```

```
            // Once that's done, do work on the main queue

        }
    }
```

An operation queue runs as many operations as it can simultaneously. The number of concurrent operations that can be run depends on several conditions, including the number of processor cores available and the different priorities that other operations may have.

By default, an operation queue determines the number of operations that it can run at the same time on its own. However, you can specify a maximum number of concurrent operations by using the `maxConcurrentOperationCount` property.

1.14 Performing a Task in the Future

Problem

You want to run some code, but you want it to happen a couple of seconds from now.

Solution

Use the `DispatchQueue` class's `asyncAfter` method to schedule a closure of code to run in the future:

```
// Place a bomb, but make it explode in 10 seconds
PlaceBomb()

let deadline = DispatchTime.now() + 10

DispatchQueue.main.asyncAfter(deadline: deadline, execute: {
    // Time's up. Kaboom.
    ExplodeBomb()
})
```

Discussion

`OperationQueue` is actually a higher-level wrapper around the lower-level features provided by the C-based *Grand Central Dispatch* API. Grand Central Dispatch, or GCD, works mostly with objects called "dispatch queues," which are basically `Opera tionQueues`. You do work with GCD by putting closures onto a queue, which runs the closures. Just as with `OperationQueue`, there can be many queues operating at the same time, and they can be serial or concurrent queues.

1.15 Making Operations Depend on Each Other

Problem

You want to run some operations, but they need to run only after certain other operations are done.

Solution

To make an operation wait for another operation to complete, store each individual operation in a variable, and then use the `addDependency:` method to indicate which operations need to complete before a given operation begins:

```swift
let firstOperation = BlockOperation { () -> Void in
    print("First operation")
}

let secondOperation = BlockOperation { () -> Void in
    print("Second operation")
}

let thirdOperation = BlockOperation { () -> Void in
    print("Third operation")
}

// secondOperation will not run until firstOperation and
// thirdOperation have finished
secondOperation.addDependency(firstOperation)
secondOperation.addDependency(thirdOperation)

let operations = [firstOperation, secondOperation, thirdOperation]

backgroundQueue.addOperations(operations, waitUntilFinished: true)
```

Discussion

You can add an operation to another operation as a *dependency*. This is useful for cases where you want one closure to run only after one or more operations have completed.

To add a dependency to an operation, you use the `addDependency:` method. Doing this doesn't run the operation, but just links the two together.

Once the operation dependencies have been set up, you can add the operations to the queue in any order that you like; operations will not run until all of their dependencies have finished running.

1.16 Filtering an Array with Closures

Problem

You have an array, and you want to filter it with your own custom logic.

Solution

Use the `filtered` method to create an array that only contains objects that meet certain conditions:

```
let array = ["One", "Two", "Three", "Four", "Five"]

print("Original array: \(array)")

let filteredArray = array.filter { (element) -> Bool in

    if element.range(of: "e") != nil {
        return true
    } else {
        return false
    }
}

print("Filtered array: \(filteredArray)")
```

Discussion

The closure that you provide to the `filter` method is called multiple times. Each time it's called, it takes an item in the array as its single parameter, and returns `true` if that item should appear in the filtered array, and false if it shouldn't.

1.17 Loading New Assets During Gameplay

Problem

You want to load new resources without impacting the performance of the game.

Solution

For each resource that needs loading, run an operation that does the loading into memory, and do it in the background. Then run a subsequent operation when all of the loads have completed.

You can do this by scheduling load operations on a background queue, and also running an operation on the main queue that depends on all of the load operations. This means that all of your images will load in the background, and you'll run code on the main queue when it's complete:

```swift
let imagesToLoad = ["Image 1.jpg", "Image 2.jpg", "Image 3.jpg"]

let imageLoadingQueue = OperationQueue()

// We want the main queue to run at close to regular speed, so mark this
// background queue as running in the background

// (Note: this is actually the default value, but it's good to know about
// the qualityOfService property.)
imageLoadingQueue.qualityOfService = QualityOfService.background

// Allow loading multiple images at once
imageLoadingQueue.maxConcurrentOperationCount = 10

// Create an operation that will run when all images are loaded - you may want
// to tweak this
let loadingComplete = BlockOperation { () -> Void in
    print("Loading complete!")
}

// Create an array for storing our loading operations
var loadingOperations : [Operation] = []

// Add a load operation for each image

for imageName in imagesToLoad {
    let loadOperation = BlockOperation { () -> Void in

        print("Loading \(imageName)")

    }

    loadingOperations.append(loadOperation)

    // Don't run the loading complete operation until
    // this load (and all other loads) are done
    loadingComplete.addDependency(loadOperation)
}

imageLoadingQueue.addOperations(loadingOperations, waitUntilFinished: false)
imageLoadingQueue.addOperation(loadingComplete)
```

Discussion

When you create an `OperationQueue`, you can control its quality of service. By default, operation queues you create have the *background* quality of service, which indicates to the operating system that it's OK for higher-priority operations to take precedence. This is generally what you want for your asset-loading routines, because it's important that you keep your application responsive to user input.

Depending on how much memory the rest of your game takes, you can also use this technique to load assets while the user is busy doing something else. For example, once the user reaches the main menu, you could start loading the resources needed for actual gameplay while you wait for the user to tap the New Game button.

1.18 Adding Unit Tests to Your Game

Problem

You want to test different parts of your game's code in isolation, so that you can ensure that each part is working.

Solution

You can write code that tests different parts of your app in isolation using unit tests. By default, all newly created projects come with an empty set of unit tests, in which you can add isolated testing functions.

 If you're working with an existing project, you can create a new set of unit tests by choosing File→New→Target and creating an iOS Unit Testing Bundle.

You'll find your unit test files in a group whose name ends with Tests. For example, if your Xcode project is called MyAwesomeGame, your testing files will be in a group named MyAwesomeGameTests, and it will by default come with a file called *MyAwesomeGameTests.swift*.

When you want to add a test, open your test file (the *.swift* file) and add a method whose name begins with test:

```
func testDoingSomethingCool() {

    let object = SomeAwesomeObject()

    let succeeded = object.doSomethingCool()

    if succeeded == false {
        XCTFail("Failed to do something cool");
    }
}
```

When you want to run the tests, choose Product→Test or press Command-U. All of the methods in your testing classes that begin with test will be run, one after the other.

You can also add additional collections of tests, by creating a new *test suite*. You do this by choosing File→New→File and creating a new Swift test case class. When you create this new class, don't forget to make it belong to your testing target instead of your game target, or you'll get compile errors.

Discussion

Unit testing is the practice of writing small tests that test specific features of your code. In normal use, your code is used in a variety of ways, and if there's a bug, it can be difficult to track down exactly why your code isn't behaving the way you want it to. By using unit tests, you can run multiple tests of your code and check each time to see if the results are what you expect. If a test fails, the parts of your game that use your code in that particular way will also fail.

Each test is actually a method in a *test case*. Test cases are subclasses of XCTestCase whose names begin with test. The XCTestCase objects in a testing bundle make up a *test suite*, which is what's run when you tell Xcode to test your application.

When tests run, Xcode performs the following tasks for each test method, in each test case, in each test suite:

- Call the test case's setUp method.
- Call the test method itself, and note if the test succeeds or fails.
- Call the test case's tearDown method.
- Show a report showing which tests failed.

As you can see, the test case's setUp and tearDown methods are called for *each* test method. The idea behind this is that you use setUp to create whatever conditions you want to run your test under (e.g., if you're testing the behavior of an AI, you could use setUp to load the level in which the AI needs to operate). Conversely, the tearDown method is used to dismantle whatever resources are set up in setUp. This means that each time a test method is run, it's operating under the same conditions.

The contents of each test method are entirely up to you. Typically, you create objects that you want to test, run methods, and then check to see if the outcomes were what you expected. The actual way that you check the outcomes is through a collection of dedicated *assertion methods*, which flag the test as failing if the condition you pass in evaluates to false. The assertion methods also take a string parameter, which is shown to the user if the test fails.

For example:

```
// Fails if X is not nil
XCTAssertNil(X, "X should be nil")

// Fails if X IS nil
XCTAssertNotNil(X, "X should not be nil")

// Fails if X is not true
XCTAssertTrue(1 == 1, "1 really should be equal to 1")

// Fails if X is not false
XCTAssertFalse(2 != 3, "In this universe, 2 equals 3 apparently")

// Fails if X and Y are not equal (tested by calling X.equals(Y)])
XCTAssertEqualObjects((2), (1+1), "Objects should be equal")

// Fails if X and Y ARE equal (tested by calling X.equals(Y))
XCTAssertNotEqualObjects("One", "1", "Objects should not be equal")

// Fails, regardless of circumstances
XCTFail("Everything is broken")
```

There are several other assertion methods available for you to use that won't fit in this book; for a comprehensive list, see the documentation for the XCTest framework (*https://apple.co/2Dz0NVK*).

1.19 2D Grids

Problem

You want to represent your game's layout as a 2D grid.

Solution

Use a GKGridGraph to represent a grid of a fixed size. Subclass the GKGridGraphNode class to store custom objects, like the position of a game entity, on the graph.

The GKGridGraph represents a 2D grid of nodes, each of which has a coordinate that defines its position on the grid, as well as connections to other nodes on the grid.

For example, let's define a subclass of GKGridGraphNode that allows you to store some additional information, like a string:

```
class GameNode : GKGridGraphNode {
    var name : String

    init (name: String, gridPosition: vector_int2) {
        self.name = name
        super.init(gridPosition: gridPosition)
```

```
    }

    override var description: String {
        return self.name
    }

    required init?(coder aDecoder: NSCoder) {
        fatalError("not implemented")
    }
}
```

We can now create a grid using this node, like so:

```
let graph = GKGridGraph<GameNode>(
    fromGridStartingAt: [0,0], width: 6, height: 6, diagonalsAllowed: false)
```

You can remove nodes from the grid, and add new nodes. Note that a node is not considered *part* of the grid unless it is attached to other nodes, which you can do using the connectToAdjacentNodes method:

```
func add<NodeType>(node: NodeType, to graph: GKGridGraph<NodeType>) {

    // If there's a node at this position here already, remove it
    if let existingNode = graph.node(atGridPosition: node.gridPosition) {
        graph.remove([existingNode])
    }

    // Add the new node, and connect it to the other nodes on the graph
    graph.connectToAdjacentNodes(node: node)
}
```

When you add a node to the grid, you specify its position:

```
// Add two
let playerNode = GameNode(name: "Player", gridPosition: [0,2])
let exitNode   = GameNode(name: "Exit", gridPosition: [0,3])

add(node: playerNode, to: graph)
add(node: exitNode, to: graph)
```

You can also retrieve a node from the grid by specifying a position:

```
graph.node(atGridPosition: [0,2])?.name // "Player"
```

Finally, you can get *all* nodes on the grid, and filter them based on whatever properties you desire:

```
// Get all GameNodes on the grid of a certain type
let allNodes = graph.nodes?.filter { $0 is GameNode }
```

Discussion

Nodes on a GKGridGraph class can also be used for pathfinding, which is discussed in Recipe 9.10.

1.20 Using Randomization

Problem

You want to make use of random numbers in your game, in a way that makes for satisfying gameplay.

Solution

Use a random number generator from `GameplayKit`. The framework offers several different types, each producing a different distribution of random numbers.

The `GKRandomDistribution` generator produces a sequence of numbers where every value has an equally likely chance of appearing:

```
// Random distributions generate a random value every time
let dice = GKRandomDistribution(forDieWithSideCount: 6)

// Getting values from a random source
dice.nextBool()
dice.nextUniform()
dice.nextInt()
```

An example of a stream of random numbers from this generator looks like this:

```
4, 4, 6, 6, 4, 2, 3, 3, 6, 3
```

 As you can see, some numbers appear multiple times, and sometimes appear twice in a row. This is because each value's probability in the stream is entirely independent of any other number.

The `GKGaussianDistribution` is a *weighted* random distribution. Numbers coming out of this random number generator are more likely to be in the center of the distribution, and will rarely be at the lowest or highest values in the range:

```
// Gaussian distributions produce values that tend to be around the middle,
// and rarely produce values that tend to be at the edges
let gaussian = GKGaussianDistribution(forDieWithSideCount: 20)
```

An example of a stream of random numbers coming from this generator is:

```
14, 10, 13, 8, 7, 14, 19, 15, 13, 11
```

Notice how the numbers in this example tend to be close to the 8-to-12 range, and it's rare to see numbers near 1 or 20.

Finally, the `GKShuffledDistribution` generator produces a stream of values that tries to avoid repeating the same value:

```
// Shuffled distributions avoid repeating the same element
let shuffled = GKShuffledDistribution.d6()
```

An example of a stream of random numbers from this generator is:

```
2, 4, 3, 6, 1, 5, 1, 6, 4, 3
```

Discussion

True randomness, such as numbers coming from a GKRandomDistribution generator, can feel "unfair" to the player, since humans have trouble understanding probability. The *gambler's fallacy* is a famous example, in which people playing a game of chance who notice a trend of losses keep playing, feeling that a win will happen "soon," when in reality, each win and loss exists entirely independently of the others.

Two common types of dice are six-sided dice and twenty-sided dice. To quickly create a random number generator that produces numbers between zero and six or zero and twenty, use the d6 and d20 functions:

```
let d6 = GKRandomDistribution.d6()
let d20 = GKRandomDistribution.d20()
```

1.21 Building a State Machine

Problem

You want to use a state machine to manage the different states a part of your game can be in.

Solution

State machines are systems in which you define multiple *states* that a system can be in. The system is always in one state at a time; additionally, each state has a list of *other* states that the system can transition to.

For example, imagine a system where there are three states: sitting, standing, and walking. You can transition from sitting to standing (and vice versa), and you can transition from standing to walking. However, you can't transition directly from sitting to walking; you need to go via standing first.

Every time you transition to another state, you have the opportunity to run code. To continue this example, when you transition to the standing state, you might make your character display a standing up animation.

State machines are useful for managing the states that a system can be in, and in navigating between different states.

GameplayKit provides the `GKStateMachine` class, which you can use to manage and transition between different states. To work with `GKStateMachine`, you create subclasses of `GKState`, which handle the logic of entering, updating, and leaving a state.

For example, consider the following four states:

```swift
// The 'Building Up an Army' state
class BuildUpState : GKState {

    override func didEnter(from previousState: GKState?) {
        print("Now building up!")
    }

    // Called every time the state machine is updated
    override func update(deltaTime seconds: TimeInterval) {
        print("Building in progress!")
    }

    // Called when we leave this state
    override func willExit(to nextState: GKState) {
        print("Stopping buildup!")
    }


}

// The 'Attacking with the Army' state
class AttackState : GKState {

    override func didEnter(from previousState: GKState?) {
        // Called when we enter this state
        print("Now attacking the enemy!")
    }

    override func update(deltaTime seconds: TimeInterval) {
        // Called every time the state machine is updated
        print("Attack in progress!")
    }
}

// The 'Withdrawing the Army from Attack' state
class WithdrawState : GKState {

}

// The 'Defeated' state
class DefeatedState : GKState {
    override func didEnter(from previousState: GKState?) {
        // Called when we enter this state
        print("I'm defeated!")

        // Use 'previousState' to learn about the state we entered from
```

```
        if previousState is BuildUpState {
            print("I was in the middle of building up, too!")
        }
    }
}
```

To use these states in a state machine, you create an instance of each of the states, put them in an array, and then provide that array to the initializer of GKStateMachine:

```
// Create instances of the states
let states = [
    BuildUpState(),
    AttackState(),
    WithdrawState(),
    DefeatedState()
]

let stateMachine = GKStateMachine(states: states)
```

You can then tell the state machine to transition between different states:

```
stateMachine.enter(BuildUpState.self)
stateMachine.enter(AttackState.self)
stateMachine.enter(BuildUpState.self)
stateMachine.enter(DefeatedState.self)
```

When you transition between states, each state has an opportunity to run code when it enters and exits. In this example, telling the state machine to enter these states results in the following being printed:

```
Now building up!
Stopping buildup!
Now attacking the enemy!
Now building up!
Stopping buildup!
I'm defeated!
I was in the middle of building up, too!
```

You can also run the update method on a state machine's current state by calling update on the state machine:

```
stateMachine.update(deltaTime: 0.033)
```

You can also get the actual state object itself:

```
stateMachine.currentState
```

If you want to get the state object for a certain *class* of state, you can use the state(forClass:) method:

```
let state = stateMachine.state(forClass: BuildUpState.self)
```

Finally, you can place restrictions on which states can transition to others by implementing the isValidNextState on your GKState subclass. This method receives a class as a parameter, and returns `true` if the state should transition to a state of this class, and `false` otherwise:

```
// Limiting which states we can proceed to from here
override func isValidNextState(_ stateClass: AnyClass) -> Bool {

    if stateClass == AttackState.self || stateClass == DefeatedState.self {
        return true
    } else {
        return false
    }
}
```

You can then ask the state machine if it's possible to transition from the current state to a class you specify:

```
stateMachine.enter(BuildUpState.self)
stateMachine.canEnterState(WithdrawState.self)
// = false
```

The `enter` function returns `true` if the state transition was allowed, and `false` otherwise.

Discussion

State machines are great for several problems, because they help to encapsulate a lot of the logic that comes up around objects that need to switch between modes. Additionally, by adding constraints on which states can transition to other states, you can reduce the number of bugs caused by invalid transitions.

CHAPTER 2

Views and Menus

When you fire up a game, you don't often get immediately dropped into the action. In most games, there's a lot of "nongame" stuff that your game will need to deal with first, such as showing a settings screen to let your player change volume levels and the like, or a way to let the player pick a chapter in your game to play.

Though it's definitely possible to use your game's graphics systems to show this kind of user interface, there's often no reason to recreate the built-in interface libraries that already exist on iOS.

UIKit is the framework that provides the code that handles controls like buttons, sliders, image views, and checkboxes. Additionally, UIKit has tools that let you divide up your game's screens into separate, easier-to-work-with units called *view controllers*. These view controllers can in turn be linked together using *storyboards*, which let you see how each screen's worth of content connects to the others.

The controls available to you in UIKit can also be customized to suit the look and feel of your game, which means that UIKit can fit right into your game's visual design. In addition to simply tinting the standard iOS controls with a color, you can use images and other material to theme your controls. This means that you don't have to reimplement standard stuff like sliders and buttons, which saves you a lot of time in programming your game.

To work with menus, it's useful to know how to work with storyboards. So, before we get into the meat of this chapter, we'll first talk about how to set up a storyboard with the screens you want.

2.1 Working with Storyboards

Problem

You need a way to organize the different screens of your game, defining how each screen links to other screens and what content is shown on each screen.

Solution

You can use storyboards to organize your screens:

1. Create a new single-view application. Call it whatever you like.

2. Open the *Main.storyboard* file. You're now looking at an empty screen.

3. Click the Object Library button, and the Object Library will appear (see Figure 2-1). The button looks like a circle containing a square. Alternatively, press Command-Shift-L.

4. Scroll down in the Object Library until you find the button, as shown in Figure 2-2. You can also type "button" into the search field at the bottom of the Object Library.

5. Drag a button into the center of the window.

6. Center the button in the window by holding down the Control key and dragging from the button to the view in which it's contained. A list of constraints will appear; hold Shift, and click Center Horizontally In Container and Center Vertically In Container (see Figure 2-3). Press Enter, and Xcode will add centering constraints to the button, which will center it on the screen no matter how big or small the screen is.

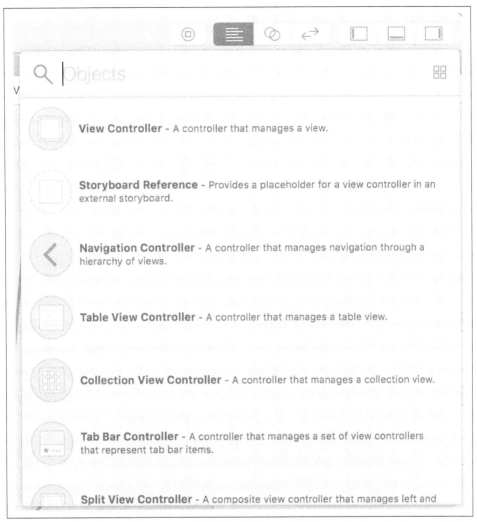

Figure 2-1. The Object Library, available by clicking the leftmost button in the top-right corner of the window

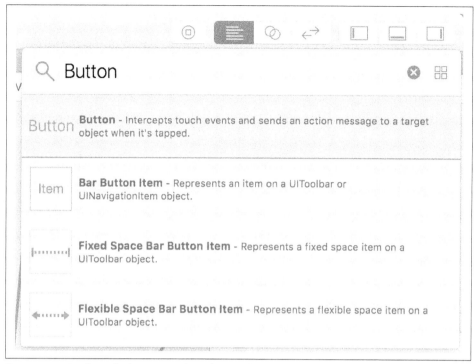

Figure 2-2. Finding the button in the Object Library

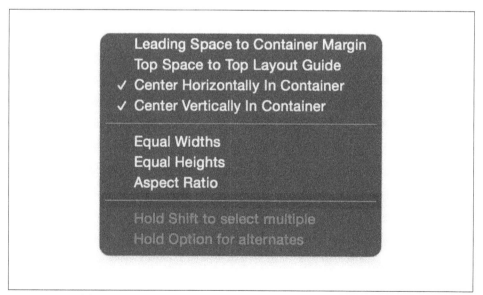

Figure 2-3. Adding the two centering constraints to the button

7. Run the application. A button will appear on the screen, as shown in Figure 2-4. You can tap it, but it won't do anything yet.

   Next, we'll set up the application so that tapping the button displays a new screen.

8. Find the navigation controller in the Object Library by typing "navigation" into the search field. Drag one into the storyboard.

   Navigation controllers come with an attached Table View. We don't want this—select it and delete it.

9. The original screen currently has a small arrow attached to it. This indicates that it's the screen that will appear when the application begins. Drag this arrow from where it is right now to the navigation controller.

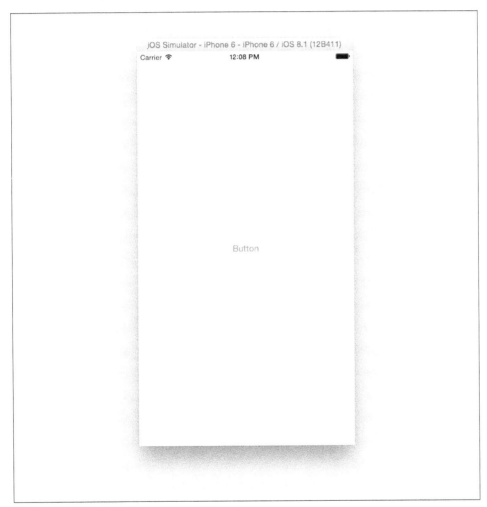

Figure 2-4. A button shown on the iPhone's screen

10. Hold down the Control key, and drag from the navigation controller to the first screen.

11. A window containing a list of possible "segues" will appear. Choose the "root view controller" option. When you do this, the two view controllers will be linked together, as shown in Figure 2-5.

Figure 2-5. The linked view controllers

When the application starts up, the navigation controller will appear, and inside it, you'll see the screen you designed. Next, we'll make it so that the button shows an additional screen when it's tapped:

1. Drag a new view controller into the storyboard.

   A new, empty screen will appear.

2. Hold down the Control key, and drag from the button to the new screen.

   Another list of possible segues will appear, as shown in Figure 2-6. Choose "show."

3. The two screens will appear linked with a line, which indicates that it's possible to go from one screen to the next.

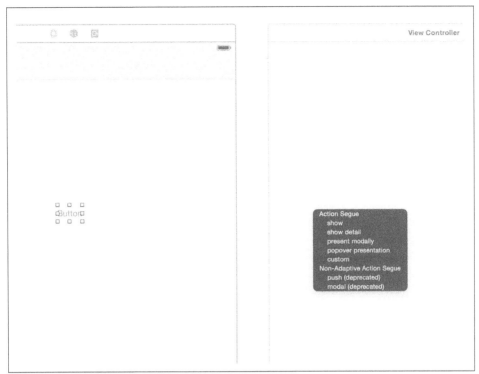

Figure 2-6. Selecting a segue

Because view controllers take up quite a bit of space on the screen, you might want to zoom out to get a bigger picture. Note that when you're zoomed out, you can't work with the views and controls inside a view controller.

4. Run the application.

When you tap the button, a new screen will appear. A Back button will also appear in the navigation bar at the top of the screen.

When you create a new project, it will come with a storyboard file. *Storyboards* are files that define what *view controllers* are used in your application, and how those view controllers are linked together via *segues*.

A view controller is an object that contains the logic that controls an individual screen. Typically, you have one view controller per screen. For each type of screen that the user will see, you create a subclass of the UIViewController class, and you instruct the storyboard to use that subclass for specific screens. (For information on how to do this, see Recipe 2.2.)

In a storyboard, screens can be linked together using segues. A segue is generally a transition from one screen to the next. For example, a *show* segue tells the system that, when the segue is activated, the current view's *presentation context* should present a new view controller. Because the presentation context is a navigation controller, the navigation controller shows the new screen using a push animation.

Segues are also used to indicate relationships between different view controllers. For example, navigation controllers need to know which screen they should display when they're first shown; you do this by creating a *root view controller* segue.

2.2 Creating View Controllers

Problem

You have a project that has a storyboard, and you want to keep all of the logic for your screens in separate, easily maintainable objects. For example, you want to keep your main menu code separate from the high scores screen.

Solution

Follow these steps to create a new view controller:

1. Create a subclass of `UIViewController`.

   Choose New → File from the File menu. Select the Source category, and choose to make a Cocoa Touch class, as shown in Figure 2-7.

2. Create the new `UIViewController` subclass.

   Name the class `MainMenuViewController`, and set "Subclass of" to `UIView Controller`.

   Make sure that "Also create XIB file" is unchecked, as shown in Figure 2-8.

3. Create the file.

   Xcode will ask you where to put the newly created file. Choose somewhere that suits your particular purpose.

   Once this is done, a new file will appear in the Project Navigator: *MainMenu-ViewController.swift*. To actually use this new class, you need to indicate to the storyboard that it should be used on one of the screens. In this example, there's only one screen, so we'll make it use the newly created `MainMenuViewController` class.

Figure 2-7. Creating a new Cocoa Touch subclass

Figure 2-8. Setting up the new file

4. Open the storyboard.

   Find *Main.storyboard* in the Project Navigator, and click it.

5. Open the outline view.

   The outline view lists all of the parts making up your user interface. You can open it either by choosing Show Document Outline from the Editor menu, or by clicking the Show Outline button at the bottom left of the Interface Builder.

6. Select the view controller.

   You'll find it at the top of the outline view.

 If you just click the large blank white rectangle in the storyboard, what you're actually selecting is just the *view* that the view controller manages, instead of the *view controller* itself. To select the view controller, click the little yellow circle icon, which you can find above the view or in the outline view.

7. Open the Identity Inspector.

   You can do this by selecting the Identity Inspector at the top of the Utilities pane. It's the third icon from the left.

8. Change the class of the selected view controller to `MainMenuViewController`.

   At the top of the Identity Inspector, you'll find the class of the currently selected view controller. Change it to `MainMenuViewController`, as shown in Figure 2-9. Doing this means that the `MainMenuViewController` class will be the one used for this particular screen.

   Now that this is done, we'll add a text field to the screen and make the view controller class able to access its contents (on its own, a text field can't communicate with the view controller—you need an outlet for that). We'll also add a button to the screen, and make some code run when the user taps it.

9. Add a text field.

   Open the Object Library by clicking the Object Library button at the top-right of the screen, or by pressing Command-Shift-L.

   Scroll down until you find the Text Field control. Alternatively, type "text field" into the search bar at the bottom of the Object Library (as shown in Figure 2-10).

   Drag and drop a text field into the top-left of the screen.

   On its own, a text field can't communicate with the view controller—you need an *outlet* for that.

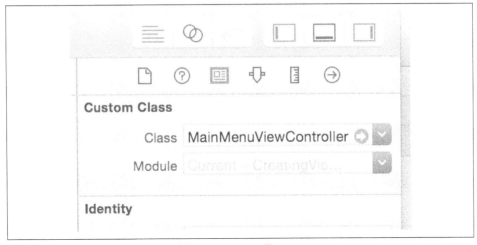

Figure 2-9. Changing the class of the view controller

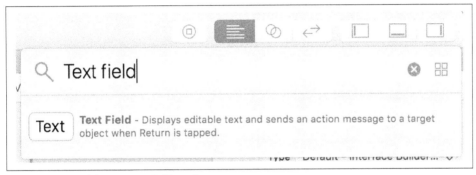

Figure 2-10. Adding a text field to the screen

10. Open the view controller's code in the Assistant editor.

    Open the Assistant editor by clicking the Assistant button at the top-right of the Xcode window or by choosing View → Assistant Editor → Show Assistant Editor.

    Once you've opened it, *MainMenuViewController.swift* should be visible in the editor. If it isn't, choose Automatic→*MainMenuViewController.swift* from the jump bar at the top of the Assistant editor (Figure 2-11).

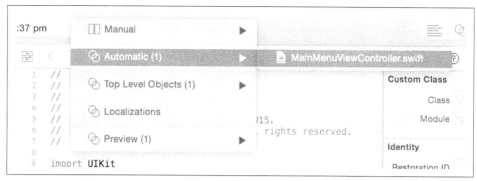

Figure 2-11. Selecting MainMenuViewController.swift in the Assistant editor

11. Add the outlet for the text field.

    Hold down the Control key, and drag from the text field into the MainMenuView
    Controller class. When you finish dragging, a dialog box will appear (see
    Figure 2-12) asking you what to name the variable.

    Type **textField**, and click the Connect button.

Figure 2-12. Creating an outlet for the text field

12. Add a button to the screen (which will run code when the button is tapped).

    Follow the same instructions for adding a text field, but this time, add a button.

13. Add the action.

    Hold down the Control key, and drag from the button into the MainMenuViewCon
    troller class.

    Another dialog will appear, as shown in Figure 2-13, asking you what to name
    the connection. Set the connect's type to Action, name it buttonPressed, and
    click Connect. A new method will be added to MainMenuViewController.

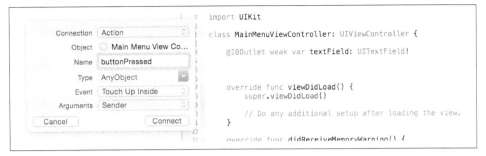

Figure 2-13. Creating an action

14. Add some code to the newly created `buttonPressed` method.

    We'll use the following code:

```
let alert = UIAlertController(title: "Button tapped",
    message: "The button was tapped",
    preferredStyle: UIAlertController.Style.alert)

alert.addAction(UIAlertAction(title: "OK",
                          style: UIAlertAction.Style.default,
    handler: nil))

self.present(alert,
    animated: true, completion: nil)
```

Discussion

In almost every single case, different screens perform different tasks. A "main menu" screen, for example, has the task of showing the game's logo, and probably a couple of buttons to send the player off to a new game, to continue an existing game, to view the high scores screen, and so on. Each one of these screens, in turn, has its own functionality.

The easiest way to create an app that contains multiple screens is via a storyboard. However, a storyboard won't let you define the behavior of the screens—that's the code's job. So, how do you tell the application what code should be run for different screens?

Every view controller that's managed by a storyboard is an instance of the `UIView Controller` class. `UIViewControllers` know how to be presented to the user, how to show whatever views have been placed inside them in the Interface Builder, and how to do a few other things, like managing their lifecycle (i.e., they know when they're about to appear on the screen, when they're about to go away, and when other important events are about to occur, like the device running low on memory).

However, `UIViewControllers` don't have any knowledge of what their role is—they're designed to be empty templates, and it's your job to create subclasses that perform the work of being a main menu, or of being a high scores screen, and so on.

When you subclass `UIViewController`, you override some important methods:

- `viewDidLoad` is called when the view has completed loading and all of the controls are present, but before the view is visible on screen.

- `viewWillAppear` is called when the view is about to appear on the screen, but is not yet visible.

- `viewDidAppear` is called when the view has finished appearing on the screen and is now visible.

- `viewWillDisappear` is called when the view is about to disappear from the screen, but is currently still visible.

- `viewDidDisappear` is called when the view is no longer visible.

- `applicationReceivedMemoryWarning` is called when the application has received a memory warning and will be force-quit by iOS if memory is not freed up. Your `UIViewController` subclass should free any objects that can be recreated when needed.

Additionally, your `UIViewController` is able to respond to events that come from the controls it's showing, and to manipulate those controls and change what they're doing.

This is done through outlets and actions. An *outlet* is a property on the `UIView Controller` that is connected to a view; once `viewDidLoad` has been called, each outlet property has been connected to a view object. You can then access these properties as normal.

To define an outlet, you create a property that uses the special keyword `IBOutlet`, like so:

```
@IBOutlet weak var textField: UITextField!
```

Actions are methods that are called as a result of the user doing something with a control on the screen. For example, if you want to know when a button has been tapped, you create an action method and connect the button to that method. You create similar action methods for events such as the text in a text field changing, or a slider changing position.

Action methods are defined in the `@interface` of a class, like this:

```
@IBAction func buttonPressed(_ sender: AnyObject) {
```

Xcode uses the `IBAction` attribute to identify methods that can be connected to views in the Interface Builder.

In the preceding example, the action method takes a single parameter: an object called `sender`. This object will be the object that triggered the action: the button that was tapped, the text field that was edited, and so on.

If you don't care about the sender of the action, you can just define the method with no parameters, like so:

```
@IBAction func actionWithNoParameters() {

}
```

2.3 Using Segues to Move Between Screens

Problem

You want to use segues to transition between different screens.

Solution

We'll step through the creation of two view controllers, and show how to create and use segues to move between them:

1. Create a new single-view project.

2. Open *Main.storyboard*.

3. Add a new view controller.

   You can do this by searching for "view controller" in the Object Library.

4. Add a button to the first view controller.

   Label it "Automatic Segue."

5. Add a segue from the button to the second view controller.

   Hold down the Control key, and drag from the button to the second view controller. A menu will appear when you finish dragging, which shows the possible types of segues you can use. Choose "present modally."

6. Run the application.

   When you tap the button, the second (empty) view controller will appear.

Currently, there's no way to return to the first one. We'll now address this:

1. Open *ViewController.swift*.

   This is the class that powers the first screen.

2. Add an exit method.

   Add the following method to ViewController's code:

   ```
   @IBAction func closePopup(_ segue: UIStoryboardSegue) {
       NSLog("Second view controller was closed!")
   }
   ```

3. Add an exit button to the second view controller.

   Add a button to the second view controller, and label it "Exit."

   Then, hold down the Control key, and drag from the button to the Exit icon above the screen. It looks like a little orange rectangle.

   A menu will appear, listing the possible actions that can be run. Choose "closePopupWithSegue."

4. Run the application.

   Open the pop-up screen, and then tap the Exit button. The screen will disappear, and the console will show the "Second view controller was closed!" text.

Finally, we'll demonstrate how to manually trigger a segue from code. To do this, we'll first need a named segue in order to trigger it. One already exists—you created it when you linked the button to the second view controller:

1. Give the segue an identifier.

   In order to be triggered, a segue must have a name. Click the segue you created when you linked the button to the second view controller (i.e., the line connecting the first view controller to the second).

   In the Attributes Inspector (choose View→Utilities→Show Attributes Inspector, or press Command-Option-4), set the identifier of the segue to "ShowPopup," as shown in Figure 2-14.

Figure 2-14. Naming the segue

Make sure you use the same capitalization as we've used here. "ShowPopup" isn't the same as "showpopup" or even "ShowPopUp."

2. Add a button that manually triggers the segue.

Add a new button to the first view controller. Label it "Manual Segue."

Open *ViewController.swift* in the Assistant editor.

Hold down the Control key, and drag from the new button into the View Controller's code. Using the dialog box that appears, create a new action method called showPopup—note the capitalization.

Add the following code to this new method:

```
@IBAction func showPopup(_ sender: AnyObject) {
    self.performSegue(withIdentifier: "ShowPopup",
        sender: self)
}
```

3. Run the application.

Now, tapping the Manual Segue button shows the second screen.

Discussion

A segue is an object that describes a transition from one view controller to the next.

When you run a segue, the segue takes care of presenting the new view controller for you. For example, if you create a push segue, the segue will handle creating the view controller and pushing the new view controller onto the navigation controller's stack.

A segue performs its work of transitioning between view controllers when it's *triggered*. There are two ways you can trigger a segue: you can connect it to a button in the Interface Builder, or you can trigger it from code.

When you hold down the Control key and drag from a button to a different screen, you create a segue. This new segue is set up to be triggered when the button is tapped.

Triggering a segue from code is easy. First, you need to give the segue an *identifier*, which is a string that uniquely identifies the segue. In our example, we set the identifier of the segue to "ShowPopup."

Once that's done, you use the `performSegue(withIdentifier:, sender:)` method. This method takes two parameters—the name of the segue you want to trigger, and the object that was responsible for triggering it.

You can trigger any segue from code, as long as it has an identifier. You don't need to create multiple segues from one view controller to the next.

When a view controller is about to segue to another, the view controller that's about to disappear is sent the `prepare(for:, sender:)` message. When you want to know about the next screen that's about to be shown to the user, you implement this method, like so:

```
override func prepare(for segue: UIStoryboardSegue, sender: Any?) {
    if let identifier = segue.identifier {
        NSLog("About to run \(identifier)")
    }
}
```

The method has two parameters: the segue that's about to run, and the object that triggered the segue. The segue object itself contains two particularly useful properties: the `identifier` of the segue, which allows you to differentiate between segues; and the `destinationViewController`, which is the view controller that's about to be displayed by the segue. This gives you an opportunity to send information to the screen that's about to appear.

Finally, *exit segues* are segues that allow you to return to a previously viewed view controller. You don't create these segues yourself; rather, you define an action method in the view controller that you'd like to return *to*, and then connect a control to the "exit" segue in the Interface Builder.

2.4 Using Constraints to Lay Out Views

Problem

You have a screen with another view (such as a button) inside it. You want the views to stay in the correct places when the screen rotates.

Solution

You use *constraints* to position views, as illustrated here:

1. Drag the view into the place you'd like to put it.

2. Add the constraint.

   Select the view, and open the Add New Constraints menu. This is the second button from the right, in the group of buttons at the bottom right of the Interface Builder canvas. It looks like a little square with in between two vertical lines.

3. Apply the values you want to use for the new constraints.

   Let's assume that you want the view to always be 20 pixels from the top edge of the screen and 20 points from the left edge of the screen. Additionally, you want the righthand edge of the label to always be *at least* 20 points from the right edge, but if the text is short (or the screen is wide), then a distance of more than 20 pixels is allowed. This will have the effect of aligning the label to the lefthand edge of the screen, while preventing it from running off the edge of the screen if the text is too long. This is shown in Figure 2-15.

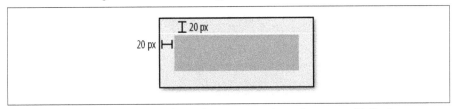

Figure 2-15. The view should always be 20 points from the top and left edges

Type **20** into the top field, **20** into the right field, and **20** into the left field (Figure 2-16).

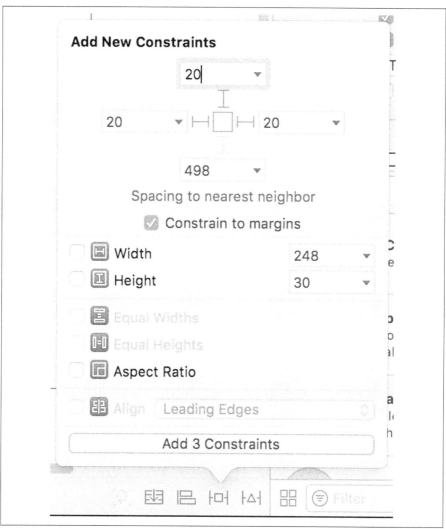

Figure 2-16. Creating the constraints

4. Add the constraints.

   The button at the bottom of the menu should now read "Add 3 Constraints." Click it, and the button will be locked to the upper-right corner.

5. Adjust the trailing constraint.

   As it currently stands, the view's top, left, and right edges are constrained to always be 20 points away from the screen edge. This has the effect of making the view grow in width to fit the screen; for example, if the screen rotates, then the screen's width grows, and the view will grow with it. Depending on your circumstances, this may be what you want, but if you want the view to remain the *same* width, you'll need to tell either the left or right constraint that it should grow. In this example, let's make the view left-aligned, which means indicating that the right constraint should grow.

Select the righthand constraint, and go to Attributes Inspector (the fourth icon at the top of the righthand pane). Change the constraint's Relation to Greater Than or Equal (Figure 2-17).

 You can now verify the behavior of your constraints by changing the presentation of the canvas. To do this, click the View As button at the lower-left of the canvas, and choose a different device or orientation. The canvas will update to show how the views would be positioned and sized under the new circumstances.

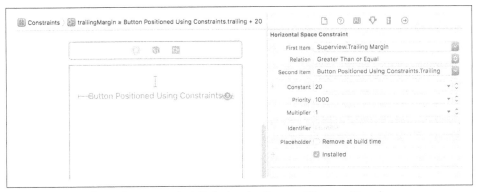

Figure 2-17. Making the constraint's Relation be Greater Than or Equal

Discussion

To control the positioning and sizing of views, you use constraints. Constraints are rules that are imposed on views, along the lines of "Keep the top edge 10 points beneath the top edge of the container," or "Always be half the width of the screen." Without constraints, views don't change position when the size and shape of their superview changes shape (such as when the screen rotates).

Constraints can modify both the position and the size of a view, and will change these in order to make the view fit the rules.

Another way that you can add constraints to views is to Control-drag from the view you want to constrain to another view. A pop-up menu will appear that lets you select the specific type of constraint you want to add. The specific types available for selection depend on the position of the two views; for example, when you have two buttons side by side, if you Control-drag from one to the other, you will be offered the option to constrain the horizontal space between the two.

2.5 Adding Images to Your Project

Problem

You want to add images to your game's project in Xcode, so that they can be used in your menu interface.

Solution

When you create a new project in Xcode, an *asset catalog* is created, which contains your images. Your code can then get images from the catalog, or you can use them in your interface.

By default, projects come with an asset catalog called `Assets.xcassets`. If your project doesn't have one, or if you want a new one, choose File→New→File, choose Resource, and choose Asset Catalog.

Select the asset catalog in the Project Navigator, and then drag and drop your image into the catalog.

You can rename individual images by double-clicking the name of the image in the left pane of the asset catalog.

The easiest way to display an image is through a `UIImageView`. To add an image view, search for "image view" in the Object Library, and add one to your screen. Then, select the new image view, open the Attributes Inspector, and change the Image property to the name of the image you added (Figure 2-18).

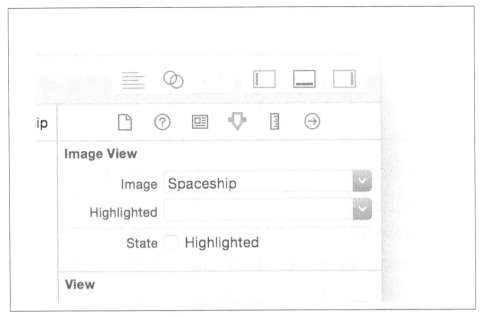

Figure 2-18. Setting the image for a UIImageView

You can also use images in your code. For example, if you've added an image called "Spaceship" to an asset catalog, you can use it in your code as follows:

```
let image = UIImage(named: "Spaceship")
```

Once you have this image, you can display it in a `UIImageView`, display it as a sprite, or load it as a texture.

Discussion

It's often the case that you'll need to use different versions of an image under different circumstances. The most common example of this is when dealing with apps that target larget iPhone devices, such as the iPhone 6 Plus, 7 Plus and 8 Plus, which have a larger and denser screen. On these devices, one point is three pixels, while on other devices, one point is two pixels.

Fortunately, asset catalogs make this rather straightforward. When you add an image to the catalog, you can add alternative representations of the same image, making available both 2x and 3x versions of the image. You can also add specific versions of an image for the iPhone and iPad; when you get the image by name, the correct version of the image is returned to you, which saves you having to write code that checks to see which platform your game is running on.

2.6 Slicing Images for Use in Buttons

Problem

You want to customize a button with images. Additionally, you want the image to not get distorted when the button changes size.

Solution

To apply an image to a button, you can use any image file that's in your project, including images in asset catalogs. If an image is inside an asset catalog, you can mark which parts of the image are allowed to be stretched, by *slicing* the image. This helps to prevent distortions when the button isn't exactly the same size as the image.

To customize your button, perform the following steps:

1. Add the image you want to use to an asset catalog.

    See Recipe 2.5 to learn how to do this.

2. Select the newly added image, and click Show Slicing.

    The button is at the bottom right of the asset catalog's view.

3. Click Start Slicing.

    Choose one of the slicing options. You can slice the image horizontally, vertically, or both horizontally and vertically, as shown in Figure 2-19.

4. Open your storyboard and select the button you want to theme.

5. Open the Attributes Inspector and set the background.

    Select the name of the image that you added to the Xcode catalog. The button will change to use the new background image. You can also resize the image, and the background image will scale appropriately.

Discussion

One of the most effective ways to customize the look and feel of your game's user interface is to use custom images for buttons and other controls, which you can do by setting the Background property of your buttons.

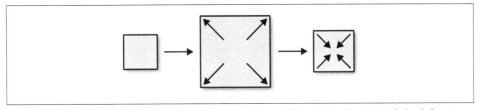

Figure 2-19. The available slicing options are, from left to right, horizontal, both horizontal and vertical, and vertical

However, if you want to use background images, you need to take into account the size of the controls you're theming: if you create an image that's 200 pixels wide and try to use it on a button that's only 150 pixels wide, your image will be squashed. Do the reverse, and you'll end up with a repeating background, which may look worse.

To solve this issue, you can *slice* your images. Slicing divides your image into multiple regions, of which only some are allowed to squash and stretch or repeat. When a sliced image is resized, only the central regions of the image - as defined by you in the image editor - will stretch. The rest will remain the same size, and won't stretch.

In this solution, we looked at customizing a button; however, the same principles apply to other controls as well.

2.7 Using UI Dynamics to Make Animated Views

Problem

You want to make the views on your screen move around the screen realistically.

Solution

You can add physical behaviors to any view inside a view controller, using UIDynamicAnimator. In these examples, we'll assume that you've got a view called animatedView. It can be of any type—button, image, or anything else you like.

First, create a UIDynamicAnimator object in your view controller. Add this property to your view controller's class:

```
var animator : UIDynamicAnimator?
```

Then, in your view controller's viewDidLoad method, add the following code:

```
self.animator = UIDynamicAnimator(referenceView: self.view)
```

We'll now talk about how you can add different kinds of physical behaviors to your views. Because these behaviors interact with each other, we'll go through each one and, in each case, assume that the previous behaviors have been added.

Adding gravity to views

Add the following code to your `viewDidLoad` method:

```
let gravity = UIGravityBehavior(items: [self.animatedView])

self.animator?.addBehavior(gravity)
```

Run the application. The view will move down the screen (and eventually fall off!).

Adding collision

Add the following code to your `viewDidLoad` method:

```
let collision = UICollisionBehavior(items: [self.animatedView])

collision.translatesReferenceBoundsIntoBoundary = true

self.animator?.addBehavior(collision)
```

Run the application. The button will fall to the bottom of the screen.

 By default, the collision boundaries will be the same as the boundaries of the container view. This is what's set when `translatesReferenceBoundsIntoBoundary` is changed to `true`. If you would prefer to create boundaries that are inset from the container view, use `setTranslatesReferenceBoundsIntoBoundary( with:)` instead:

```
collision.setTranslatesReferenceBoundsIntoBoundary(
    with: UIEdgeInsets(top: 10,
                       left: 10,
                       bottom: 10,
                       right: 10))
```

Adding attachment

Add the following code to your `viewDidLoad` method:

```
// Anchor = top of the screen, centered
let anchor = CGPoint(x: self.view.bounds.width / 2, y: 0)

let attachment = UIAttachmentBehavior(item: self.animatedView,
    attachedToAnchor: anchor)

self.animator?.addBehavior(attachment)
```

Run the application. The button will swing down and hit the side of the screen.

Move your button to the left or right side of the screen before running. If it's right in the middle of the screen, it won't have anywhere to swing to.

When you create a `UIAttachmentBehavior`, you can attach your views to specific points, or to other views. If you want to attach your view to a point, you should use `UIAttachmentBehavior(item:, attachedToAnchor:)`, as shown in the previous example. If you want to attach a view to another view, you use `UIAttachmentBehavior(item:, attachedToItem:)`, and provide another view as the second parameter.

Discussion

UIKit has a physics engine in it, which you can use to create a complex set of physically realistic behaviors.

The dynamic animation system is designed for user interfaces, rather than games—if you're interested in using physics simulation for games, use SpriteKit (see Chapter 6).

Keep in mind that controls that move around too much may end up being disorienting for users, who are used to buttons generally remaining in one place. Additionally, if you're displaying your UI content on top of your game, you may end up with performance problems if you have lots of controls that use the dynamic animation system.

2.8 Moving an Image with Core Animation

Problem

You want an image to move around the screen, and smoothly change its position over time.

Solution

To animate your image, follow these steps:

1. Create a new single-view application for iPhone, named `ImageAnimation`.
2. Add an image of a ball to the project (one has been provided as part of the sample code):
   - Open *Main.storyboard*.
   - Add an image view to the screen. Set it to display the image you dragged in.

- Connect the image view to an outlet called `ball` in your view controller's code (see Recipe 2.2).

- Open *ViewController.swift*.

- Add the following method to the `viewDidLoad` method:

```
UIView.animate(withDuration: 2.0, animations: { () -> Void in
    self.ball.center = CGPoint(x: 0, y: 0)
})
```

3. Run the application.

When the app starts up, the ball will slowly move up to the upper-left corner of the screen.

Discussion

This application instructs a `UIImageView` to change its position over the course of two seconds.

Image views, being completely passive displays of images, have no means (nor any reason) to move around on their own, which means that something else needs to do it for them. That "something else" is the view controller, which is responsible for managing each view that's displayed on the screen.

For the view controller to be able to tell the image view to move, it first needs an outlet to that image view. An outlet is a variable in an object that connects to a view. When you hold the Control key and drag and drop from the image view into the code, Xcode recognizes that you want to add a connection and displays the "add connection" dialog.

When the application launches, the first thing that happens is that all connections that were created in the Interface Builder are set up. This means that all of your code is able to refer to properties like `self.ball` without having to actually do any of the work involved in setting them up.

Once the connection is established, the real work of moving the ball around on the screen is done in the `viewWillAppear:` method. This method is called, as you can probably tell from the name, when the view (i.e., the screen) is about to appear to the user. This snippet of code is where the actual work is done:

```
UIView.animate(withDuration: 2.0, animations: { () -> Void in
    self.ball.center = CGPoint(x: 0, y: 0)
})
```

The `animate(withDuration:, animations:)` method takes two parameters: the duration of the animation, and a block that performs the changes that should be seen during the animation.

In this case, the animation being run takes two seconds to complete, and a single change is made: the `center` property of whatever view `self.ball` refers to is changed to the point (0,0). Additional changes can be included as well. For example, try adding the following line of code between the two curly braces ({}):

```
self.ball.alpha = 0.0
```

This change causes the view's alpha setting (its opacity) to change from whatever value it currently is to zero, which renders it fully transparent. Because this change is run at the same time as the change to the view's position, it will fade out while moving.

2.9 Rotating an Image View

Problem

You want to rotate an image on the screen.

Solution

To rotate an image view, use the `transform` property:

```
self.transformedView.transform =
    CGAffineTransform(rotationAngle: CGFloat(Double.pi / 2))
```

In this example, `self.transformedView` is a `UIImageView`. Any view can be rotated, though, not just image views.

Discussion

The `transform` property allows you to modify a view's presentation without affecting its contents. This allows you to rotate, shift, squash, and stretch a view however you want.

The value of `transform` is a `CGAffineTransform`, which is a 3-by-3 matrix of numbers. This matrix is multiplied against the four vertices that define the four corners of the view. The default transform is the identity transform, `CGAffineTransformIdentity`, which makes no changes to the presentation of the view.

To create a transform matrix that rotates a view, you use the `CGAffineTransform(rotationAngle:)` method. This method takes a single parameter: the amount to rotate by, measured in radians. There are 2π radians in a circle; therefore, a rotation of one-quarter of a circle is $2\pi/4 = \pi/2$.

In our example, we have created a transform matrix using the `CGAffine Transform(rotationAngle:)` function. Other initializers you can use include:

`CGAffineTransform(translationX: , y: )`
> Adjusts the position of the view.

`CGAffineTransform(scaleX:, y: )`
> Scales the view on the horizontal or vertical axis.

In addition to creating transform matrices that apply a rotation, translation or scale, you can also modify an existing matrix. For example, you can create a matrix that scales, and modify it to include rotation, which produces a single matrix that scales *and* rotates.

You can do this using the `scaledBy(x:, y: )`, `translatedBy(x:, y: )`, and `rota ted(by:)` functions, which each take an existing transform and modify it. Once you're done making changes to the transform, you can then apply it.

For example:

```
var transform = CGAffineTransform.identity ❶
transform = transform.translatedBy(x: 50, y: 0) ❷
transform = transform.rotated(by: CGFloat(Double.pi / 2)) ❸
transform = transform.scaledBy(x: 0.5, y: 2) ❹

self.transformedView.transform = transform ❺
```

This code does the following:

❶ Start with the default identity transform.

❷ Translate the transform 50 pixels to the right.

❸ Rotate the transform one quarter-circle clockwise.

❹ Scale the transform by 50% on the horizontal axis and 200% on the vertical axis.

❺ Apply the transform to a view.

The `transform` property of a view can be animated, just like its opacity and position. This lets you create animations where views rotate or squash and stretch.

2.10 Animating a Popping Effect on a View

Problem

You want the main menu of your game to feature buttons that appear with a visually appealing "pop" animation, which draws the player's eye (the object starts small, expands to a large size, and then shrinks back down to its normal size, as shown in Figure 2-20).

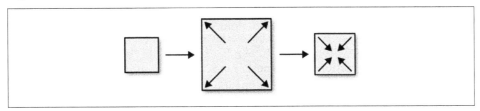

Figure 2-20. A "pop" animation

Solution

The solution to this problem makes use of features available in the Quartz Core framework. To use this framework, add this line near the top of your code:

```
import QuartzCore
```

Finally, add the following code at the point where you want the popping animation to happen:

```
let keyframeAnimation = CAKeyframeAnimation(keyPath: "transform.scale")

keyframeAnimation.keyTimes = [0.0, 0.7, 1.0]

keyframeAnimation.values = [0.0, 1.2, 1.0]

keyframeAnimation.duration = 0.4

keyframeAnimation.timingFunction =
    CAMediaTimingFunction(name: CAMediaTimingFunctionName.easeOut)

self.poppingView.layer.add(keyframeAnimation, forKey: "pop")
```

In this example, `self.poppingView` is a `UIView`, but any view can be animated in this way.

Discussion

Every single view on the screen can be animated using Core Animation. These animations can be very simple, such as moving an item from one location to another, or they can be more complex, such as a multiple-stage "pop" animation.

You can achieve this behavior using a `CAKeyframeAnimation`. `CAKeyframeAnimations` allow you to change a visual property of any view over time, and through multiple stages. You do this by creating a CAKeyframeAnimation, providing it with the values that the property should animate through, and providing corresponding timing information for each value. Finally, you give the animation object to the view's CALayer, and the view will perform the animation.

Every animation object must have a "key path" that indicates what value should change when the animation runs. The key path used for this animation is transform.scale, which indicates that the animation should be modifying the scale of the view.

The values property is an array that contains the values that the animation should move through. In this animation, there are three values: 0, 1.2, and 1.0. These will be used as the scale values: the animation will start with a scale of zero (i.e., scaled down to nothing), then expand to 1.2 times the normal size, and then shrink back down to the normal size.

The keyTimes property is another array that must contain the same number of numbers as there are values in the values array. Each number in the keyTimes array indicates at which point the corresponding value in the values array will be reached. Each key time is given as a value from 0 to 1, with 0 being the start of the animation and 1 being the end.

In this case, the second value (1.2) will be reached at 70% of the way through the animation, because its corresponding key time is 0.7. This is done to make the first phase of the animation, in which the button expands from nothing, take a good amount of time, which will look more natural.

The duration of the animation is set to 0.4 seconds, and the timing function is set to "ease out." This means that the "speed" of the animation will slow down toward the end. Again, this makes the animation feel more organic and less mechanical.

Lastly, the animation is given to the view's layer using the addAnimation(_, forKey:) method. The "key" in this method is any string you want—it's an identifier to let you access the animation at a later time.

2.11 Theming UI Elements with UIAppearance

Problem

You want to change the color of views, or use background images to customize their look and feel.

Solution

You can set the color of a view by changing its tint color or by giving it a background image:

```
self.button.tintColor = UIColor.red

let image = UIImage(named: "Ball")
self.button.setBackgroundImage(image,
                          for: UIControl.State.normal)
```

You can also set the tint color for most views in the Attributes Inspector.

Discussion

Many controls can be themed. There are two main ways you can change a control's appearance:

- Set a *tint color*, which sets the overall color of the control.
- Set a *background image*, which sets a background image.

To set a tint color for a specific control, you call one of the `setTintColor:` methods. Some controls have a single tint color, which you set with `setTintColor:`, while other controls can have multiple tint colors, which you set independently. For example, to tint a `UIProgressView`, do the following:

```
self.progressView.progressTintColor = UIColor.orange
```

You can also set the tint color for *all* controls of a given type, by accessing its *appearance proxy*. The appearance proxy is an object that you get from a class that has all of the same appearance-controlling properties—things like tint colors and background images—but applies those properties to *all* instances of that class. For example, to set *all* progress views to use purple as their progress tint color:

```
UIProgressView.appearance().progressTintColor = UIColor.purple
```

Background images for navigation bars work similarly:

```
UINavigationBar.appearance()
    .setBackgroundImage(image,
                        for: UIBarMetrics.default)
```

2.12 Rotating a UIView in 3D

Problem

You want to make a view rotate in 3D, and have a perspective effect as it does so (i.e., as parts of the view move away from the user, they get smaller, and as they get closer, they get larger).

Solution

To implement this functionality, you'll need to import the QuartzCore module at the top of your source code, just as in Recipe 2.10.

Then, when you want the animation to begin, you do this:

```
let animation = CABasicAnimation(keyPath: "transform.rotation.y")

animation.fromValue = 0.0
animation.toValue = .pi * 2.0

animation.repeatCount = Float.infinity
animation.duration = 2.0

self.rotatingView.layer.add(animation, forKey: "spin")

var transform = CATransform3DIdentity
transform.m34 = 1.0 / 500.0
self.rotatingView.layer.transform = transform
```

To stop the animation, you do this:

```
self.rotatingView.layer.removeAnimation(forKey: "spin")
```

 In this example code, `self.rotatingView` is a `UIView` that's on the screen. This technique can be applied to any view, though—buttons, image views, and so on.

Discussion

`CABasicAnimation` allows you to animate a property of a view from one value to another. In the case of rotating a view, the property that we want to animate is its rotation, and the values we want to animate from and to are angles.

When you use `CABasicAnimation(keyPath:)` to create the animation, you specify the property you want to animate. In this case, the one we want is the rotation around the y-axis:

```
let animation = CABasicAnimation(keyPath: "transform.rotation.y")
```

The animation is then configured. In this example, we made the rotation start from zero, and proceed through to a full circle. In Core Animation, angles are measured in radians, and there are 2π radians in a full circle. So, the fromValue and toValue are set thusly:

```
animation.fromValue = 0.0
animation.toValue = .pi * 2.0
```

Next, the animation is told that it should repeat an infinite number of times, and that the full rotation should take two seconds:

```
animation.repeatCount = Float.infinity
animation.duration = 2.0
```

You start the animation by adding it to the view's layer, using the add(animation:, forKey:) method. This method takes two parameters, the animation object that you want to use and a key (or name) to use to refer to the animation:

```
self.rotatingView.layer.add(animation, forKey: "spin")
```

Don't be confused by the similarity between the "key" that you use when you add the animation and the "key path" you use when creating the animation. The former is just a name you give the animation, and can be anything; the key path describes exactly what the animation modifies.

The last step is to give the rotating view a little perspective. If you run the code while omitting the last few lines, you'll end up with a view that appears to horizontally squash and stretch. What you want is for the edge that's approaching the user's eye to appear to get bigger, while the edge that's moving away from the user's eye appears to get smaller.

You do this by modifying the view's 3D transform. By default, all views have a transform matrix applied to them that makes them all lie flat over each other. When you want something to have perspective, though, this doesn't apply, and you need to override it:

```
var transform = CATransform3DIdentity
transform.m34 = 1.0 / 500.0
self.rotatingView.layer.transform = transform
```

The key to this part of the code is the second line: the one where the m34 field of the transform is updated. This part of the transform controls the sharpness of the perspective. (It's basically how much the z coordinate gets scaled toward or away from the vanishing point as it moves closer to or farther from the "camera.")

2.13 Overlaying Menus on Top of Game Content

Problem

You want to overlay controls and views on top of your existing game content. For example, you want to overlay a pause menu, or put UIButtons on top of sprites. Additionally, you want to keep the interface for the pause menu in a separate file.

Solution

You can overlay any UIView you like on top of any other UIView. Additionally, both OpenGL views and SpriteKit views are actually UIViews, which means anything can be overlaid on them.

To create a view that you can show, you can use *nibs*. A nib is like a storyboard, but only contains a single view.

To make a nib, choose File→New→File from the menu, choose User Interface, and choose View. Save the new file wherever you like. You can then edit the file and design your interface.

To instantiate the nib and use the interface you've designed, you first create a UINib object by loading it from disk, and then ask the nib to instantiate itself. This is typically done in viewDidLoad, because it's your first opportunity to prepare the contents of a view after the main view has loaded.

```
// Load the nib
let nib = UINib(nibName: "PauseMenu", bundle: nil)

// Instantiate a copy of the objects stored in the nib
let loadedObjects = nib.instantiate(withOwner: self,
    options: nil)
```

 The name of the nib file must be the same as the nibName string parameter (which doesn't include the .xib file extension).

The instantiate(withOwner:, options:) method returns an array that contains the objects that you've designed. If you've followed these instructions and created a nib with a single view, this array will contain a single object—the UIView object that you designed. Once you have this, you can add this view to your view controller using the addSubview: method:

```
// Try to get the first object, as a UIView
if let pauseMenuView = loadedObjects[0] as? UIView {
```

```
        // Add it to the screen and center it
        self.view.addSubview(pauseMenuView)
        pauseMenuView.center = self.view.center
    }
```

Discussion

Keep in mind that if you overlay a view on top of SpriteKit or OpenGL, you'll see a performance decrease. This is because the Core Animation system, which is responsible for compositing views together, has to do extra work to combine UIKit views with raw OpenGL.

That's not to say that you shouldn't ever do it, but be mindful of the possible performance penalty.

Additionally, keep in mind that the default background color for views is white, which will cover up everything behind it. If you want the view to be transparent, don't forget to change the background color to clear.

2.14 Designing Effective Game Menus

Problem

You want to build a game that uses menus effectively.

Solution

You should make your menus as simple and easy to navigate as possible. There's nothing worse than an iOS game that has an overly complicated menu structure, or tries to present too many options to the player. Menus should be simple and have the minimum amount of options required to make your game work.

Including only the minimum required set of options will make players feel more confident and in control of the game—ideally they'll be able to play through your entire game without ever using any menus beyond those necessary to start and end the game. And those menus should be super simple too!

Discussion

It's important to keep your game menus as simple as possible. When your game is the app running on a device, a simple and clear menu will ensure that the user is more likely to be playing the game than trying to configure it. You're building a game, not an elaborate set of menus!

CHAPTER 3
Input

Without a way to collect input from the user, your game is nothing but a pretty graphics demo. In this chapter, we'll look at common tasks that games often need to perform in order to get input from their players. The only way that a game can know about what the user wants to do is via the input that it collects, and the main way that the player provides that input is through the device's built-in touchscreen.

Behind the scenes, a touchscreen is a very complex piece of technology. However, the information that it provides to your game is rather simple: you get told when a touch lands on the screen, when a touch moves, and when a touch is lifted from the screen. This might not sound like much—everyone knows you can detect taps, for example— but the touch system built into iOS is able to use this information to determine when the user is dragging, pinching, rotating, and flicking, all of which can be used to interpret the user's will.

In addition to the touch system, iOS devices have a number of built-in sensors that detect the current state of the hardware. These include an accelerometer (which detects force and movement), a gyroscope (which detects rotation), a magnetometer (which detects magnetic fields), and a receiver for the Global Positioning System, or GPS (which can calculate where on the planet the device is).

You can combine all of this information to learn a great deal about what the user's doing with the device, which can be used as input to your game. For example, it's possible to determine the user's speed by observing the distance traveled over time, which can give you an idea of whether the player is in a vehicle—which you can then use as part of your game's input.

3.1 Detecting When a View Is Touched

Problem

You want to know when the user touches a view.

Solution

You can override certain UIView methods that get called when a touch begins, moves, ends, and is cancelled.

Put this code in your view controller, or in your UIView subclasses:

```
override func touchesBegan(_ touches: Set<UITouch>, with event: UIEvent?) {
    for touch in touches {
        NSLog("A touch began at \(touch.location(in: self.view))")
    }
}

override func touchesMoved(_ touches: Set<UITouch>, with event: UIEvent?) {
    for touch in touches {
        NSLog("A touch moved at \(touch.location(in: self.view))")
    }
}

override func touchesEnded(_ touches: Set<UITouch>, with event: UIEvent?) {
    for touch in touches {
        NSLog("A touch ended at \(touch.location(in: self.view))")
    }
}

override func touchesCancelled(_ touches: Set<UITouch>, with event: UIEvent?) {
    for touch in touches {
        NSLog("A touch was cancelled at \(touch.location(in: self.view))")
    }
}
```

Discussion

A touch can be in one of four states:

Began
: The touch just landed on the screen.

Moved
: The touch moved from one location to another. (The related method is often called multiple times over the life of a touch.)

Ended
: The touch was lifted from the screen.

Cancelled
> The touch was interrupted by something, such as a gesture recognizer claiming the touch for itself (Recipe 3.2).

When a touch lands on the screen, iOS first determines which view should be responsible for handling that touch. It does this by first determining where the touch landed on the screen, and which view happens to contain that point; second, it determines if this view, or any of its subviews, is capable of handling the touch. This is determined by checking to see if the view (or any of its subviews) has implemented any of the touchesBegan, touchesMoved, touchesEnded, or touchesCancelled methods.

Each of these methods is called when a touch that belongs to the view changes state; because several touches can change state at the same time (e.g., two fingers being moved simultaneously over a view), each of the methods takes a Set that contains each of the UITouch objects that recently changed state.

3.2 Responding to Tap Gestures

Problem

You want to detect when the user taps a view.

Solution

A tap is when a finger lands on a view, and then lifts back up without having moved.

Use a UIGestureRecognizer (specifically, UITapGestureRecognizer):

```
override func viewDidLoad() {
    super.viewDidLoad()

    let tap = UITapGestureRecognizer(target: self,
        action: #selector(ViewController.tap(tapRecognizer:)))

    // In this case, we're adding it to the view controllers'
    // view, but you can add it to any view
    self.view.addGestureRecognizer(tap)
}

@objc func tap(tapRecognizer : UITapGestureRecognizer) {
    if tapRecognizer.state == UIGestureRecognizer.State.ended {
        NSLog("View was tapped!")
    }
}
```

Discussion

Gesture recognizers are objects that you can attach to views that look for specific patterns of touches, such as pinches, taps, and drags.

`UITapGestureRecognizer` is a gesture recognizer that looks for taps—that is, a touch landing and then being lifted up quickly, without moving. Taps are the most common gesture performed on the iPhone or iPad.

When the gesture recognizer detects that the user has performed the gesture that it's looking for, it sends a message to a target object. You specify the message and the target object when you create the recognizer.

In this example, the message that's sent is `tap`. This method needs to be implemented on the target object (in this example, `self`). The method takes one parameter, which is the gesture recognizer itself.

By default, a Tap Gesture Recognizer looks for a single finger that taps one time. However, you can configure the recognizer so that it looks for multiple taps (such as double taps, triple taps, or even the fabled quadruple tap), or taps with more than one finger at the same time (e.g., two-finger taps). These can also be combined to create, for example, double-fingered double-taps:

```
tap.numberOfTapsRequired = 2 // double tap
tap.numberOfTouchesRequired = 2 // with two fingers
```

 If you set up a gesture recognizer as in Recipe 3.1, you can see touches transitioning to the Canceled state when a touch recognizer claims them.

3.3 Dragging an Image Around the Screen

Problem

You want to let the user directly manipulate the position of an image on the screen by dragging it around.

Solution

In this example, `self.draggedView` is a property that connects to a `UIView`. It can be any type of view that you like, but image views work particularly well:

```
override func viewDidLoad() {
    super.viewDidLoad()

    self.draggedView.isUserInteractionEnabled = true
```

```
    let dragged = #selector(ViewController.dragged(dragGesture:))

    let drag = UIPanGestureRecognizer(target: self,
                                      action: dragged)
    self.draggedView.addGestureRecognizer(drag)
}

@objc func dragged(dragGesture: UIPanGestureRecognizer) {

    if dragGesture.state == .began ||
        dragGesture.state == .changed {

        var newPosition = dragGesture.translation(in: dragGesture.view)

        newPosition.x += dragGesture.view!.center.x
        newPosition.y += dragGesture.view!.center.y

        dragGesture.view!.center = newPosition

        dragGesture.setTranslation(CGPoint.zero,
                                   in: dragGesture.view)
    }

}
```

Discussion

This code uses a gesture recognizer to detect and handle the user dragging a finger over the screen (a drag is when the user places a single finger on the screen within the bounds of the view, and then begins moving that finger).

The first thing that happens in this code is this:

```
    self.draggedView.isUserInteractionEnabled = true
```

It's possible that the view may have interaction disabled by default. Some views do this, including UIImageViews. So, to be sure that it's going to work correctly, the view is set to allow user interaction.

The next two lines create and add the gesture recognizer:

```
    let dragged = #selector(ViewController.dragged(dragGesture:))

    let drag = UIPanGestureRecognizer(target: self,
                                      action: dragged)
    self.draggedView.addGestureRecognizer(drag)
```

The dragged method is called when the recognizer changes state. For dragging, there are two states that we want to know about: when the drag begins, and when the drag changes. In both cases, we need to do the following:

---

1. Determine how much the drag has moved by.

2. Figure out where the view is on the screen.

3. Decide where it should now be, by adding the movement to the current position.

4. Make the view's position be this new position.

Pan gesture recognizers expose a value called *translation*, which is the amount of movement that they've seen. This value allows your code to work out a new position for the view:

```swift
@objc func dragged(dragGesture: UIPanGestureRecognizer) {

    if dragGesture.state == .began ||
        dragGesture.state == .changed {

        var newPosition = dragGesture.translation(in: dragGesture.view)

        newPosition.x += dragGesture.view!.center.x
        newPosition.y += dragGesture.view!.center.y

        dragGesture.view!.center = newPosition

        dragGesture.setTranslation(CGPoint.zero,
                                    in: dragGesture.view)
    }

}
```

The translation value needs to be manually reset once you've done this, because when the gesture recognizer next updates, you want to update the view's position from its current position rather than its starting position.

3.4 Detecting Rotation Gestures

Problem

You want to let the user use two fingers to rotate something on the screen.

Solution

Use a `UIRotationGestureRecognizer`:

```swift
class ViewController: UIViewController {

    @IBOutlet weak var rotationView: UIView!
    @IBOutlet weak var rotationStatusLabel: UILabel!

    // The current angle of the rotation, in radians
    var angle : Float = 0.0
```

```swift
    // Converts self.angle from radians to degrees,
    // and wrap around at 360 degrees
    var angleDegrees : Float {
        get {
            return (self.angle * 180.0 / .pi)
                .truncatingRemainder(dividingBy: 360)
        }
    }

    override func viewDidLoad() {
        super.viewDidLoad()

        let rotated = #selector(ViewController.rotated(rotationGesture:))

        // Set up the rotation gesture
        let rotationGesture = UIRotationGestureRecognizer(target: self,
                                                          action: rotated)

        self.rotationView.isUserInteractionEnabled = true
        self.rotationView.addGestureRecognizer(rotationGesture)

        self.rotationStatusLabel?.text = "\(self.angleDegrees)°"
    }

    // When the rotation changes, update self.angle
    // and use that to rotate the view
    @objc func rotated(rotationGesture : UIRotationGestureRecognizer) {

        switch rotationGesture.state {

        case .changed:
            self.angle += Float(rotationGesture.rotation)

            rotationGesture.rotation = 0.0

            self.rotationView.transform =
                CGAffineTransform(rotationAngle: CGFloat(self.angle))

        default: () // do nothing

        }

        // Display the rotation
        self.rotationStatusLabel?.text = "\(self.angleDegrees)°"

    }

}
```

Discussion

The `UIRotationGestureRecognizer` is a *continuous* gesture recognizer (in other words, unlike a tap, rotation starts, changes over time, and then ends).

When a rotation gesture recognizer realizes that the user has begun a rotation—that is, when the user has placed two fingers on the view and begun to rotate them around a central point—it sends its target the message that it was configured with when it was created.

This method then checks the current state of the recognizer, and reacts accordingly. Recognizers can be in several different states. The states relevant to the rotation gesture recognizer are the following:

`UIGestureRecognizerState.began`
> The recognizer enters this state when it determines that a rotation gesture is in progress.

`UIGestureRecognizerState.changed`
> This state is entered when the angle of the rotation that the user is performing changes.

`UIGestureRecognizerState.ended`
> This state is entered when the fingers are lifted from the screen, ending the rotation gesture.

`UIGestureRecognizerState.cancelled`
> This state is entered when the gesture is interrupted by a system-wide event, such as a phone call or an alert box appearing. This can also occur when another gesture recognizer interrupts the gesture recognizer. For example, a long press gesture recognizer might be cancelled by a pan recognizer once the user starts moving his finger.

The `UIRotationGestureRecognizer`'s key property is `rotation`, which is a measure of how far the rotation has changed since it was last reset, in radians.

In the example code, whenever the gesture changes, the rotation is measured and used to update an angle. Once that's done, the `rotation` property of the gesture recognizer is reset to zero.

 Don't forget that the pivot point that the view rotates around is the center of the view itself, and not the point in the center of the two fingers that are rotating.

3.5 Detecting Pinching Gestures

Problem

You want to track when the user pinches or spreads her fingers on the screen.

Solution

Use a `UIPinchGestureRecognizer` to detect when the user is pinching her fingers together, or spreading them apart:

```swift
class ViewController: UIViewController {

    @IBOutlet weak var scalingView: UIView!
    @IBOutlet weak var scalingStatusLabel: UILabel!

    // The current scale of the view (1.0 = normal scale)
    var scale : Float = 1.0

    override func viewDidLoad() {
        super.viewDidLoad()

        let pinched = #selector(ViewController.pinched(pinchGesture:))

        // Set up the rotation gesture
        let rotationGesture = UIPinchGestureRecognizer(target: self,
                                                       action: pinched)

        self.scalingView.isUserInteractionEnabled = true
        self.scalingView.addGestureRecognizer(rotationGesture)

        self.scalingStatusLabel?.text = "\(self.scale)x"
    }

    // When the rotation changes, update self.angle
    // and use that to rotate the view
    @objc func pinched(pinchGesture : UIPinchGestureRecognizer) {

        switch pinchGesture.state {

        case .changed:
            self.scale *= Float(pinchGesture.scale)

            pinchGesture.scale = 1.0

            self.scalingView.transform =
                CGAffineTransform(scaleX: CGFloat(self.scale),
                                  y: CGFloat(self.scale))

        default: () // do nothing
```

```
        }

        // Display the current scale factor
        self.scalingStatusLabel?.text = "\(self.scale)x"

    }

}
```

Discussion

`UIPinchGestureRecognizer` is your friend in this situation. A pinch gesture recognizer looks for fingers moving away from each other, or closer to each other.

The key property for `UIPinchGestureRecognizer` is `scale`. This starts at 1 when the gesture begins, and moves toward 0 when the fingers get closer together, or toward infinity when the fingers move away from each other. This value is always relative to the *initial* scale—so, for example, if the user spreads her fingers so that the scale becomes 2, and then pinches *again*, the scale will reset to 1 when the pinch begins.

To see this in action, comment out the following line of code:

```
pinchGesture.scale = 1.0
```

3.6 Creating Custom Gestures

Problem

You want to create a gesture recognizer that looks for a gesture that you define.

Solution

Creating a new gesture recognizer means subclassing `UIGestureRecognizer`. To get started, create a new class that's a subclass of `UIGestureRecognizer`.

In this example, we'll create a new gesture recognizer that looks for a gesture in which the finger starts moving down, moves back up, and then lifts from the screen (see Figure 3-1). However, there's nothing stopping you from creating simpler or more complex gestures of your own.

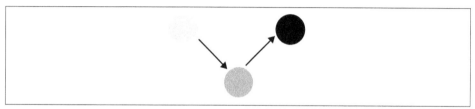

Figure 3-1. The gesture first goes down, then up again

This example shows a new `UIGestureRecognizer` called `DownUpGestureRecognizer`.

Create a file called *DownUpGestureRecognizer.swift* with the following contents:

```swift
import UIKit.UIGestureRecognizerSubclass

class DownUpGestureRecognizer: UIGestureRecognizer {

    // Represents the two phases that the gesture can be in:
    // moving down, or moving up after having moved down
    enum DownUpGesturePhase : CustomStringConvertible {
        case movingDown, movingUp

        // The 'CustomStringConvertible' protocol above means
        // that this type can be turned into a string.
        // This means you can say "\(somePhase)" and it will
        // turn into the correct string.
        // The following property adds support for this.
        var description: String {
            get {
                switch self {
                case .movingDown:
                    return "Moving Down"
                case .movingUp:
                    return "Moving Up"
                }
            }
        }
    }

    var phase : DownUpGesturePhase = .movingDown

    override func touchesBegan(_ touches: Set<UITouch>, with event: UIEvent) {

        // The gesture begins in the moving down phase.
        self.phase = .movingDown

        if self.numberOfTouches > 1 {

            // If there's more than one touch, this is not the type of gesture
            // we're looking for, so fail immediately
            self.state = .failed
        } else {

            // Else, this touch could possible turn into a down-up gesture
            self.state = .possible
        }
    }

    override func touchesMoved(_ touches: Set<UITouch>, with event: UIEvent) {

        // We know we only have one touch, beacuse touchesBegan will stop
        // recognizing when more than one touch is detected
```

```
guard let touch = touches.first else {
    return
}

// Get the current and previous position of the touch
let position = touch.location(in: touch.view)
let lastPosition = touch.previousLocation(in: touch.view)

// If the state is Possible, and the touch has moved down, the
// gesture has Begun
if self.state == .possible && position.y > lastPosition.y {
    self.state = .began
}

// If the state is Began or Changed, and the touch has moved, the
// gesture will change state
else if self.state == .began ||
    self.state == .changed {

    // If the phase of the gesture is MovingDown, and the touch moved
    // down, the gesture has Changed
    if self.phase == .movingDown && position.y >
        lastPosition.y {
            self.state = .changed
    }
    // If the phase of the gesture is MovingDown, and the touch moved
    // up, the gesture has Changed also, change the phase to MovingUp
    else if self.phase == .movingDown && position.y <
        lastPosition.y {
            self.phase = .movingUp
            self.state = .changed
    }
    // If the phase of the gesture is MovingUp, and the touch moved
    // down, then the gesture has Failed
    else if self.phase == .movingUp && position.y >
        lastPosition.y {
        self.state = .failed
    }

}
}

override func touchesEnded(_ touches: Set<UITouch>, with event: UIEvent) {

    // If the touch ends while the phase is MovingDown, the gesture
    // has Failed.
    if self.phase == .movingDown {
        self.state = .failed
    }
    // If the touch ends while the phase is MovingUp, the gesture has
    // Ended.
    else if self.phase == .movingUp {
```

```
            self.state = .ended
        }
    }

}
```

 The `UIKit.UIGestureRecognizerSubclass` import is required for making `self.state` writable. Without it, `self.state` is read-only, making it impossible to actually modify the state of your gesture recognizer.

You can now use this gesture recognizer like any other. For example, here's a view controller that uses it:

```
class ViewController: UIViewController {

    @IBOutlet weak var customGestureView : UIView!
    @IBOutlet weak var customGestureStatusLabel : UILabel!

    override func viewDidLoad() {
        super.viewDidLoad()

        let downUp = #selector(ViewController.downUp(downUpGesture:))

        let downUpGesture = DownUpGestureRecognizer(target:self, action:downUp)

        self.customGestureView.isUserInteractionEnabled = true

        self.customGestureView.addGestureRecognizer(downUpGesture)

    }

    @objc func downUp(downUpGesture: DownUpGestureRecognizer) {

        switch downUpGesture.state {
        case .began:
            self.customGestureStatusLabel.text = "Gesture began"

        case .changed:
            self.customGestureStatusLabel.text = "Gesture changed, phase = " +
            "\(downUpGesture.phase)"

        case .ended:
            self.customGestureStatusLabel.text = "Gesture ended"

        case .cancelled:
            self.customGestureStatusLabel.text = "Gesture cancelled"

        case .possible:
            self.customGestureStatusLabel.text = "Gesture possible"
```

```
        case .failed:
            self.customGestureStatusLabel.text = "Gesture failed"


        }
    }

}
```

Discussion

The first step in creating a new `UIGestureRecognizer` is to import the `UIKit.UIGestureRecognizerSubclass` module. This module contains code that redefines the `state` property of the `UIGestureRecognizer` class as `readwrite`, which lets your subclass modify its own state. Everything else is simply watching touches, and changing state based on that.

A gesture recognizer works by receiving touches, via the `touchesBegan`, `touchesMoved`, `touchesEnded`, and `touchesCancelled` methods (much like a `UIView` does). A recognizer is responsible for keeping track of whatever information it needs to determine the state of the gesture.

Recognizers don't communicate directly with their targets; instead, they change the value of the `state` property, which controls whether they're in the `began`, `changed`, `ended`, `cancelled`, or other states.

When your recognizer decides that it's seen a gesture, it changes its state to `UIGestureRecognizer.State.began`. This causes the gesture recognition system to send the recognizer's target object its action message. Similarly, your recognizer changes the `state` property to `changed` when it decides that the gesture has changed.

An important state that you can set your recognizer to is `failed`. For complex gestures, it's possible that the sequences of touches that the recognizer has been observing won't turn out to actually constitute the kind of gesture you're looking for. For example, if a drag gesture recognizer sees a touch land on the screen, it's possible that it's the start of a drag gesture, but it can't be sure—it's not a drag until the touch starts moving. If the touch immediately lifts up, the drag gesture recognizer changes to the `failed` state. This allows other gesture recognizers to step in, if applicable.

3.7 Receiving Touches in Custom Areas of a View

Problem

By default, a `UIView` detects all touches that fall within its bounds. You want a view to receive touches in a different region.

Solution

To tell iOS that a point should be considered to be within the bounds of a view, you override the `point(inside:, withEvent:)` method.

In a `UIView` subclass:

```
override func point(inside point: CGPoint, with event: UIEvent?) -> Bool {

    // A point is inside this view if it falls inside a rectangle that's 40pt
    // larger than the bounds of the view

    return self.bounds.insetBy(dx: -40, dy: -40).contains(point)
}
```

Discussion

When a touch lands on the screen, iOS starts checking all views to find out which view was touched. It does this by calling `point(inside:, with:)` on the top-level view, and finding out whether the touch is considered "inside" that view. It then begins asking each of the subviews inside that view whether the touch should be considered inside it, proceeding until the lowest-level view is reached.

By default, a point is considered "inside" the view if it's within the view's bounds rectangle. However, you can override this by providing your own implementation of `pointInside(_, withEvent:)`.

`point(inside:, with:)` takes a `CGPoint` in the coordinate space of the view, and returns `true` if the point should be considered inside the view and `false` if the point is outside of the view.

3.8 Detecting Shakes

Problem

You want to detect when the user's device is shaking.

Solution

Add this code to a view controller:

```
override func motionBegan(_ motion: UIEvent.EventSubtype, with event: UIEvent?) {
    // Show a label when shaking begins
    self.shakingLabel.isHidden = false
}

override func motionEnded(_ motion: UIEvent.EventSubtype, with event: UIEvent?) {
    // Hide the label 1 second after shaking ends
    let delayInSeconds : Double = 1.0
```

```
    DispatchQueue.main.asyncAfter(deadline: DispatchTime.now() + delayInSeconds) {
        self.shakingLabel.isHidden = true
    }

}


override var canBecomeFirstResponder: Bool {
    return true
}
```

Discussion

Shaking is a kind of gesture that views and view controllers can detect. If you want a view controller to detect it, you first need to indicate to the system that your view controller is capable of becoming the "first responder"—that is, that it's able to receive motion gestures like shaking.

When shaking begins, the view controller receives the `motionBegan(_, with:)` message. When shaking ends, the `motionEnded(_, with:)` message is sent.

In the case of the example code, all we're doing is making a label become visible when shaking begins, and making it invisible two seconds after shaking ends.

3.9 Detecting Device Tilt

Problem

You want to detect how the device has been tilted. For example, if you're making a driving game, you want to know how far the device is being turned, so that you can figure out how the user's car is being steered.

Solution

You get information about how the device is being moved and rotated by using the Core Motion framework. To add this framework to your code, you just need to `import` the `CoreMotion` module in the files you want to use it in.

```
import CoreMotion
```

You can then create a `CMMotionManager`, and use it to receive updates whenever the device's orientation changes:

```
@IBOutlet weak var pitchLabel : UILabel!
@IBOutlet weak var yawLabel : UILabel!
@IBOutlet weak var rollLabel : UILabel!

var motionManager = CMMotionManager()
```

```swift
override func viewDidLoad() {
    let mainQueue = OperationQueue.main

    motionManager.startDeviceMotionUpdates(to: mainQueue) {
        (motion, error) in

        // Ensure that we have a CMDeviceMotion to work with
        guard let motion = motion else {
            if let error = error {
                print("Failed to get device motion: \(error)")
            }
            return
        }

        let roll = motion.attitude.roll
        let rollDegrees = roll * 180 / .pi

        let yaw = motion.attitude.yaw
        let yawDegrees = yaw * 180 / .pi

        let pitch = motion.attitude.pitch
        let pitchDegrees = pitch * 180 / .pi

        self.rollLabel.text = String(format:"Roll: %.2f°", rollDegrees)
        self.yawLabel.text = String(format: "Yaw: %.2f°", yawDegrees)
        self.pitchLabel.text = String(format: "Pitch: %.2f°", pitchDegrees)
    }

}
```

Discussion

Objects can be tilted in three different ways. As illustrated in Figure 3-2, they can *pitch*, *yaw*, and *roll*: that is, rotate around three different imaginary lines. When an object pitches, it rotates around a line drawn from its left edge to its right edge. When it yaws, it rotates around a line drawn from the top edge to the bottom edge. When it rolls, it rotates around a line drawn from the middle of its front face to the middle of the back face.

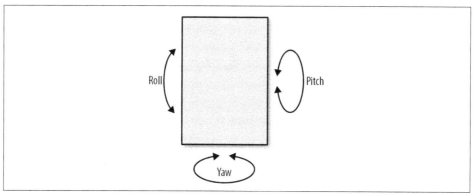

Figure 3-2. The three axes of rotation

Your app can get information regarding how the device is angled through the Core Motion framework. The main class in this framework is CMMotionManager, which allows you to sign up to be notified when the device is moved or tilted. So, to get started, you first need to create a CMMotionManager.

It's important to keep a reference to your CMMotionManager around. Without one, the automatic reference counting system will notice that there's no reason to keep the CMMotionManager in memory, and it'll be deallocated. This won't lead to a crash, but it will mean that you won't get any information from it when the device is rotated or moved.

That's why, in the example, we store the CMMotionManager in an instance variable. Doing this means that the view controller has a strong reference to the CMMotionManager, which will keep it in memory.

Once you've created your motion manager, you can start receiving information about the device's movement. To receive this information, you need to call startDeviceMotionUpdates(to: , withHandler:) on your CMMotionManager.

This method takes two parameters: an OperationQueue and a block. Every time the device moves, the motion manager will call the block, using the operation queue you provide. In our example, we're using the main queue (i.e., OperationQueue.mainQueue), so that the block is able to update the user interface.

Every time the block is called, it receives two parameters: a CMMotion object and an Error object. The CMMotion object contains information about how the device is currently moving, and the Error object either is nil if nothing's gone wrong, or contains information about what's gone wrong and why.

A `CMMotion` object contains a *lot* of information for you to work with:

- You can access accelerometer information, which tells you how the device is moving and in which direction gravity is, through the `userAcceleration` and `gravity` properties.
- You can access calibrated gyroscope information, which tells you how the device is oriented and how fast it's currently rotating, through the `attitude` and `rotationRate` properties.
- You can access calibrated magnetic field information, which tells you about the total magnetic field that the device is in (minus device bias), through the `magneticField` property.

The `magneticField` property is really cool. It's not too tricky to write an app that watches the magnetic field—once you've made that, wave your device near something made of iron or steel. Congratulations, you've just turned your phone into a metal detector! See Recipe 3.18.

In this particular example, we care most about the device's *attitude*. The attitude of an object means how it's oriented in space. The attitude of a device is represented by three angles, *pitch*, *yaw*, and *roll*, measured in radians—if you remember your high school math, there are 2π radians in a circle.

To convert from radians to degrees, and vice versa, use these formulas:

```
degrees = radians / Double.pi * 180.0

radians = degrees * Double.pi / 180.0
```

This recipe talks about how you can access tilt across all axes; to use this information for steering, take a look at Recipe 3.18.

When you're done receiving motion updates, you can call `stopDeviceMotionUpdates()` on your `CMMotionManager` to stop it.

It's worth noting that Apple's documentation warns against using the main queue due to the possibility of events arriving at a high rate. We're using the main queue here for the purposes of discussion; for better performance, consider using a background queue, which we discuss in Recipe 1.13.

3.10 Getting the Compass Heading

Problem

You want to know which direction the user is facing, relative to north.

Solution

First, add the Core Motion framework to your project and set up a `CMMotionManager`, as per Recipe 3.9.

When you ask the system to start delivering device motion information to your application, use the `startDeviceMotionUpdates(using:, to:, withHandler:)` method and pass in `CMAttitudeReferenceFrame.xTrueNorthZVertical` as the first parameter:

```
motionManager.startDeviceMotionUpdates(
    using: CMAttitudeReferenceFrame.xTrueNorthZVertical,
    to: mainQueue) { (motion, error) in

        // Ensure that we have a CMDeviceMotion to work with
        guard let motion = motion else {
            if let error = error {
                print("Failed to get motion: \(error)")
            }
            return
        }

        let yaw = motion.attitude.yaw

        let yawDegrees = yaw * 180 / .pi

        self.directionLabel.text = String(format:"Direction: %.0f°", yawDegrees)

}
```

Discussion

When you begin receiving device motion information, all attitude information is relative to a *reference frame*. The reference frame is your "zero point" for orientation.

By default, the zero point is set when you activate the device motion system. That is, the first attitude information you receive will indicate that the device is oriented at the zero point. As you rotate the device, the attitude information will change relative to the zero point.

The default reference frame is able to determine the device's pitch and roll by measuring the direction of gravity. That is, it's always possible to know what direction "down" is. However, it isn't possible for a gyroscope and accelerometer to measure the *yaw*, for the same reason that you don't have a constant, innate knowledge of which direction is north.

To get this information, a magnetometer is needed. Magnetometers sense magnetic fields, which allows you to figure out where the north pole of the strongest magnet near you is. In other words, a magnetometer is able to function as a compass.

Magnetometers require additional power to use, as well as additional CPU resources necessary to integrate the magnetic field data with the accelerometer and gyroscope data. By default, therefore, the magnetometer is turned off. However, if you need to know where north is, you can indicate to the Core Motion system that you need this information.

With the `startDeviceMotionUpdates(using:, toQueue:, withHandler:)` method, you have a choice regarding what reference frame you can use. The options available are as follows:

`CMAttitudeReferenceFrame.xArbitraryZVertical`
: Yaw is set to zero when the device motion system is turned on.

`CMAttitudeReferenceFrame.xArbitraryCorrectedZVertical`
: Yaw is set to zero when the device motion system is turned on, and the magnetometer is used to keep this stable over time (i.e., the zero point won't drift as much).

`CMAttitudeReferenceFrame.xMagneticNorthZVertical`
: The zero yaw point is magnetic north.

`CMAttitudeReferenceFrame.xTrueNorthZVertical`
: The zero yaw point is true north. The system needs to use the location system to figure this out.

If you need the most accuracy, `CMAttitudeReferenceFrame.xTrueNorthZVertical` should be used. This uses the most battery power, and takes the longest time to get a fix. If you don't really care about which direction north is, go with `CMAttitudeReferenceFrame.XArbitraryZVertical` or `CMAttitudeReference Frame.xArbitraryCorrectedZVertical`.

3.11 Accessing the User's Location

Problem

You want to determine where on the planet the user currently is.

Solution

When you want to work with user location data, you need to explain to the user for what purpose the location data is going to be used:

1. Go to the project's information screen by clicking the project at the top of the Project Navigator (at the left of the Xcode window).
2. Select the project target in the list of Targets.
3. Go to the Info tab.
4. Add a new entry in the list of settings that appears: "Privacy - Location When In Use Usage Description." In the Value column, add some text that explains what the user location will be used for. (In this example, it can be something like "the app will display your coordinates.")

The method for specifying your location usage justification depends on how you'll be using location data.

- If your app will use the user's location only when the app is running—that is, it's running in the foreground—you add an entry with the key "Privacy - Location When In Use Usage Description".

- To give the user the choice between letting the app have access to their location at all times, when in use, or never, add an entry with the key `Privacy - Location Always and When In Use Usage Description`.

- If your app supports iOS 10 and earlier, and will use the user's location even when the app is closed, add an entry with the key `Privacy - Location Always Usage Description`.

Adding this information is mandatory. If you don't explain why you need access to the user's location, you can't access it. Additionally, your explanation needs to be reasonable and truthful, or else your app may not pass App Store Review.

The reason for this is that the user's location is private information, and your app needs to have a good reason for using it. That's not to say that you shouldn't make games that ask for the user's location—far from it! But don't get the user's location just so that you can gather statistics about where your users live.

To actually get the user's location and work with it, you import the `CoreLocation` module and use a `CLLocationManager`:

```
import UIKit
import CoreLocation

class ViewController: UIViewController, CLLocationManagerDelegate {
```

```
    var locationManager = CLLocationManager()

    @IBOutlet weak var latitudeLabel : UILabel!
    @IBOutlet weak var longitudeLabel : UILabel!
    @IBOutlet weak var locationErrorLabel : UILabel!

    override func viewDidLoad() {
        super.viewDidLoad()

        locationManager.delegate = self

        locationManager.requestWhenInUseAuthorization()

        locationManager.startUpdatingLocation()

        self.locationErrorLabel.isHidden = true

    }

    func locationManager(_ manager: CLLocationManager,
        didUpdateLocations locations: [CLLocation]) {
        self.locationErrorLabel.isHidden = true

        let location = locations.last!

        let latitude = location.coordinate.latitude
        let longitude = location.coordinate.longitude

        self.latitudeLabel.text = String(format: "Latitude: %.4f", latitude)
        self.longitudeLabel.text = String(format: "Longitude: %.4f", longitude)
    }

    func locationManager(_ manager: CLLocationManager,
        didFailWithError error: Error) {
        self.locationErrorLabel.isHidden = false
        self.locationErrorLabel.text = error.localizedDescription
    }

}
```

Discussion

A CLLocationManager, once set up and configured, sends messages to a delegate object, notifying it of the user's location.

To receive messages from a CLLocationManager, an object needs to conform to the CLLocationManagerDelegate protocol:

```
class ViewController: UIViewController, CLLocationManagerDelegate {
```

To set up a CLLocationManager, you create an instance of the class. You'll also need to create and keep a strong reference to the CLLocationManager object, to keep it from being freed from memory, and indicate to it what object should receive location updates. Finally, you need to tell the CLLocationManager that it should activate the GPS system, request permission from the user, and begin telling the delegate object about the user's location:

```
locationManager.delegate = self

locationManager.requestWhenInUseAuthorization()

locationManager.startUpdatingLocation()
```

Once you've told the location manager that you want to start receiving location information, you then need to implement one of the methods in the CLLocationManager Delegate protocol: locationManager(_, didUpdateLocations:). This method is called every time the location manager decides that the user has changed location. It receives two parameters: the CLLocationManager itself, and an array containing one or more CLLocation objects.

There can be more than one CLLocation object in the array. This can happen when, for some reason, your application hasn't been able to receive location updates (e.g., it may have been in the background). In these cases, you'll receive a bunch of CLLocations, which are delivered in the order in which they occurred. The last object in the array is always the most recent location at which the device was observed. You can access it through the array's last method:

```
let location = locations.last!
```

A CLLocation object represents the user's current location on the planet. It contains, among other information, the user's latitude, longitude, and altitude.

The user's latitude and longitude, which are almost always the only things you want to know about, can be accessed through the CLLocation's coordinate property, which is a CLLocationCoordinate2D. A CLLocationCoordinate2D contains two things:

```
let latitude = location.coordinate.latitude
let longitude = location.coordinate.longitude
```

The user's location is not guaranteed to be precise—the GPS system is good, but it's not accurate enough to pinpoint the location down to the nearest centimeter (unless you're in the US military, in which case, greetings!).

Therefore, each CLLocation object contains a horizontalAccuracy property, which represents the "radius of uncertainty" of the location, measured in meters.

For example, if the horizontalAccuracy of a CLLocation is 5, this means that the user is within 5 meters of the location indicated by the latitude and longitude.

Sometimes, you just want to get the user's current location, and don't want to track him over a period of time. To do this, you can use the requestLocation method on CLLocationManager:

```
locationManager.requestLocation()
```

This doesn't return a location - it returns immediately, and when it has the current location, it dispatches it via a delegate callback, just like if you use startRequestingLocation. The difference is that requestLocation gets a single location, and then turns it off.

3.12 Calculating the User's Speed

Problem

You want to determine how fast the user is moving.

Solution

This information can be gained through the Core Location framework.

First, set up a CLLocationManager, as discussed in the previous recipe, and start receiving updates to the user's location:

```swift
func locationManager(_ manager: CLLocationManager,
    didUpdateLocations locations: [CLLocation]) {

    guard let lastLocation = locations.last else {
        return
    }

    if lastLocation.speed > 0 {
        self.speedLabel.text = String(
            format: "Currently moving at %.0f meters/second",
            lastLocation.speed
        )
    }
}
```

Discussion

CLLocation objects contain a speed property, which contains the speed at which the device is traveling. This is measured in meters per second.

If you want to convert meters per second to kilometers per hour, you can do this:

```
var kPH = location.speed * 3.6
```

If you want to convert meters per second to miles per hour, you can do this:

```
var mPH =  location.speed * 2.236936
```

3.13 Pinpointing the User's Proximity to Landmarks

Problem

You want to calculate how far away the user is from a location.

Solution

We'll assume that you already know the user's location, represented by a `CLLocation` object. If you don't already have this information, see Recipe 3.11.

We'll also assume that you have the latitude and longitude coordinates of the location from which you want to measure the distance. You can use this information to determine the proximity:

```
var userLocation : CLLocation = ... // get the user's location from CoreLocation
var latitude : Float = ... // latitude of the other location
var longitude : Float = ... // longitude of the other location

var otherLocation = CLLocation(latitude:latitude
                                longitude:longitude)

var distance = userLocation.distance(from: otherLocation)
```

Discussion

The `distance(from:)` method returns the distance from the other location, measured in meters.

It's important to note that the distance is not a direct straight-line distance, but rather takes into account the curvature of the earth. Also keep in mind that the distance traveled doesn't take into account any mountains or hills between the user's location and the other location.

3.14 Receiving Notifications When the User Changes Location

Problem

You want to be notified when the user enters a specific region, or exits it.

Solution

Your application can receive updates to the user's location even when it's not running. To enable this, follow these steps:

1. Go to your project's Info screen by clicking the project at the top of the Project Navigator (at the left of the Xcode window; see Figure 3-3).

Figure 3-3. The project, at the top of the Project Navigator

2. Select the project's target in the Target list.
3. Click the Capabilities tab.
4. Turn on Background Modes.
5. Check the "Location updates" checkbox, as shown in Figure 3-4.

Figure 3-4. Adding the "Location updates" background mode

Additionally, you will need to add the key NSLocationAlwaysUsageDescription to your app's Info dictionary, and provide an explanation of how the app will be using the user's location.

Make *ViewController.swift* look like the following code:

```swift
import UIKit
import CoreLocation

class ViewController: UIViewController, CLLocationManagerDelegate {

    var locationManager = CLLocationManager()
    var regionToMonitor : CLCircularRegion?


    override func viewDidLoad() {
        locationManager.delegate = self;

        locationManager.requestAlwaysAuthorization()

        locationManager.startUpdatingLocation()


    }
```

```swift
func locationManager(_ manager: CLLocationManager,
    didUpdateLocations locations: [CLLocation]) {

    // Only start monitoring a region when we first get
    // a location
    guard regionToMonitor == nil else {
        return
    }

    // Ensure we have a location
    guard let location = locations.last else {
        return
    }

    let region = CLCircularRegion(center: location.coordinate,
        radius: 20.0, identifier: "StartingPoint")

    locationManager.startMonitoring(for: region)

    print("Now monitoring region \(region)")

    regionToMonitor = region


}

func locationManager(_ manager: CLLocationManager,
                     monitoringDidFailFor region: CLRegion?,
                     withError error: Error) {
    print("Failed to start monitoring region!")

}

func locationManager(_ manager: CLLocationManager,
                     didEnterRegion region: CLRegion) {
    print("Entering region!")
}

func locationManager(_ manager: CLLocationManager,
                     didExitRegion region: CLRegion) {
    print("Exiting region!")
}


}
```

Discussion

Your application can be notified when the user enters or exits a region. A region is defined by a central point and a radius—that is to say, regions are always circular.

You register a region by creating a `CLRegion` object and giving it a center point (latitude and longitude) and radius, as well as a name (a string that you will use to refer to the region):

```
var latitude  : Float = ...  // latitude
var longitude : Float = ...  // longitude
var radius    : Float = ...  // radius
var name = "My Region"       // something to call the region

var coordinate = CLCoordinate2D(latitude: latitude, longitude: longitude)

var region = CLCircularRegion(center:coordinate,
              radius: radius, identifier: name)
```

The maximum allowed radius for a region might vary from device to device. You can check what the maximum allowed radius is by asking the `CLLocationManager` class for its `maximumRegionMonitoringDistance` property:

```
var maximumRegionRadius
    = locationManager.maximumRegionMonitoringDistance
```

If you attempt to start monitoring a region with a distance that's larger than this value, the location manager will send an error to your `CLLocationManagerDelegate`.

Once the region has been created, you indicate to your `CLLocationManager` that you want to be notified when the user enters and exits the region:

```
locationManager.startMonitoring(for: regionToMonitor)
```

Once this is done, the `CLLocationManager`'s delegate will receive a `locationManager(_, didEnterRegion:)` message when the user enters the region, and a `locationManager(_, didExitRegion:)` message when the user exits.

You can only register 20 regions at a time. You can ask the location manager to give you an array of all of the `CLRegion`s you've registered via the `monitoredRegions` method:

```
var monitoredRegions = locationManager.monitoredRegions
```

When you no longer want to receive notifications regarding a region, you send the `CLLocationManager` the `stopMonitoringForRegion` message:

```
locationManager.stopMonitoring(for: regionToMonitor)
```

More tend to be more precise. Additionally, when the user enters or exits a region, it generally takes about 3 to 5 minutes for the device to notice it and send a notification to your application. This means that using smaller regions may mean that your app receives notifications well after the user has left the area. To report region changes in a timely manner, the region monitoring service requires network connectivity.

3.15 Looking Up GPS Coordinates for a Street Address

Problem

You have a street address, and you want to get latitude and longitude coordinates for it. For example, you have a game that involves players moving from one named location to another, and you want to get the coordinates so you can monitor when they get close.

Solution

iOS has a built-in system that lets you convert between coordinates and street addresses. *Geocoding* is the process of converting a human-readable address (like "1 Infinite Loop, Cupertino, California") into latitude and longitude coordinates, which you can then use with the location system.

First, import the `CoreLocation` module (see Recipe 3.9).

Next, create a `CLGeocoder` instance variable:

```
var geocoder = CLGeocoder()
```

When you want to convert an address to a coordinate pair, call `geocodeAddressString`:

```
let addressString = self.addressTextView.text ?? "" // get the address
                                                     // from somewhere

geocoder.geocodeAddressString(addressString) { (placemarks, error) -> Void in

    if error != nil {
        self.latitudeLabel.text = "Error!"
        self.longitudeLabel.text = "Error!"
    } else {

        guard let placemark = placemarks?.last else {
            print("No placemarks provided!")
            return
        }

        guard let location = placemark.location else {
            print("Placemark has no location data!")
            return
        }

        let latitude = location.coordinate.latitude
```

```
        let longitude = location.coordinate.longitude

        self.latitudeLabel.text = String(format: "Latitude: %.4f", latitude)
        self.longitudeLabel.text = String(format: "Longitude: %.4f", longitude)
    }
}
```

Discussion

To use geocoding, you create a CLGeocoder object. A CLGeocoder object communicates with Apple's geocoding server, and runs the completion handler block that you provide when the geocoding request returns. This means that your device needs to be on the network in order to use geocoding.

When the geocoding request returns, you'll either receive an array that contains CLPlacemark objects, or an Error that describes what went wrong. You might get more than one CLPlacemark object; for example, if the geocoding server is unsure about the exact location you meant, it may return a few different options.

CLPlacemark objects describe a location, and they contain quite a lot of information for you to use. The specific contents available for each placemark vary, but they include things like the name of the location, the street name, the town or city, country, and so on.

Additionally, every CLPlacemark contains a property called location, a CLLocation object that you can use to get the latitude and longitude.

3.16 Looking Up Street Addresses from the User's Location

Problem

You know the user's location, and you want to find the street address using his coordinates.

Solution

Create a CLGeocoder instance variable (in this example, we've named it geocoder), and call reverseGeocodeLocation on it:

```
func locationManager(_ manager: CLLocationManager,
                     didUpdateLocations locations: [CLLocation]) {

    guard let location = locations.last else {
        return
    }

    geocoder.reverseGeocodeLocation(location, completionHandler: {
        (placemarks, error) -> Void in
```

```
            guard let placemark = placemarks?.first else {
                if let error = error {
                    print("Failed to get a placemark! \(error)")
                }
                return
            }

            let addressString = placemark.name

            self.labelTextView.text = addressString

        })
    }
```

Discussion

A `CLGeocoder` object is able to perform both geocoding and *reverse* geocoding. Whereas geocoding involves taking a street address and returning coordinates, reverse geocoding means taking coordinates and providing a street address.

Reverse geocoding works similarly to geocoding: you create a `CLGeocoder`, provide it with input data and a block that you want to run when the work is complete, and set it off.

Also like with normal geocoding, reverse geocoding returns an array of `CLPlacemark` objects. However, there's no built-in method for converting a `CLPlacemark` into a string (not counting `description`, which includes all kinds of information that the user doesn't care about). It's therefore up to you to pull the information out of the `CLPlacemark` object and format it into a string for the user to see.

3.17 Using the Device as a Steering Wheel

Problem

You want to let the user use the device as a steering wheel, and get information on how far he's steering.

Solution

You can get information about how far the user is steering by deciding which axis you want to define as the "steering" axis, and using Core Motion to work out the rotation around that axis.

In most cases, games that involve steering are played in landscape mode. To make sure your game only appears in landscape, select the project at the top of the Project

Navigator, and scroll down to Device Orientation. Make sure that only Landscape Left and Landscape Right are selected.

Next, import the Core Motion framework (see Recipe 3.9). Finally, add a `CMMotion Manager`, and add the following code to watch for device motion updates:

```
motionManager.startDeviceMotionUpdates(to: OperationQueue.main) {
    (motion, error) -> Void in

    // Ensure that we have a CMDeviceMotion to work with
    guard let motion = motion else {
        if let error = error {
            print("Error: \(error)")
        }
        return
    }

    // Maximum steering left is -50 degrees, maximum steering right is
    // 50 degrees
    let maximumSteerAngle = 50.0

    // When in landscape,
    let rotationAngle = motion.attitude.pitch * 180.0 / .pi

    // -1.0 = hard left, 1.0 = hard right
    var steering = 0.0

    let orientation = UIApplication.shared.statusBarOrientation

    if orientation == UIInterfaceOrientation.landscapeLeft  {
        steering = rotationAngle / -maximumSteerAngle
    } else if orientation == UIInterfaceOrientation.landscapeRight {
        steering = rotationAngle / maximumSteerAngle
    }

    // Limit the steering to between -1.0 and 1.0
    steering = fmin(steering, 1.0)
    steering = fmax(steering, -1.0)

    print("Steering: \(steering)")
}
```

Discussion

In this solution, the code figures out how the device is being held and generates a number to represent how the user is "steering" the device: –1.0 means the device is being steered hard left, and 1.0 means hard right.

In landscape mode, "steering" the device means changing its pitch—that is, changing the angle of the line that extends from the left of the screen to the right of the screen. However, "landscape" can mean that the device is being held in two different ways:

"landscape left" means that the home button is to the left of the screen, and "landscape right" means that the home button is to the right. In other words, landscape right is an upside-down version of landscape left.

This means that if we want −1.0 to always mean left, we have to know the orientation in which the device is being held. You can check this by asking the shared UIApplication object for the current statusBarOrientation.

3.18 Detecting Magnets

Problem

You want your game to detect when the device is near a magnet or other ferrous material.

Solution

First, you need to import the Core Motion framework. See Recipe 3.9 for instructions. Use the CMMotionManager class's startMagnetometerUpdates(to:, withHandler:) method to register to receive information from the device's built-in magnetometer:

```
motionManager.startMagnetometerUpdates(to: OperationQueue.main) {
    (magnetometerData, error) -> Void in

    // Ensure that we have a CMMagnetometerData to work with
    guard let magnetometerData = magnetometerData else {
        if let error = error {
            print("Failed to get magnetometer data: \(error)")
        }
        return
    }

    let magneticField = magnetometerData.magneticField

    let xValue = String(format:"%.2f", magneticField.x)
    let yValue = String(format:"%.2f", magneticField.y)
    let zValue = String(format:"%.2f", magneticField.z)

    let average = (magneticField.x + magneticField.y + magneticField.z) / 3.0

    let averageValue = String(format:"%.2f", average)

    self.magneticFieldXLabel.text = xValue
    self.magneticFieldYLabel.text = yValue
    self.magneticFieldZLabel.text = zValue
    self.magneticFieldAverageLabel.text = averageValue

}
```

Discussion

The built-in magnetometer in all devices shipped since the iPhone 3GS is used to find the heading of the device (i.e., the direction in which it's pointing). By getting a reading on the magnetic fields surrounding the device, the iPhone can determine which direction is north.

However, this isn't the only reason why magnetometers are cool. The magnetometer can be accessed directly, which gives you information on the presence of magnets (as well as ferromagnetic metals, like steel and iron) near the device.

When you want to start getting information about nearby magnetic fields, you use the CMDeviceMotion class's startMagnetometerUpdates(to:, withHandler) method. This method works in a manner very similar to when you want to get overall device motion (see Recipe 3.9); however, instead of receiving a CMDeviceMotion object, you instead get a CMMagnetometerData object.

The CMMagnetometerData object contains two properties: a TimeInterval that represents when the information was sampled, and a CMMagneticField structure that contains the data itself.

The information stored in the CMMagneticField is represented in microteslas, which are a measurement of magnetic flux density—that is, the strength of the magnetic field currently affecting the device.

When the device is near a planet—which, at the time of writing, is very likely to be the case—it will be subjected to that planet's magnetic field. Earth has a particularly strong magnetic field, which means that the measurements that come from the magnetometer will never be zero. Additionally, some components in the device itself are slightly magnetic, which contributes to the readings. Finally, the readings that you'll get from the magnetometer will be stronger when the sensor is *moving* through a magnetic field, as opposed to remaining stationary within one.

This means that you can't treat the information that comes from the magnetometer as absolute "near magnet"/"not near magnet" data. Instead, you need to interpret the information over time: if the values you're getting from the magnetometer are rising or falling quickly, the device is near something magnetic.

Magnetometers haven't seen much use in games to date, which means that there's a huge potential area for new kinds of gameplay. This is left as an exercise for the reader —what kind of gameplay can you create that's based on detecting metal?

3.19 Utilizing Inputs to Improve Game Design

Problem

You want to effectively utilize the inputs (some of them unique) that are available on iOS to make a better game.

Solution

When you're considering how your game is controlled, it pays to look at the environment in which iOS games are frequently played. The iPhone and iPad are, obviously, inherently mobile devices—they are used by people who are often out and about, or at work, lying in front of the television, or commuting to work on a loud train.

Because of this, iOS games should be simple and easy to control, and should use as much direct manipulation—dragging, touching, gestures—as possible. People are distracted, and they don't want to think about the myriad ways in which they could control something. If the obvious doesn't work, they'll go and play a different game—it's hard enough trying to play a game on the train anyway!

If a player can directly drag her character around, rather than using an on-screen directional control, you should enable that feature. If your game requires the player to shake loose enemy boarders from a spacecraft, why not let her shake the device instead of tapping a button marked "shake"?

Discussion

Give users direct control and your game will feel more responsive, be more entertaining, and end up getting played a whole lot more often.

CHAPTER 4

Sound

Sound is a frequently overlooked part of games. Even in big-name titles, sound design and programming are sometimes left until late in the game development process. This is especially true on mobile devices—the user might be playing the game in a crowded, noisy environment and might not even hear the sounds and music you've put into it, so why bother putting in much effort?

However, sound is an incredibly important part of games. When a game sounds great, and makes noises in response to the visible parts of the game, the player gets drawn in to the world that the game's creating.

In this chapter, you'll learn how to use iOS's built-in support for playing both sound effects and music. You'll also learn how to take advantage of the speech synthesis features built into iOS.

Sound good?[11]

4.1 Playing Sound with AVAudioPlayer

Problem

You want to play back an audio file, as simply as possible and with a minimum of work.

---

1 We apologize for this pun and have fired Jon, who wrote it.

Solution

The simplest way to play a sound file is using AVAudioPlayer, which is a class available in the AVFoundation framework. To use this feature, you first need to import the AVFoundation module in each file that uses the AVFoundation classes:

```
import AVFoundation
```

You create an AVAudioPlayer by providing it with the location of the file you want it to play. This should generally be done ahead of time, before the sound needs to be played, to avoid playback delays. To get the location of the file, you use the Bundle class's url(forResource:, withExtension:) method, which allows you to access the location of any resource that's been added to your app's target in Xcode (for example, by dragging and dropping it into the Project navigator.)

In this example, audioPlayer is an optional AVAudioPlayer instance variable:

```
guard let soundFileURL = Bundle.main.url(forResource: "TestSound",
                                         withExtension:"wav") else {
                        print("URL not found")
                        return
}

do {
    audioPlayer = try AVAudioPlayer(contentsOf: soundFileURL)
} catch let error {
    print("Failed to load the sound: \(error)")
}

audioPlayer?.prepareToPlay()
```

To begin playback, you use the play method:

```
audioPlayer?.play()
```

To make playback loop, you change the audio player's numberOfLoops property. To make an AVAudioPlayer play one time and then stop:

```
audioPlayer?.numberOfLoops = 0
```

To make an AVAudioPlayer play twice and then stop:

```
audioPlayer?.numberOfLoops = 1
```

To make an AVAudioPlayer play forever, until manually stopped:

```
audioPlayer?.numberOfLoops = -1
```

By default, an AVAudioPlayer will play its sound one time only. After it's finished playing, a second call to play will rewind it and play it again. By changing the number OfLoops property, you can make an AVAudioPlayer play its file a single time, a fixed number of times, or continuously until it's sent a pause or stop message.

To stop playback, you use the `pause` or `stop` method (the `pause` method just stops playback, and lets you resume from where you left off later; the `stop` method stops playback completely, and unloads the sound from memory):

```
// To pause:
audioPlayer?.pause()
// To stop:
audioPlayer?.stop()
```

To rewind an audio player, you change the `currentTime` property. This property stores how far playback has progressed, measured in seconds. If you set it to zero, playback will jump back to the start:

```
audioPlayer.currentTime = 0
```

You can also set this property to other values to jump to a specific point in the audio.

Discussion

If you use an `AVAudioPlayer`, you need to keep a strong reference to it (using an instance variable) to avoid it being released from memory. If that happens, the sound will stop.

If you have multiple sounds that you want to play at the same time, you need to keep references to each (or use an array to contain them all). This can get cumbersome, so it's often better to use a dedicated sound engine instead of managing each player yourself.

Preparing an `AVAudioPlayer` takes a little bit of preparation. You need to either know the location of a file that contains the audio you want the player to play, or have a `Data` object that contains the audio data.

`AVAudioPlayer` supports a number of popular audio formats. The specific formats vary slightly from device to device; the iPhone X supports the following formats:

- AAC-LC
- HE-AAC
- HE-AAC v2
- Protected AAC
- MP3
- Linear PCM (`.wav`)
- Apple Lossless
- FLAC
- Dolby Digital (AC-3),

- Dolby Digital Plus (E-AC-3)
- Audible (formats 2, 3, 4, Audible Enhanced Audio, AAX, and AAX+)

You shouldn't generally have problems with file compatibility across devices, but it's usually best to go with AAC, MP3, or WAV.

In this example, it's assumed that there's a file called *TestSound.wav* in the project. You'll want to use a different name for your game, of course.

Use the Bundle's `url(forResource:, withExtension:)` method to get the location of a resource on disk:

```
guard let soundFileURL = Bundle.main.url(forResource: "TestSound",
                                  withExtension:"wav") else {
                                      print("URL not found")
                                      return
}
```

This returns an `URL` object that contains the location of the file, which you can give to your `AVAudioPlayer` to tell it where to find the sound file.

Finally, the `AVAudioPlayer` can be told to preload the audio file before playback. If you don't do this, it's no big deal—when you tell it to play, it loads the file and then begins playing back. However, for large files, this can lead to a short pause before audio actually starts playing, so it's often best to preload the sound as soon as you can. Note, however, that if you have many large sounds, preloading everything can lead to all of your available memory being consumed, so use this feature with care.

4.2 Recording Sound with AVAudioRecorder

Problem

You want to record sound made by the player, using the built-in microphone.

Solution

`AVAudioRecorder` is your friend here. Like its sibling `AVAudioPlayer` (see Recipe 4.1), `AVAudioRecorder` lives in the AVFoundation framework, so you'll need to import that module in any files where you want to use it. You can then create an `AVAudio Recorder` as follows:

```
// destinationURL is the location of where we want to store our recording

do {
    audioRecorder = try AVAudioRecorder(url:destinationURL, settings: [:])
} catch let error {
    print("Couldn't create a recorder: \(error)")
}
```

```
audioRecorder?.prepareToRecord()
```

To begin recording, use the `record` method:

```
audioRecorder?.record()
```

To stop recording, use the `stop` method:

```
audioRecorder?.stop()
```

When recording has ended, the file pointed at by the URL you used to create the `AVAudioRecorder` contains a sound file, which you can play using `AVAudioPlayer` or any other audio system.

Discussion

Like an `AVAudioPlayer`, an `AVAudioRecorder` needs to have at least one strong reference made to it in order to keep it in memory.

To record audio, you first need to have the location of the file where the recorded audio will end up. The `AVAudioRecorder` will create the file if it doesn't already exist; if it does, the recorder will erase the file and overwrite it. So, if you want to avoid losing recorded audio, either never record to the same place twice, or move the recorded audio somewhere else when you're done recording.

The recorded audio file needs to be stored in a location where your game is allowed to put files. A good place to use is your game's *Documents* directory; any files placed in this folder will be backed up when the user's device is synced.

To get the location of your game's *Documents* folder, you can use the `FileManager` class:

```
let documentsURL = FileManager.default
    .urls(for: FileManager.SearchPathDirectory.documentDirectory,
        in:FileManager.SearchPathDomainMask.userDomainMask).last!
```

Once you have the location of the directory, you can create a URL relative to it. Remember, the URL doesn't have to point to a real file yet; one will be created when recording begins:

```
return documentsURL.appendingPathComponent("RecordedSound.wav")
```

4.3 Working with Multiple Audio Players

Problem

You want to use multiple audio players, but reuse players when possible.

Solution

Create a manager object that manages a collection of AVAudioPlayers. When you want to play a sound, you ask this object to give you an AVAudioPlayer. The manager object will try to give you an AVAudioPlayer that's not currently doing anything, but if it can't find one, it will create one.

To create your manager object, create a file called *AVAudioPlayerPool.swift* with the following contents:

```
// An array of all players stored in the pool; not accessible
// outside this file
private var players : [AVAudioPlayer] = []

class AVAudioPlayerPool: NSObject {

    // Given the URL of a sound file, either create or reuse an audio player
    class func player(url : URL) -> AVAudioPlayer? {

        // Try and find a player that can be reused and is not playing
        let availablePlayers = players.filter { (player) -> Bool in
            return player.isPlaying == false && player.url == url
        }

        // If we found one, return it
        if let playerToUse = availablePlayers.first {
            print("Reusing player for \(url.lastPathComponent)")
            return playerToUse
        }

        // Didn't find one? Create a new one

        do {
            let newPlayer = try AVAudioPlayer(contentsOf: url)
            players.append(newPlayer)
            return newPlayer
        } catch let error {
            print("Couldn't load \(url.lastPathComponent): \(error)")
            return nil
        }

    }

}
```

You can then use it as follows:

```
if let url = Bundle.main.url(forResource: "TestSound",
                                       withExtension: "wav") {
    let player = AVAudioPlayerPool.player(url: url)
```

```
        player?.play()
    }
```

Discussion

AVAudioPlayers are allowed to be played multiple times, but aren't allowed to change the file that they're playing. If you want to reuse a single player, you have to use the same file; if you want to use a different file, you'll need a new player.

This means that the AVAudioPlayerPool object shown in this recipe needs to know which file you want to play.

Our AVAudioPlayerPool object does the following things:

1. It keeps a list of AVAudioPlayer objects in an array.

2. When a player is requested, it checks to see if it has an available player with the right URL; if it does, it returns that.

3. If there's no AVAudioPlayer that it can use—either because all of the suitable AVAudioPlayers are playing, or because there's no AVAudioPlayer with the right URL—it creates one, prepares it with the URL provided, and adds it to the list of AVAudioPlayers. This means that when this new AVAudioPlayer is done playing, it can be reused.

4.4 Cross-Fading Between Tracks

Problem

You want to blend multiple sounds by smoothly fading one out and another in.

Solution

This method slowly fades an AVAudioPlayer from a starting volume to an end volume, over a set duration:

```swift
func fade(player: AVAudioPlayer,
             fromVolume startVolume : Float,
             toVolume endVolume : Float,
             overTime time : TimeInterval) {

    let stepsPerSecond = 100

    // Update the volume every 1/100 of a second
    let fadeSteps = Int(time * TimeInterval(stepsPerSecond))
    // Work out how much time each step will take
    let timePerStep = TimeInterval(1.0 / Double(stepsPerSecond))
```

```
player.volume = startVolume;

// Schedule a number of volume changes
for step in 0...fadeSteps {

    let delayInSeconds : TimeInterval = TimeInterval(step) * timePerStep

    let deadline = DispatchTime.now() + delayInSeconds

    DispatchQueue.main.asyncAfter(deadline: deadline, execute: {
        let fraction = (Float(step) / Float(fadeSteps))

        player.volume = startVolume + (endVolume - startVolume) * fraction
    })

    }
}
```

To use this method to fade in an AVAudioPlayer, use a startVolume of 0.0 and an endVolume of 1.0:

```
fade(player: audioPlayer!, fromVolume: 0.0, toVolume: 1.0, overTime: 1.0)
```

To fade out, use a startVolume of 1.0 and an endVolume of 0.0:

```
fade(player: audioPlayer!, fromVolume: 1.0, toVolume: 0.0, overTime: 1.0)
```

To make the fade take longer, increase the overTime parameter.

Discussion

When you want the volume of an AVAudioPlayer to slowly fade out, what you really want is for the volume to change very slightly but very often. In this recipe, we've created a method that uses Grand Central Dispatch to schedule the repeated, gradual adjustment of the volume of a player over time.

To determine how many individual volume changes are needed, the first step is to decide how many times per second the volume should change. In this example, we've chosen 100 times per second—that is, the volume will be changed 100 times for every second the fade should last:

```
let stepsPerSecond = 100

// Update the volume every 1/100 of a second
let fadeSteps = Int(time * TimeInterval(stepsPerSecond))
// Work out how much time each step will take
let timePerStep = TimeInterval(1.0 / Double(stepsPerSecond))
```

Feel free to experiment with this number. Bigger numbers will lead to smoother fades, whereas smaller numbers will be more efficient but might sound worse.

The next step is to ensure that the player's current volume is set to be the start volume:

```
player.volume = startVolume;
```

We then repeatedly schedule volume changes. We're actually scheduling these changes all at once; however, each change is scheduled to take place slightly after the previous one.

To know exactly when a change should take place, all we need to know is how many steps into the fade we are, and how long the total fade should take. From there, we can calculate how far in the future a specific step should take place:

```
// Schedule a number of volume changes
for step in 0...fadeSteps {

    let delayInSeconds : TimeInterval = TimeInterval(step) * timePerStep
```

Once this duration is known, we can get Grand Central Dispatch to schedule it:

```
let deadline = DispatchTime.now() + delayInSeconds

DispatchQueue.main.asyncAfter(deadline: deadline, execute: {
```

The next few lines of code are executed when the step is ready to happen. At this point, we need to know exactly what the volume of the audio player should be:

```
let fraction = (Float(step) / Float(fadeSteps))

player.volume = startVolume + (endVolume - startVolume) * fraction
```

When the code runs, the `for` loop creates and schedules multiple blocks that set the volume, with each block reducing the volume a little. The end result is that the user hears a gradual lessening in volume—in other words, a fade out!

4.5 Synthesizing Speech

Problem

You want to make your app speak.

Solution

First, import the `AVFoundation` in your file (see Recipe 4.1).

Then, create an instance of AVSpeechSynthesizer:

```
var speechSynthesizer = AVSpeechSynthesizer()
```

When you have text you want to speak, create an AVSpeechUtterance:

```
let utterance = AVSpeechUtterance(string: textToSpeak)
```

You then give the utterance to your AVSpeechSynthesizer:

```
self.speechSynthesizer.speak(utterance)
```

Discussion

The voices you use with AVSpeechSynthesizer are the same ones seen in the Siri personal assistant that's built into all devices released since the iPhone 4S, and in the VoiceOver accessibility feature.

You can send more than one AVSpeechUtterance to an AVSpeechSynthesizer at the same time. If you call speak while the synthesizer is already speaking, it will wait until the current utterance has finished before moving on to the next.

 Don't call speak with the same AVSpeechUtterance twice—you'll cause an exception, and your app will crash.

Once you start speaking, you can instruct the AVSpeechSynthesizer to pause speaking, either immediately or at the next word:

```
// Stop speaking immediately
self.speechSynthesizer.pauseSpeaking(at: AVSpeechBoundary.immediate)
// Stop speaking after the current word
self.speechSynthesizer.pauseSpeaking(at: AVSpeechBoundary.word)
```

Once you've paused speaking, you can resume it at any time:

```
self.speechSynthesizer.continueSpeaking()
```

If you're done with speaking, you can clear the AVSpeechSynthesizer of the current and pending AVSpeechUtterances by calling stopSpeaking(at:). This method works in the same way as pauseSpeaking(at:), but once you call it, anything the synthesizer was about to say is forgotten.

4.6 Getting Information About What the Music App Is Playing

Problem

You want to find out information about whatever song the Music application is playing.

Solution

To do this, you'll need to add the Media Player framework to your code by importing the `MediaPlayer` module in your file.

First, get an `MPMusicPlayerController` from the system, which contains information about the built-in music library. Next, get the currently playing `MPMediaItem`, which represents a piece of media that the Music app is currently playing. Finally, call `value ForProperty` to get specific information about that media item:

```
let musicPlayer = MPMusicPlayerController.systemMusicPlayer

let currentTrack : MPMediaItem? = musicPlayer.nowPlayingItem
let title = currentTrack?.value(forProperty: MPMediaItemPropertyTitle)
    as? String ?? "None"
let artist = currentTrack?.value(forProperty: MPMediaItemPropertyArtist)
    as? String ?? "None"
let album = currentTrack?.value(forProperty: MPMediaItemPropertyAlbumTitle)
    as? String ?? "None"

self.titleLabel.text = title
self.artistLabel.text = artist
self.albumLabel.text = album
```

Once you've got this information, you can do whatever you like with it, including displaying it in a label, showing it in-game, and more.

Finally, because the contents of the user's media library is private information, you need to justify why you need permission to access it. When you request the `systemMu sicPlayer`, iOS will use the text you provide to ask the user for permission to access the library.

To do this, go to the Project navigator, and select the project at the top. In the Targets list that appears, select the app target. Click the Info tab, and add a new entry for "Privacy - Media Library Usage Description". In the Value column for this new entry, write the justification for why your app needs access to the user's media library.

Discussion

An `MPMusicPlayerController` represents the music playback system that's built into every iOS device. Using this object, you can get information about the currently playing track, set the currently playing queue of music, and control the playback (such as by pausing and skipping backward and forward in the queue).

There are actually *two* `MPMusicPlayerControllers` available to your app. The first is the *system music player*, which represents the state of the built-in Music application. The system music player is shared across all applications, so they all have control over the same thing.

The second music player controller that's available is the *application music player*. The application music player is functionally identical to the system music player, with a single difference: each application has its own application music player. This means that they each have their own playlist.

Only one piece of media can be playing at a single time. If an application starts using its own application music player, the system music player will pause and let the application take over. If you're using an app that's playing music out of the application music player, and you then exit that app, the music will stop.

To get information about the currently playing track, you use the `nowPlayingItem` property of the `MPMusicPlayerController`. This property returns an `MPMediaItem`, which is an object that represents a piece of media. Media means music, videos, audiobooks, podcasts, and more—not just music!

To get information about an `MPMediaItem`, you use the `valueForProperty` method. This method takes one of several possible property names. Here are some examples:

`MPMediaItemPropertyAlbumTitle`
> The name of the album.

`MPMediaItemPropertyArtist`
> The name of the artist.

`MPMediaItemPropertyAlbumArtist`
> The name of the album's main artist (for albums with multiple artists).

`MPMediaItemPropertyGenre`
> The genre of the music.

`MPMediaItemPropertyComposer`
> The composer of the music.

`MPMediaItemPropertyPlaybackDuration`
> The length of the music, in seconds.

The media library is only available on iOS devices—it's not available on the iOS Simulator. If you try to use these features on the simulator, it just plain won't work.

4.7 Detecting When the Currently Playing Track Changes

Problem

You want to detect when the currently playing media item changes.

Solution

Use a `NotificationCenter` to subscribe to the `MPMusicPlayerControllerNowPlayingItemDidChangeNotification` notification. First, create a property of type `AnyObject?` to store a reference to the *observer object*:

```
var trackChangedObserver : AnyObject?
```

When you want to begin tracking when the now playing item changes, ask the `NotificationCenter` to begin observing the notification:

```
trackChangedObserver = NotificationCenter.default
    .addObserver(forName: .MPMusicPlayerControllerNowPlayingItemDidChange,
        object: nil, queue: OperationQueue.main) { (notification) -> Void in
            self.updateTrackInformation()
}
```

Next, get a reference to the `MPMusicPlayerController` that you want to get notifications for, and call `beginGeneratingPlaybackNotifications` on it:

```
let musicPlayer = MPMusicPlayerController.systemMusicPlayer

musicPlayer.beginGeneratingPlaybackNotifications()
```

When you begin observing notifications using `addObserver(forName:, object: queue, handler:)`, you're given a reference to an object: the *observer object*. You need to keep a reference to this object around, because when you want to tell the notification system to stop notifying you (and you *must* do this, or else you'll get bugs and crashes), you pass the object back to the `NotificationCenter` and call the `removeObserver` method. A common place to do this is in the view controller's `deinit` method:

```
deinit {
    NotificationCenter.default.removeObserver(trackChangedObserver!)
}
```

Discussion

Notifications regarding the current item won't be sent unless `beginGeneratingPlay backNotifications` is called. If you stop being interested in the currently playing item, call `endGeneratingPlaybackNotifications`.

Note that you might not receive these notifications if your application is in the background. It's generally a good idea to manually update your interface whenever your game comes back from the background, instead of just relying on the notifications to arrive.

4.8 Controlling Music Playback

Problem

You want to control the track that the Music application is playing.

Solution

Use the `MPMusicPlayerController` to control the state of the music player:

```
let musicPlayer = MPMusicPlayerController.systemMusicPlayer

musicPlayer.play()
musicPlayer.pause()
musicPlayer.skipToBeginning()
musicPlayer.skipToNextItem()
musicPlayer.skipToPreviousItem()
musicPlayer.beginSeekingForward()
musicPlayer.beginSeekingBackward()
musicPlayer.stop()
```

Discussion

Don't forget that if you're using the shared system music player controller, any changes you make to the playback state apply to all applications. This means that the playback state of your application might get changed by *other* applications—usually the Music application, but possibly by other apps.

You can query the current state of the music player by asking it for the `playback State`, which is one of the following values:

`MPMusicPlaybackState.stopped`
    The music player isn't playing anything.

`MPMusicPlaybackState.playing`
    The music player is currently playing.

`MPMusicPlaybackState.paused`

   The music player is playing, but is paused.

`MPMusicPlaybackState.interrupted`

   The music player is playing, but has been interrupted (e.g., by a phone call).

`MPMusicPlaybackState.seekingForward`

   The music player is fast-forwarding.

`MPMusicPlaybackState.seekingBackward`

   The music player is fast-reversing.

You can get notified about changes in the playback state by registering for the `MPMu sicPlayerControllerPlaybackStateDidChange` notification, in the same way `MPMu sicPlayerControllerNowPlayingItemDidChange` allows you to get notified about changes in the currently playing item.

4.9 Allowing the User to Select Music

Problem

You want to allow the user to choose some music to play.

Solution

You can display an `MPMediaPickerController` to let the user select music.

First, make your view controller conform to the `MPMediaPickerControllerDelegate`:

```
class ViewController: UIViewController, MPMediaPickerControllerDelegate {
```

Next, add the following code at the point where you want to display the media picker:

```
let picker = MPMediaPickerController(mediaTypes:MPMediaType.anyAudio)

picker.allowsPickingMultipleItems = true
picker.showsCloudItems = true

picker.delegate = self

self.present(picker, animated:false, completion:nil)
```

Then, add the following two methods to your view controller:

```
func mediaPicker(_ mediaPicker: MPMediaPickerController,
    didPickMediaItems mediaItemCollection: MPMediaItemCollection) {

    for item in mediaItemCollection.items {
        if let itemName = item.value(forProperty: MPMediaItemPropertyTitle)
            as? String {
```

```
                print("Picked item: \(itemName)")
            }

        }

        let musicPlayer = MPMusicPlayerController.systemMusicPlayer

        musicPlayer.setQueue(with: mediaItemCollection)

        musicPlayer.play()

        self.dismiss(animated: false, completion:nil)
    }

    func mediaPickerDidCancel(_ mediaPicker: MPMediaPickerController) {
        self.dismiss(animated: false, completion:nil)
    }
```

Discussion

An MPMediaPickerController uses the exact same user interface as the one you see
in the built-in Music application. This means that your player doesn't have to waste
time learning how to navigate a different interface.

When you create an MPMediaPickerController, you can choose what kinds of media
you want the user to pick. In this recipe, we've gone with MPMediaTypeAnyAudio,
which, as the name suggests, means the user can pick any audio: music, audiobooks,
podcasts, and so on. Other options include:

- MPMediaType.music
- MPMediaType.podcast
- MPMediaType.audioBook
- MPMediaType.audioITunesU
- MPMediaType.movie
- MPMediaType.tvShow
- MPMediaType.videoPodcast
- MPMediaType.musicVideo
- MPMediaType.videoITunesU
- MPMediaType.homeVideo
- MPMediaType.anyVideo
- MPMediaType.anyAudio

- `MPMediaType.any`

In addition to setting what kind of content you want the user to pick, you can also set whether you want the user to be able to pick multiple items or just one:

```
picker.allowsPickingMultipleItems = true
```

Finally, you can decide whether you want to present media that the user has purchased from iTunes, but isn't currently downloaded onto the device. Apple refers to this feature as "iTunes in the Cloud," and you can turn it on or off through the `show sCloudItems` property. Apple Music content is also displayed, if the user is a subscriber.

```
picker.showsCloudItems = true
```

When the user finishes picking media, the delegate of the `MPMediaPickerController` receives the `mediaPicker(_, didPickMediaItems:)` message. The media items that were chosen are contained in an `MPMediaItemCollection` object, which is basically an array of `MPMediaItems`.

In addition to getting information about the media items that were selected, you can also give the `MPMediaItemCollection` directly to an `MPMusicPlayerController`, and tell it to start playing:

```
let musicPlayer = MPMusicPlayerController.systemMusicPlayer

musicPlayer.setQueue(with: mediaItemCollection)

musicPlayer.play()
```

Once you're done getting content out of the media picker, you need to dismiss it, by using the `dismiss(animated:, completion:)` method. This also applies if the user taps the Cancel button in the media picker: in this case, your delegate receives the `mediaPickerDidCancel` message, and your application should dismiss the view controller in the same way.

4.10 Cooperating with Other Applications' Audio

Problem

You want to play background music only when the user isn't already listening to something.

Solution

You can find out if another application is currently playing audio by using the `AVAudioSession` class:

```
let session = AVAudioSession.sharedInstance()

if (session.isOtherAudioPlaying) {
    // Another application is playing audio. Don't play any sound that might
    // conflict with music, such as your own background music.
} else {
    // No other app is playing audio - crank the tunes!
}
```

Discussion

The AVAudioSession class lets you control how audio is currently being handled on the device, and gives you considerable flexibility in terms of how the device should handle things like the ringer switch (the switch on the side of the device) and what happens when the user locks the screen.

By default, if you begin playing back audio using AVAudioPlayer and another application (such as the built-in Music app) is playing audio, the other application will stop all sound, and the audio played by your game will be the only thing audible.

However, you might want the user to be able to listen to her own music while playing your game—the background music might not be a very important part of your game, for example.

To change the default behavior of muting other applications, you need to set the audio session's *category*. For example, to indicate to the system that your application should not cause other apps to mute their audio, you need to set the audio session's category to AVAudioSession.Category.ambient:

```
do {
    try AVAudioSession.sharedInstance()
        .setCategory(AVAudioSession.Category.ambient),
} catch {
    println("Problem setting audio session: \(error)")
}
```

There are several categories of audio session available. The most important to games are the following:

AVAudioSession.Category.soloAmbient
> Audio is reasonably important to your game. If other apps are playing audio, they'll stop. However, the audio session will continue to respect the ringer switch and the screen locking. This is the default session category.

AVAudioSession.Category.ambient
> Audio isn't the most important part of your game, and other apps should be able to play audio alongside yours. When the ringer switch is set to *mute*, your audio is silenced, and when the screen locks, your audio stops.

`AVAudioSession.Category.playback`

Audio is very important to your game. Other apps are silenced, and your app *ignores* the ringer switch and the screen locking.

 When using `AVAudioSession.Category.playback`, your app will still be stopped when the screen locks. To make it keep running, you need to mark your app as one that plays audio in the background. To do this, follow these steps:

1. Open your project's information page by clicking the project at the top of the Project Navigator.

2. Select the application's target from the Targets list.

3. Go to the Capabilities tab.

4. Turn on "Background Modes," and then turn on "Audio and AirPlay."

Your app will now play audio in the background, as long as the audio session's category is set to `AVAudioSession.Category.play back`.

4.11 Determining How to Best Use Sound in Your Game Design

Problem

You want to make optimal use of sound and music in your game design.

Solution

It's really hard to make an iOS game that relies on sound. For one, you can't count on the user wearing headphones, and sounds in games (and everything else, really) don't sound their best coming from the tiny speakers found in iOS devices.

Many games "get around" this by prompting users to put on their headphones as the game launches, or suggesting that they are "best experienced via headphones" in the sound and music options menu, if it has one. We think this is a suboptimal solution.

The best iOS games understand and acknowledge the environment in which the games are likely to be played: typically a busy, distraction-filled environment, where your beautiful audio might not be appreciated due to background noise or the fact that the user has the volume turned all the way down.

The solution is to make sure your game works with, or without, sound. Don't count on the user hearing anything at all, in fact.

Discussion

Unless you're building a game that is based around music or sound, you should make it completely playable without sound. Your users will thank you for it, even if they never actually thank you for it!

CHAPTER 5

Data Storage

Games are apps, and apps run on data. Whether it's just resources that your game loads or saved-game files that you need to store, your game will eventually need to work with data stored on the flash chips that make up the storage subsystems present on all iOS devices.

In this chapter, you'll learn how to convert objects into saveable data, how to work with iCloud, how to load resources without freezing up the rest of the game, and more.

5.1 Storing Structured Information

Problem

You want to store and load your game's information in a way that produces data that's easy to read and write.

Solution

Make the objects that you want to store and load conform to the `Codable` class, and use one of the `Encoder` and `Decoder` classes to convert the objects to raw data that you can save and load.

For example, let's assume that you want to store a saved game. Saved games contain three things: the level number the player is on, the name of the player, and the set of achievements that they've earned in this game. The achievements themselves are represented as an enumeration:

```
// The list of achievements that the player can get.
enum Achievements : String, Codable {
    case startedPlaying
```

```
        case finishedGameInTenMinutes
        case foundAllSecretRooms
    }

    // The data that represents a saved game.
    class SavedGame : Codable {

        var levelNumber = 0
        var playerName = ""

        var achievements : Set<Achievements> = []
    }

    let savedGame = SavedGame()

    // Store some data
    savedGame.levelNumber = 3
    savedGame.playerName = "Grabthar"
    savedGame.achievements.insert(Achievements.foundAllSecretRooms)
```

Note that both the Achievements and SavedGame types conform to the Codable property. This is important, since it means that these types can be converted to and from an encoded representation, like JavaScript Object Notation (JSON).

To convert this savedGame variable into data that can be written to disk, use an encoder. One such encoder is JSONEncoder, which converts any object that conforms to Codable into the JSON, which is a quite common text-based format. When you use the encode method on an encoder, it produces a Data object that you can write to disk:

```
    do {
        // Encode the data
        let encoder = JSONEncoder()

        let data = try encoder.encode(savedGame)

        // We can now write the data to disk
        print(String(data: data, encoding: .utf8)!)
    } catch let error {
        print("Failed to encode the saved game! \(error)")
    }
```

This produces a Data object that contains the following text:

```
    {"achievements":["foundAllSecretRooms"],"levelNumber":3,"playerName":"Grabthar"}
```

To perform the reverse, you use a decoder. For example, if you have a Data object that contains encoded JSON data, you can create a JSONDecoder, and use its decode method:

```
    var decodedSavedGame : SavedGame?
```

```
do {
    let decoder = JSONDecoder()

    decodedSavedGame = try decoder.decode(SavedGame.self, from: data)
} catch let error {
    print("Failed to decode the saved game! \(error)")
}

// 'decodedSavedGame' will now be either nil or contain a SavedGame object
decodedSavedGame?.playerName // = "Grabthar"
```

Discussion

When you mark a type as Codable, the Swift compiler will automatically generate methods that make it encodable and decodable, as long as all of the type's stored properties are themselves Codable.

In this example, the data stored inside the SavedGame type contains three Codable properties: a string and an integer, which are defined as Codable in the Swift Standard Library, and the enumeration Achievement, which is explicitly marked as Codable, and doesn't need any further work because its underlying type is a string.

If you're working with a type that can't be made Codable (because its stored properties are themselves not Codable), you can implement the encoding and decoding manually. However, this topic is a little complex and beyond the scope of this book; for more information about it, see "Encoding and Decoding Custom Types" in Apple's documentation (*https://apple.co/2QVqrXr*).

5.2 Storing Data Locally

Problem

You want to store encoded data, such as a saved game or a list of high scores, in a file on disk.

Solution

First, store your data using an object that conforms to the Codable protocol, and encode that object into a Data object, by using the techniques found in Recipe 5.1.

Next, determine the location on disk where these scores can be placed:

```
let fileManager = FileManager.default
guard let documentsURL = fileManager.urls(
    for: FileManager.SearchPathDirectory.documentDirectory,
    in:FileManager.SearchPathDomainMask.userDomainMask).last else {

    fatalError("Failed to find the documents folder!")
```

```
    }

    let savedGameURL = documentsURL
        .appendingPathComponent("SavedGame.json")
```

Finally, write out the data to this location:

```
do {
    try data.write(to: savedGameURL)
} catch let error {
    print("Error writing: \(error)")
}
```

You can load the data from disk by reading from the location:

```
var loadedData : Data?

do {
    loadedData = try Data(contentsOf: savedGameURL)
} catch let error {
    print("Error reading: \(error)")
}
```

Discussion

An application in iOS is only allowed to read and write files that are inside the app's *sandbox*. Each app is limited to its own sandbox and is generally not allowed to access any files that lie outside of it. To get the location of an app's *Documents* folder, which is located inside the sandbox, you use the `FileManager` class to give you the URL. You can then construct an URL based on that, and give *that* URL to the array, using it to write to the disk.

5.3 Using iCloud to Save Games

Problem

You want to save the player's game in iCloud.

Solution

 To work with iCloud, you'll need to have an active iOS Developer Program membership.

First, activate iCloud support in your app. To do this, select the project at the top of the Project Navigator, select the game's target from the Target list, and ensure that your developer team is selected (and isn't None). If you happen to be a member of multiple developer teams, make sure the right one is selected, because enabling iCloud support means registering a new App ID with your developer team.

Next, switch to the Capabilities tab. Turn on the "iCloud" switch. Follow the prompts to add iCloud support.

 In iCloud, you store your app's information in *iCloud containers*. Usually, each of your apps has its own container, but you can make multiple apps share a single container. For example, if you have a Mac game and an iOS game, you can have them share their saved games by making them use the same iCloud container.

When you first enable iCloud support, only *key-value storage* is turned on by default. Turn on iCloud Documents as well, to enable support for saving files in iCloud. Xcode will do a little more work to add support for storing files in an iCloud container.

Saving the player's game in iCloud really means saving game data. This means that you need to have your data stored in a `Data` object of some kind.

First, you need to check to see if iCloud is available. It may not be; for example, if the user hasn't signed in to an Apple ID or has deliberately disabled iCloud on the device. You can check to see if iCloud is available by doing the following:

```
// Get the saved data from somewhere
let saveData : Data = self.saveGameData()

// If we aren't signed in to iCloud, then we must save locally
if FileManager.default.ubiquityIdentityToken == nil {
    saveGameLocally(data: saveData)
}
```

 If you're testing this on an iOS Simulator, don't forget to sign into an iCloud account. You can do this inside the Settings app.

To put a file in iCloud, you do this:

```
// This must always be done in the background, because
// locating the iCloud container on disk can involve
// setting it up, which can take time.
OperationQueue().addOperation { () -> Void in

    let fileName = "Documents/MySavedGame.save"
```

```
    if let containerURL = FileManager.default
        .url(forUbiquityContainerIdentifier: nil) {

        let fileURL = containerURL.appendingPathComponent(fileName)

        do {
            try saveData.write(to: fileURL,
                                    options: Data.WritingOptions.atomic
            )

        } catch let error {
            print("Error saving file to iCloud! \(error)")
        }
    }
}
```

To find files that are in iCloud, you use the NSMetadataQuery class. This returns information about files that have been stored in iCloud, either by the current device or by another device the user owns. NSMetadataQuery works like a search—you tell it what you're looking for, and register to be notified when the search completes:

```
lazy var metadataQuery : NSMetadataQuery = {
    let query = NSMetadataQuery()

    // Search for all files whose name end in .save in the iCloud
    // container's documents folder
    query.searchScopes = [NSMetadataQueryUbiquitousDocumentsScope]
    query.predicate = NSPredicate(format: "%K LIKE '*.save'",
                                    NSMetadataItemFSNameKey)

    let notificationCenter = NotificationCenter.default

    // Call the searchComplete method when this query
    // finds content (either initially, or when new
    // changes are discovered after the app starts)
    notificationCenter.addObserver(self,
                        selector: #selector(ViewController.searchComplete),
                        name: .NSMetadataQueryDidFinishGathering,
                        object: nil)
    notificationCenter.addObserver(self,
                        selector: #selector(ViewController.searchComplete),
                        name: .NSMetadataQueryDidUpdate,
                        object: nil)

    return query
}()

deinit {
    // When this object is going away, tidy up after
    // the metadata query

    metadataQuery.stop()
```

```
let notificationCenter = NotificationCenter.default
notificationCenter.removeObserver(self)
}
```

 When a property is lazy, its value is computed the first time it's accessed. So, when the metadataQuery property is accessed, its value - which is the result of defining a closure that creates and returns an NSMetadataQuery, and then immediately calling that closure - is calculated, stored, and then returned. All future use of the metadataQuery property will return that NSMetadataQuery object. Lazy properties can only be declared at the class level - they can't be declared inside a method.

When your app starts, you tell the query to start running:

```
metadataQuery.start()
```

You then implement a method that's run when the search is complete:

```
@objc func searchComplete() {

    guard let results = metadataQuery.results as? [NSMetadataItem] else {
        fatalError("Metadata query results are not an array of NSMetadataItem")
    }

    for item in results {
        // Find the URL for the item
        guard let url = item.value(forAttribute: NSMetadataItemURLKey)
            as? URL else {
                continue
        }

        if item.value(forAttribute:
            NSMetadataUbiquitousItemHasUnresolvedConflictsKey)
            as! Bool == true {
            // Another device has got a conflicting version
            // of this file, and we need to resolve it.
            self.resolveConflictsForItemAtURL(url: url)
        }

        // Has the file already been downloaded?
        if let status = item.value(
                forAttribute: NSMetadataUbiquitousItemDownloadingStatusKey)
                    as? String,
                status == NSMetadataUbiquitousItemDownloadingStatusCurrent {
            // This file is downloaded and is the most current version;
            // do something with it (like offer to let the user load
            // the saved game)
            self.saveGameWasUpdated(url: url)
```

```
    } else {
        // The file is either not downloaded at all, or is out of date
        // We need to download the file from iCloud; when it finishes
        // downloading, NSMetadataQuery will call this method again

        // Ask iCloud to begin downloading.
        do {
            try FileManager.default
                .startDownloadingUbiquitousItem(at: url)
        } catch let error {
            print("Problem starting download of \(url): \(error)")
        }


    }
  }
}
```

An NSMetadataQuery runs until it's stopped. If you make a change to a file that the query is watching, you'll receive a new notification.

If you're done looking for files in iCloud, you can stop the query using the stopQuery method:

```
metadataQuery.stop()
```

When a file is in iCloud and you make changes to it, iCloud will automatically upload the changed file, and other devices will receive the new copy. If the same file is changed at the same time by different devices, the file will be in conflict. You can detect this by checking the NSMetadataUbiquitousItemHasUnresolvedConflictsKey attribute on the results of your NSMetadataQuery; if this is set to true, then there are conflicts.

There are several ways you can resolve a conflict; one way is to simply say, "The version that I have locally is the correct version; ignore conflicts." To indicate this to the system, you do this:

```
func resolveConflictsForItemAtURL(url : URL) {

    // 'The version I have is correct; all others are wrong.'
    for conflictVersion in NSFileVersion
        .unresolvedConflictVersionsOfItem(at: url)! {
        // Mark these other versions as resolved; iCloud will tell other
        // devices to update their local copies
        conflictVersion.isResolved = true
    }

    // Remove our conflicted copies
    do {
        try NSFileVersion.removeOtherVersionsOfItem(at: url)
```

```
        } catch let error {
            print("Failed to remove other versions of item at \(url): \(error)")
        }

    }
```

Discussion

iCloud is a technology from Apple that syncs documents and information across the various devices that a user owns. "Devices," in this case, means both iOS devices and Macs; when you create a document and put it in iCloud, the same file appears on all devices that you're signed in to. Additionally, the file is backed up by Apple on the web.

To use iCloud, you need to have an active iOS Developer account, because all iCloud activity in an app is linked to the developer who created the app. You don't have to do anything special with your app besides have Xcode activate iCloud support for it—all of the setup is handled for you automatically.

It's worth keeping in mind that not all users will have access to iCloud. If they're not signed in to an Apple ID, or if they've deliberately turned off iCloud, your game still needs to work without it. This means saving your game files locally, and not putting them into iCloud.

Additionally, it's possible that the user might have signed out of iCloud, and a different user has signed in. You can check this by asking the FileManager for the `ubiquityIdentityToken`, which you can store; if it's different from the last time you checked, you should throw away any local copies of your saved games, and redownload the files from iCloud.

You should always perform iCloud work on a background queue. iCloud operations can frequently take several dozen milliseconds to complete, which can slow down your game if you run them on the main queue and cause it to appear as thoughh your game is hanging.

5.4 Using the iCloud Key-Value Store

Problem

You want to store small amounts of information in iCloud.

Solution

Use `NSUbiquitousKeyValueStore`, which is like a dictionary whose contents are shared across all of the user's devices.

To get values out of the key-value store, you do this:

```
// Retrieve the value from the key-value store
let store = NSUbiquitousKeyValueStore.default
return Int(store.longLong(forKey: "levelNumber"))
```

To store values in the key-value store, you do this:

```
// Store the value in the key-value store
let store = NSUbiquitousKeyValueStore.default
store.set(Int64(value), forKey: "levelNumber")

// Ensure that these changes have been saved to disk
// (note: this doesn't sync the local iCloud container
// with the server, that happens later when the system decides
// it's time)
store.synchronize()
```

It's possible that the contents of the key-value store can change remotely. For example, if your player happens to be playing the game on two devices at the same time—which you can be guaranteed will happen!—then you need to update your game accordingly. To do this, you register to receive the NSUbiquitousKeyValueStoreDid ChangeExternallyNotification:

```
// Register to be notified when the key-value store
// is changed by another device
NotificationCenter.default.addObserver(self,
    selector: #selector(ViewController.ubiquitousKeyValueStoreUpdated),
    name: NSUbiquitousKeyValueStore.didChangeExternallyNotification,
    object: nil);
```

Discussion

Many games don't need to store very much information in order to let the players keep their state around. For example, if you're making a puzzle game, you might only need to store the number of the level that the players reached. In these cases, the NSUbiquitousKeyValueStore is exactly what you need. The ubiquitous key-value store stores small amounts of data—strings, numbers, and so on—and keeps them synchronized.

You'll need to activate iCloud support in your app for NSUbiquitousKeyValueStore to work. Additionally, you must call FileManager's url(forUbiquityContainerIdentifier:) at least once before attempting to access the key-value store, in order to make sure that your app has access to the iCloud container. See Recipe 5.3 for an example on how to do this. Don't forget that url(forUbiquityContainerIdentifier:) must be called on a background queue.

Finally, you also need to handle the case of the user not being signed into iCloud: if the user is not signed in, anything you store in the key-value store will disappear, and you'll need to store the information locally.

Unlike when you're working with files, conflict resolution in the ubiquitous key-value store is handled automatically for you by iCloud: the most recent value that was set wins. This can sometimes lead to problems. For example, consider the following user experience:

1. You have a puzzle game, and the highest level that's been unlocked is stored in the key-value store.

2. You play up to level 6 on your iPhone, and iCloud syncs the key-value store.

3. Later, you play the game on your iPad, but it's offline. You get up to level 2 on your iPad. Later, your iPad is connected to the internet, and iCloud syncs this latest value. Because it's the latest value to be set, it overwrites the "older" value of 2.

4. You then play the game on your iPhone, and are very surprised to see that your progress has been "lost." You delete the app and leave a 1-star review on the App Store. The app developer goes bankrupt and dies alone in a gutter.

To solve this problem, you should keep data in the local user defaults, and update it only after comparing it to the ubiquitous store. When the store changes, compare it against the local user defaults; if the ubiquitous store's value is lower, copy the value from the local store into the ubiquitous store, overwriting it. If it's higher, copy the value from the ubiquitous store into the local store. Whenever you want to read the information, always consult the local store.

You're limited to 1 MB of data in the ubiquitous key-value store on a per-application basis. If you try to put more data than this into the key-value store, the value won't be saved. The per-value limit is 1MB; you can have a maximum of 1024 values.

5.5 Deciding When to Use Files or a Database

Problem

You want to decide whether to store information as individual files, or as a database.

Solution

Use individual files when:

- You know that you'll need the entire contents of the file all at the same time.
- The file is small.
- The file is easy to read and process, and won't take lots of CPU resources to get information out.

Use a database when:

- The file is large, and you don't need to load everything in at once.
- You only need a little bit of information from the file.
- You need to very quickly load specific parts of the file.
- You want to make changes to the file while continuing to read it.
- You need to make complex queries that make use of the relationships between different pieces of data.

Discussion

Games tend to load files for two different reasons:

- The file contains information that needs to be kept entirely in memory, because all of it is needed at once (e.g., textures, level layouts, and some sounds).
- The file contains a lot of information, but only parts of it need to be read at once (e.g., monster information, player info, dialogue).

Databases are much faster and more efficient at getting small amounts of information from a larger file, but the downside is *lots* of increased code complexity.

5.6 Managing a Collection of Assets

Problem

Your game has a large number of big files, and you want to load them into memory in the background, without the main thread getting slowed down.

Solution

Create a new class, called `AssetLoader`. Put the following code in *AssetLoader.swift*:

```swift
class AssetLoader: NSObject {

    // For convenience, define a loading result as a tuple
    // containing the URL of the resource that was loaded,
    // and either the loaded data or an error
    typealias LoadingResult = (url: URL, data: Data?, error: Error?)

    // Also define a loading result handler as a method that receives
    // a URL, and either a data or an error
    typealias LoadingResultHandler = (URL, Data?, Error?) -> Void

    class func loadAssets(at urls: [URL],
        withEnumerationBlock loadingComplete: @escaping LoadingResultHandler) {

        // Create a queue
        let loadingQueue = OperationQueue()

        // Create an array of results
        var loadingResults : [LoadingResult] = []

        // The loading complete operation runs the loadingComplete block
        // when all loads are finished
        let loadingCompleteOperation = BlockOperation { () -> Void in

            OperationQueue.main.addOperation { () -> Void in
                // Call the loadingComplete block for each result
                for result in loadingResults {
                    loadingComplete(result.url, result.data, result.error)
                }
            }
        }

        // Start loading the data at each URL
        for url in urls {

            // Create an operation that will load the data in the background
            let loadOperation = BlockOperation { () -> Void in
                // Attempt to load the data
                let result : LoadingResult
```

```
        do {
            let data = try Data(contentsOf: url, options: [])

            // If we got it, result contains the data

            result = (url: url, data: data, error:nil)
        } catch let error {
            result = (url: url, data: nil, error:error)
        }

        // On the main queue (to prevent conflicts),
        // add this operation's result to the list
        OperationQueue.main.addOperation { () -> Void in
            loadingResults.append(result)
        }
    }

    // Add a dependency to the loading complete operation,
    // so that it won't run until this load (and all others)
    // have completed
    loadingCompleteOperation.addDependency(loadOperation)

    // Add this load operation to the queue
    loadingQueue.addOperation(loadOperation)
    }

    // Add the loading complete operation to the queue.
    // Because it has dependencies on the load operations,
    // it won't run until all files have been loaded
    loadingQueue.addOperation(loadingCompleteOperation)
    }

}
```

To use this code:

```
// Get the list of all .png files in the bundles, or the empty array
let urls = Bundle.main
    .urls(forResourcesWithExtension: "png",
        subdirectory: nil) ?? []


// Load all these images
AssetLoader.loadAssets(at: urls) {
    (url, data, error) -> Void in

    // This block is called once for each URL

    if let data = data {
        print("Loaded resource \(url.lastPathComponent) (\(data.count) bytes)")
    } else if let error = error {
        print("Failed to load resource \(url.lastPathComponent): \(error)")
    } else {
```

```
            fatalError("Didn't get data or an error; this should not happen!")
        }
    }
}
```

Discussion

Large files can take a long time to load, and you don't want the player to be looking at a frozen screen while resources are loaded from disk. To address this, you can use a class that handles the work of loading resources in the background. The `AssetMan ager` in this solution handles the work for you, by creating a new operation queue and doing the resource loading using the new queue. After the loading is complete, a block that you provide to the loading function is called (on the main thread) for each URL that was provided.

5.7 Storing Information in UserDefaults

Problem

You want to store small amounts of information, like the most recently visited level in your game.

Solution

The `UserDefaults` class is a very useful tool that lets you store small pieces of data—strings, dates, numbers, and so on—in the *user defaults* database. The user defaults system is where each app keeps its preferences and settings.

There's only a single `UserDefaults` object that you work with, which you access using the `standardUserDefaults` method:

```
let defaults = UserDefaults.standard
```

Once you have this object, you can treat it like a dictionary:

```
defaults.setValue("A string", forKey: "mySetting")

let string = defaults.value(forKey: "mySetting") as? String
```

You can store the following kinds of objects in the `UserDefaults` system:

- Numbers
- Strings
- Data
- Date
- Arrays, as long as they only contain objects in this list

- Dictionaries, as long as they contain objects in this list

Discussion

When you store information into `UserDefaults`, it isn't stored to disk right away—instead, it's saved periodically, and at certain important moments (like when the user taps the home button). This means that if your application crashes before the information is saved, whatever you stored will be lost.

You can force the `UserDefaults` system to save to disk any changes you've made to `UserDefaults` by using the `synchronize` method:

```
defaults.synchronize()
```

Doing this will ensure that all data you've stored to that point has been saved. For performance reasons, you shouldn't call `synchronize` too often—it's really fast, but don't call it every frame. It's a good idea to call it in your application delegate's `application WillResignActive(_:)` method, which is called whenever the user leaves the application, or when the application is interrupted (for example, by an incoming phone call.)

Information you store in `UserDefaults` is backed up, either to iTunes or to iCloud, depending on the user's settings. You don't need to do anything to make this happen—this will just work.

Sometimes, it's useful for `UserDefaults` to provide you with a default value—that is, a value that you should use if the user hasn't already provided one of his own.

For example, let's say your game starts on level 1, and you store the level that your player has reached as `currentLevel` in `UserDefaults`. When your game starts up, you ask `UserDefaults` for the current level, and set up the game from there:

```
let levelNumber = defaults.integer(forKey: "currentLevel")
```

However, what should happen the first time the player starts the game? If no value is provided for the `currentLevel` setting, the first time this code is called, you'll get a value of 0—which is incorrect, because your game starts at 1.

To address this problem, you can register default values. This involves giving the `User Defaults` class a dictionary of keys and values that it should use if no other value has been provided:

```
let defaultValues = ["currentLevel": 1]
defaults.register(defaults: defaultValues)

let levelNumber = defaults.integer(forKey: "currentLevel")
// levelNumber will be either 1, or whatever was last stored in NSUserDefaults.
```

It's very, very easy for users to modify the information you've stored in UserDefaults. Third-party tools can be used to directly access and modify the information stored in the defaults database, making it very easy for people to cheat.

If you're making a multiplayer game, for example, and you store the strength of the character's weapon in UserDefaults, it's possible for players to modify the database and make their characters have an unbeatable weapon.

That's not to say that you shouldn't use UserDefaults, but you need to be aware of the possibility of cheating.

5.8 Implementing the Best Data Storage Strategy

Problem

You want to make sure your game stores data sensibly, and doesn't annoy your users.

Solution

The solution here is simple: don't drop data. If your game can save its state, then it should be saving its state. You can't expect the user to manually save in an iOS game, and you should always persist data at every available opportunity.

Discussion

Nothing is more annoying than losing your progress in a game because a phone call came in. Don't risk annoying your users: persist the state of the game regularly!

5.9 In-Game Currency

Problem

You want to keep track of an in-game resource, like money, which the player can earn and spend.

Solution

The requirements for this kind of functionality vary from game to game. However, having an in-game currency is a common element in lots of games, so here's an example of how you might handle it.

In this example, let's say you have two different currencies: *gems* and *gold*. Gems are permanent, and the player keeps them from game to game. Gold is temporary, and goes away at the end of a game.

To add support for these kinds of currencies, use a computed property to persist the value of the gem currency in UserDefaults, while keeping the gold currency in memory (and reset it to zero when the game ends):

```
class CurrencyManager {

    var gold : Int = 0

    var gems : Int {
        set(value) {
            // Set the updated count of gems in the user defaults system
            UserDefaults.standard.set(value, forKey: "gems")
        }

        get {
            // Ask the user defaults system for the current number of gems
            return UserDefaults.standard.integer(forKey: "gems")
        }
    }

    func endGame() {
        // When the game is over, reset gold but leave gems alone
        gold = 0
    }

}
```

Discussion

In this solution, the gems property stores its information using the UserDefaults system, rather than simply leaving it in memory (as is done with the gold property). From the perspective of other objects, the property works like everything else:

```
let currency = CurrencyManager()

currency.gold = 45
currency.gems = 21

currency.endGame()
```

When data is stored in UserDefaults, it persists between application launches. This means that your gems will stick around when the application exits—something that players will appreciate. Note that data stored in the UserDefaults system can be modified by the user, which means cheating is not impossible.

5.10 Setting Up CloudKit

Problem

You want to store game information in CloudKit, a cloud-hosted database service operated by Apple.

Solution

To begin using iCloud, you first need to enable the iCloud capability in your app, by following the steps in Recipe 5.3.

Next, you need to set up the project to use CloudKit in particular. In the iCloud settings, select the CloudKit checkbox, and Xcode will configure your application's iCloud container to use CloudKit.

> If you click the CloudKit Dashboard button, you'll be taken to the web-based CloudKit dashboard, which allows you to view and manage the data stored in CloudKit.

Discussion

Apps that use iCloud store their information in iCloud containers. A container is created for you when you enable iCloud in your app. You can create more than one if you need, though this is rare.

In CloudKit, data is stored in databases. There are two types of databases to know about: the *public* database and the *private* databases. The public database is a shared database that all users have access to (including users who are not signed in). Each user also has a private database that contains data only the current user can see, and nobody else—not even you, the developer.

> In terms of how you work with them, the two types of databases are largely the same. The only difference is who's permitted to access them.

To access a database, you ask a `CKContainer` object for the database you want. To access the container's public database, use the `publicCloudDatabase` property:

```
let database = CKContainer.default().publicCloudDatabase
```

To access the user's private database, use the `privateCloudDatabase` property:

```
let database = CKContainer.default().privateCloudDatabase
```

A database is comprised of records, which are instances of the CKRecord class. As you work with CloudKit, most of your time will be spent creating, modifying, querying, and deleting these objects; we'll be looking at doing this in the recipes that follow.

5.11 Adding Records to a CloudKit Database

Problem

You want to store information in a CloudKit database.

Solution

Create an instance of the CKRecord type, use its setObject(_, forKey:) methods to fill it with data, and use the database's save method to save the changes.

When you create a CKRecord, you specify what type it is. A record's type is simply a string; records that have the same string are considered the same type.

Once you have a CKRecord object, you save information into its fields, which are referred to by string keys.

Rather than hardcoding a string, it's generally better to use Swift language features like enumerations, which mean that the compiler will catch problems like typos for you.

So, for a simple example, let's consider a situation where you want to store plain-text notes in CloudKit. We'll create a record type called "Note," and it will store its contents in a key called "contents":

```
enum NoteRecordKey : String {
    case contents
}

let NoteRecordType = "Note"
```

With that defined, you can create your CKRecord, fill it with data, and save it into the database.

When you call the save method on your database, you provide a closure that's run when the save operation completes. This closure receives two parameters: the CKRecord that was saved, and an error. Both of these are optional values, and only one of them will actually have a value (the other will be nil). If the closure receives a CKRecord, the save operation was successful; if the closure receives an error, it was unsuccessful:

```
func saveNewMessage(text: String) {

    let record = CKRecord(recordType: NoteRecordType)

    record.setObject(text as CKRecordValue,
        forKey: NoteRecordKey.contents.rawValue)

    self.database.save(record, completionHandler: { (record, error) in

        if let record = record {
            print("Successfully saved record \(record.recordID)")

            // Indicate to the user that it's saved


        } else if let error = error {
            print("Error saving record: \(error)")
        }
    })
}
```

Discussion

Creating a new record, and updating an existing record, are both done in the same way—you update its fields and save your changes.

When developing your app, types and fields are automatically created for you when you save a CKRecord that uses them. You can also manually create types and fields through the CloudKit Dashboard. When you release your app, you migrate your databases to CloudKit's production environment, where you can *only* define types and fields through the Dashboard.

The closure that's run after the save operation completes can run on any operation queue, which means that if you want to make changes to the user interface, you'll need to ensure that work is done on the main queue. For more information, see Recipe 1.13.

5.12 Querying Records to a CloudKit Database

Problem

You want to retrieve records from a CloudKit database.

Solution

Once you have data stored in CloudKit, you can retrieve them using a *query*. A query effectively searches the database, looking for records of a certain type that pass a certain test. After a query runs, CloudKit will deliver you the CKRecord objects, which you can then use to get at the data they contain.

In order to perform queries, you need to specify to CloudKit which fields you want to search for. To do this, open the CloudKit Dashboard by opening the following URL in your web browser: *https://icloud.developer.apple.com/dashboard/*. Sign in, and you'll be presented with a list of containers that you have access to.

When you select the container, you'll be prompted to choose which area of the container you want to view (Figure 5-1).

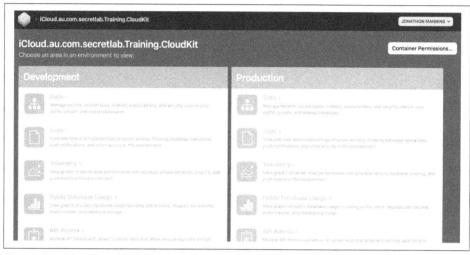

Figure 5-1. The CloudKit Dashboard

Your container is divided into two environments: production and development. While your game is under development, you prepare your database in the development environment, and when you release your game, you transfer the database's setup into production. All real-world use of the CloudKit container happens in production; meanwhile, you are free to work on the development environment while building the next version of your app.

In the development environment, click the Data button, and you'll be taken to a view of the data stored in this container.

Click the Indexes tab, and select the record type you want to do queries on. For example, if you've defined a Note type by following Recipe 5.11, you'll see *Note* in the list of Record Types.

Click the Add Index button, and choose *recordName*. Ensure that the Index Type is *Queryable* (Figure 5-2). Click Save Record Type.

Figure 5-2. Adding an index

Next, to ensure that this has been set up correctly, you can perform a test query in the CloudKit Dashboard, before writing code for your iOS app. Click Records, and choose the Public Database in the Load Records From menu. Next, select your record type in the Query for Records of Type field. Click Query Records, and the query will be run (Figure 5-3).

Figure 5-3. Running a query

Once you know that it works, you can write the code that performs the same query. When writing code that talks to CloudKit, you create a CKQuery object that represents the query you want to run. CKQuery objects need two pieces of information: the record type that you want to return, and a *predicate*.

 For more information about how to use predicates, see the Xcode documentation (*htttps://apple.co/2DyT2z3*).

A predicate is the filter that's used to determine which records should be included in the results. In this example, we'll use a predicate that always passes, which means that all records of the desired type are returned:

```
// Find all records
let allRecordsPredicate = NSPredicate(format: "TRUEPREDICATE")

// Build the query
let query = CKQuery(recordType: NoteRecordType,
                    predicate: allRecordsPredicate)


// Perform the query
self.database.perform(query, inZoneWith: nil) { (records, error) in

    if let error = error {
        print("Failed to query records: \(error)")
    } else if let records = records {
        print("Loaded \(records.count) records.")

        // We can now use these records.
    } else {
        // This shouldn't happen
        fatalError("Failed to query records, but also didn't get an error?")
    }


}
```

 The block that perform(query:, inZoneWith:) calls when the query completes is run on a background queue. If you want to update the user interface with the data you've received, you'll need to perform that work on the main queue - see Recipe 1.13 for details.

Once you've received your records, you can access information from them. Note that you'll need to perform a cast on every value you get—the object(forKey:) method doesn't know the type of the fields you're trying to access:

```
// 'record' is a CKRecord object

// Getting a string key, and fall back to the empty string
let message = record.object(forKey: "contents") as? String ?? ""

// Getting a date key, and fall back to the current date
let date = record.object(forKey: "modifiedAt") as? Date ?? Date()
```

Discussion

When you query the database, you can also specify fields that can be sorted. To do this, you'll need to add an index to them, by following the same steps, but changing the Index Type to *Sortable*. Once that's done, you can create a SortDescriptor, and provide it to the CKQuery:

```
// Sort by record modification date
let sortDescriptor = NSSortDescriptor(key: "modificationDate",
                                      ascending: false)

query.sortDescriptors = [sortDescriptor]
```

The closure that receives your results can run on any operation queue, which means that if you want to make changes to the user interface, you'll need to ensure that work is done on the main queue. For more information, see Recipe 1.13.

5.13 Deleting Records from a CloudKit Database

Problem

You want to delete a record from your CloudKit database.

Solution

To delete a record, you need to know its record ID. One way to do this is to get the record you want to delete, by performing a query (see Recipe 5.12).

Once you know the record ID, use the delete method on your database, and provide the record ID for the record you want to delete:

```
// 'record' is the CKRecord object we want to remove from
// the database; get this by doing a query
self.database.delete(withRecordID: record.recordID,
                     completionHandler: { (recordID, error) in

    if let error = error {
```

```
        print("Error removing record: \(error)")
    } else if let recordID = recordID {
        print("Removed record \(recordID)")
    } else {
        fatalError("Didn't get a record ID or an error?")
    }

})
```

Discussion

The closure you provide to delete might run on any operation queue, which means that if you want to make changes to the user interface, you'll need to ensure that work is done on the main queue. For more information, see Recipe 1.13.

CHAPTER 6

2D Graphics and SpriteKit

Just about every game out there incorporates 2D graphics on some level. Even the most sophisticated 3D games use 2D elements, such as in the menu or in the in-game interface.

Creating a game that limits itself to 2D graphics is also a good way to keep your game simple. 2D is simpler than 3D, and you'll end up with an easier-to-manage game, in terms of both gameplay and graphics. Puzzle games, for example, are a category of game that typically use 2D graphics rather than more complex 3D graphics.

2D is simpler for a number of reasons: you don't need to worry about how objects are going to look from multiple angles, you don't need to worry as much about lighting, and it's often simpler to create a great-looking scene with 2D images than it is to create a 3D version of the same scene.

iOS comes with a system for creating 2D graphics, called *SpriteKit*. SpriteKit takes care of low-level graphics tasks like creating OpenGL contexts and managing textures, allowing you to focus on game-related tasks like showing your game's sprites on the screen.

 SpriteKit was introduced in iOS 7, and is available on both iOS and OS X. The API for SpriteKit is the same on both platforms, which makes porting your game from one platform to the other easier.

In this chapter, you'll learn how to work with SpriteKit to display your game's graphics.

6.1 Getting Familiar with 2D Math

When you're working with 2D graphics, it's important to know at least a little bit of 2D math.

Coordinate System

In 2D graphics, you deal with a space that has two dimensions: *x* and *y*. The x-axis is the horizontal axis and goes from left to right, whereas the y-axis is the vertical axis and runs from top to bottom. We call this kind of space a *coordinate system*. The central point of the coordinate system used in graphics is called the *origin*.

To describe a specific location in a coordinate space, you just need to provide two numbers: how far away from the origin the location is on the horizontal axis (also known as the *x coordinate*), and how far away it is on the vertical axis (also known as the *y coordinate*). These coordinates are usually written in parentheses, like this: (*x* coordinate, *y* coordinate).

The coordinates for a location 5 units to the right of the origin and 2 units above it would be written as (5,2). The location of the origin itself is written as (0,0)—that is, zero units away from the origin on both the x- and y-axes.

 Coordinate spaces in 3D work in the exact same way as in 2D, with one difference: there's one more axis, called the *z-axis*. In this coordinate system, coordinates have one more number, as in (0,0,0).

Vectors

In the simplest terms, a *vector* is a value that contains two or more values. In games, vectors are most useful for describing two things: positions (i.e., coordinates) and velocities.

An empty 2D vector—that is, one with just zeros—is written like this: [0, 0].

When you're working in iOS, you can use the `CGPoint` structure as a 2D vector, as illustrated in Figure 6-1:

```
let myPosition = CGPoint(x: 2, y: 2)
```

You can also use vectors to store *velocities*. A velocity represents how far a location changes over time; for example, if an object is moving 2 units right and 3 units down every second, you could write its velocity as [2, 3]. Then, every second, you would add the object's velocity to its current position.

Although you can store velocities in `CGPoint` structures, it's slightly more convenient to store them in `CGVector` structures (see Figure 6-2). These are 100% identical to `CGPoints`, but the fields of the structure are named differently: x is named dx, and y is named dy. The d prefix stands for "delta," which means "amount of change of." So, "dx" means "delta x"—that is, "amount of change of x":

```
let myVector = CGVector(dx: 2, dy: 3)
```

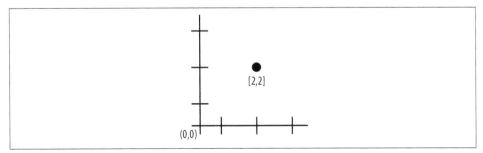

Figure 6-1. A vector used to define the position (2,2)

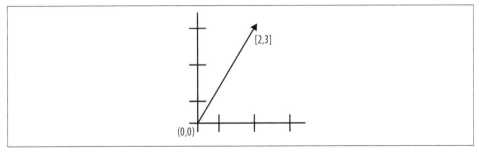

Figure 6-2. A vector used to define the direction (2,3)

Vector lengths

Let's say you've got a velocity vector [2, 3]. This means that in every second, it will move rightward 2 units and upward 3 units. In a given second, how many units will it have traveled in total?

The first thing you might think of is to add the two values together, giving a value of 5. However, this isn't correct, because the object is traveling in a straight line, not traveling a certain distance, turning, and traveling the rest of the distance.

To get the *length* of a vector (also sometimes referred to as the *magnitude*), you square each component of the vector, add them all up, and take the square root of the result:

```
let length = sqrt(myVector.dx * myVector.dx + myVector.dy * myVector.dy)
// length = 3.60555127546399
```

You can use extensions to add convenience methods to types in Swift. This includes the `CGVector` type—so, if you wanted to be able to access a vector's length using a property instead of having to type out the equation every time, you can add it like so:

```
// Add a read-only property called 'length' to all CGVectors
extension CGVector {
    var length : Double {

        get {
            let dx = Double(self.dx)
            let dy = Double(self.dy)

            return sqrt(dx * dx +
                        dy * dy)
        }
    }
}

// Use it like this:
print(myVector.length)
```

Moving vectors

When you want to move a point by a given velocity, you need to add the two vectors together.

To add two vectors together (also known as *translating* a vector), you just add the respective components of each vector—that is, you sum the *x* coordinates, then the *y* coordinates (see Figure 6-3):

```
let vector1 = CGVector(dx: 1, dy: 2)
let vector2 = CGVector(dx: 1, dy: 1)

let combinedVector = CGVector(dx: vector1.dx + vector2.dx,
                              dy: vector1.dy + vector2.dy)

// combinedVector = [2, 3]
```

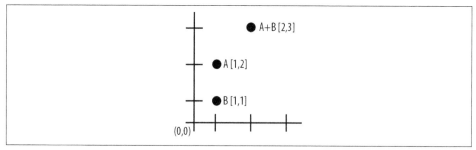

Figure 6-3. Adding vectors

You can also add an extension to the `CGVector` type that allows adding two vectors together using the + operator. You do this like so:

```
// Note: this function, like other operator functions,
// needs to be at the top level, and not in a class or extension
func + (left: CGVector, right: CGVector) -> CGVector {
    return CGVector(dx: left.dx + right.dx,
                    dy: left.dy + right.dy)
}

// Can now directly add using +:
let vectorAdding = vector1 + vector2
// = [2, 3]
```

The same thing applies to subtracting vectors: you just subtract the components, instead of adding them.

Rotating vectors

To rotate a vector, you first need to know the angle by which you want to rotate it.

In graphics, angles are usually given in *radians*. There are 2π radians in a full circle (and, therefore, π radians in half a circle, and $\pi/2$ radians in a quarter circle).

To convert from radians to degrees, multiply by 180 and divide by π:

```
let radians = 3.14159
let degrees = radians * 180.0 / .pi
// degrees ~= 180.0
```

To convert from degrees to radians, divide by 180 and multiply by π:

```
let degrees = 45.0
let radians = degrees * .pi / 180.0
// radians ~= 0.7854
```

When you have your angle in radians, you can rotate a vector like this:

```
let angle : Float = .pi / 4.0 // = 45 degrees

let point = CGPoint(x: 4, y: 4)

let x = Float(point.x)
let y = Float(point.y)

var rotatedPoint : CGPoint = point
rotatedPoint.x = CGFloat(x * cosf(angle) - y * sinf(angle))
rotatedPoint.y = CGFloat(y * cosf(angle) + x * sinf(angle))
print(rotatedPoint)
// rotatedPoint = (0, 6.283)
```

Doing this will rotate the vector counterclockwise around the origin. If you want to rotate around another point, first subtract that point from your vector, perform your rotation, and then add the first point back.

Scaling vectors

Scaling a vector is easy—you just multiply each component of the vector by a value:

```
var scaledVector = CGVector(dx: 2, dy: 7)
scaledVector.dx *= 4
scaledVector.dy *= 4

// scaledVector = [8, 28]
```

Dot product

The *dot product* is a useful way to find out how much two vectors differ in the direction in which they point.

For example, let's say you've got two vectors, [2, 2] and [2, 1], and you want to find out how much of an angle there is between them (see Figure 6-4).

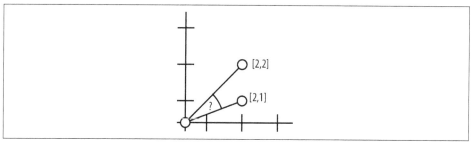

Figure 6-4. The dot product can be used to determine the angle between two vectors

You can figure this out by taking the dot product. The dot product can be calculated like this:

```
let v1 = CGPoint(x: 2, y: 2)
let v2 = CGPoint(x: 2, y: 1)

let dotProduct = (v1.x * v2.x + v1.y * v2.y)
```

In mathematical notation, the dot product operation is represented by the • character. Because Swift allows you to define entirely new operators, you can define your own operator that lets you dot two points together, like so:

```
// Declare the operator as having left associativity
// and the same level of precedence as the + operator
infix operator •
// (Typing Tip™: Press Option-8 to type the • character)
```

```
// Define what the • operator actually does
func • (left : CGPoint, right : CGPoint) -> Double {
    return Double(left.x * right.x + left.y * right.y)
}

// Use it like so:
v1 • v2
```

 Defining your own operators in Swift is powerful, because it can save a lot of duplicate code, but can lead to problems. Unless your custom operators are understood by all of the people who read your code (including future versions of you, since you can forget things!) your code may be rendered *less* readable by the inclusion of arcane symbols.

In this particular case, using the • character is *usually* okay, because it's generally understood by people who are familiar with vector math notation. But, if you're unsure, consider extending the type and adding a dotProduct method instead of defining a new operator.

An interesting property of the dot product is that the dot product of any two vectors is the same as the result of multiplying their lengths together along with the cosine of the angle between them:

```
// A and B are vectors, a is the angle between them
A • B = |A| × |B| × cos a
```

This means that you can get the cosine of the angle by rearranging the equation as follows:

```
A • B ÷ (|A| × |B|) = cos a
```

which means you can get the angle itself by taking the arc cosine, like this:

```
acos(A • B ÷ (|A| × |B|)) = a
```

Matrices

A *matrix* is a grid of numbers, as shown below:

$$M = \begin{bmatrix} 1 & 2 & 3 \\ 4 & 5 & 7 \\ 0 & 1 & 2 \end{bmatrix}$$

On their own, matrices are just a way to store numbers. However, matrices are especially useful when they're combined with vectors. This is because you can multiply a matrix with a vector, which results in a changed version of the original vector.

Additionally, if you multiply two matrices together, the result is a matrix that, if you multiply it with a vector, has the same result as if you had multiplied the vector with each matrix individually. This means that a single matrix can be used to represent a combination of operations.

Additionally, there's a single matrix that, if multiplied with a vector, returns a vector with no changes (i.e., it returns the original vector). This is referred to as the *identity matrix*, and it's a good starting point for building a matrix: you start with the identity matrix and then translate it, rotate it, and so on.

The three most useful things a matrix can do with a vector are:

Translation
    Moving the vector

Rotation
    Rotating the vector in 3D space

Scaling
    Increasing or decreasing the distance of the vector from the origin

Another common kind of matrix, called a *perspective projection transform matrix*, does the work of making objects get smaller as they move away from the origin point. You can multiply a vector with a perspective projection transform matrix, just like any other transform.

Conversely, if you use an *orthographic projection transform matrix*, objects remain the same size no matter how far away they get. In both of these cases, you define the height and width of the view area, and objects outside of the view area aren't visible.

With this math primer in mind, it's on to the recipes!

6.2 Creating a SpriteKit View

Problem

You want to display a SpriteKit view, which you can use for showing 2D graphics.

Solution

To use any element of SpriteKit, you need to import the SpriteKit module by adding this line in the files in which you want to use SpriteKit:

```
import SpriteKit
```

Go to your storyboard and select the view controller in which you want to show SpriteKit content. Select the main view inside the view controller, and change its class to SKView.

You need to have added the `import SpriteKit` line of code to at least one file. If you don't, Xcode won't add the SpriteKit framework to your code at build time, which means that when the view loads, the `SKView` class won't be found, and your app will crash.

Next, go to your view controller's implementation, and add the following code to the `viewDidLoad` method:

```
if let spriteView = self.view as? SKView {
    spriteView.showsDrawCount = true
    spriteView.showsFPS = true
    spriteView.showsNodeCount = true
}
```

Finally, run the application. You'll see an empty screen; however, as you begin to add content to your scene (which the rest of this chapter discusses!), down in the lower-right corner of the screen, you'll see additional information about how well your game is performing.

Discussion

An `SKView` is the area in which SpriteKit content is drawn. All of your drawing of 2D graphics happens inside this area.

An `SKView` is a subclass of `UIView`, which means you can work with it in the Interface Builder. Given that you'll most likely want to use the entire screen for your sprites, it makes sense to make the view used by the view controller an `SKView` (rather than, for example, adding an `SKView` as a subview of the view controller's main view).

By default, an `SKView` doesn't contain anything; you need to add content to it yourself. In this recipe, we've shown how to enable some debugging information: the frames per second (FPS), the number of draw calls that have been made, and the total number of nodes (items) in the scene. Note that these debugging displays don't appear if your scene is entirely empty—they'll only appear if your scene is actually rendering content.

6.3 Creating a Scene

Problem

You want to show a scene—that is, a collection of sprites—inside an `SKView`.

Solution

Add a new file to your Xcode project called TestScene.swift, which you'll use to define a new class. Make the new class a subclass of SKScene. Be sure to add a line to import the SceneKit framework.

Add a new property to the `TestScene` class:

```
var contentCreated = false
```

Add the following methods to *TestScene.swift*:

```
override func didMove(to view: SKView) {
    if self.contentCreated == false {
        self.createSceneContents()
        self.contentCreated = true
    }
}

func createSceneContents() {
    self.backgroundColor = SKColor.black
    self.scaleMode = SKSceneScaleMode.aspectFit
}
```

Finally, implement the `viewWillAppear` method in your view controller, and add the following code:

```
override func viewWillAppear(_ animated: Bool) {
    let scene = TestScene()
    scene.size = self.view.bounds.size
    if let spriteView = self.view as? SKView {
        spriteView.presentScene(scene)
    }
}
```

Discussion

When an `SKScene` is added to an `SKView`, it receives the `didMoveToView:` message. This is your scene's opportunity to prepare whatever content it wants to display.

However, it's important to keep in mind that an `SKScene` might be presented multiple times over its lifetime. For that reason, you should use a variable to keep track of whether the content of the scene has already been created:

```
override func didMove(to view: SKView) {
    if self.contentCreated == false {
        self.createSceneContents()
        self.contentCreated = true
    }
}
```

In the `createSceneContents` method, the actual content that appears in the scene is prepared. In this example, the scene is empty, but shows a black background:

```
self.backgroundColor = SKColor.black
```

The type of backgroundColor depends on which platform you're writing for. On OS X, it's an NSColor, and on iOS, it's a UIColor class. Both of these classes have very similar APIs, which means that it's a little easier to port code from iOS to OS X. If you use SKColor, the compiler will use the correct color class for you depending on the platform you're building for.

Additionally, the scene's scaleMode is set. The scene's scaleMode property determines how the SKView scales the scene—because your scene might appear in different sizes (e.g., on iPhone screens versus iPad screens), it's important to know how the scene should be sized to fit into the SKView.

Several options exist for this:

SKSceneScaleMode.fill
> The scene will be scaled to fill the SKView.

SKSceneScaleMode.aspectFill
> The scene will be scaled to fill the SKView, preserving the aspect ratio of the scene. Some areas of the scene might be clipped off in order to achieve this.

SKSceneScaleMode.aspectFit
> The scene will be scaled to fit inside the SKView. You might see some letterboxing (i.e., some blank areas at the top and bottom or sides).

SKSceneScaleMode.resizeFill
> The scene will be resized—*not* scaled—in order to fill the SKView.

Once a scene has been prepared, it needs to be *presented* in order to appear in an SKView. This is quite straightforward—all you need to do is call presentScene, and pass in an SKScene:

```
override func viewWillAppear(_ animated: Bool) {
    let scene = TestScene()
    scene.size = self.view.bounds.size
    if let spriteView = self.view as? SKView {
        spriteView.presentScene(scene)
    }
}
```

When you call presentScene, the currently presented scene in the SKView is replaced with whatever you provided. Note that you have to cast self.view to an SKView before you can call presentScene. The safest way to do this is to use the if-let syntax, which attempts to cast the type, and will only attempt to run code if the cast succeeded.

6.4 Adding a Sprite

Problem

You want to display a sprite - that is, a 2D image - in a SpriteKit scene.

Solution

To show a sprite to the player, you create an SKSpriteNode, configure its size and position, and then add it to your SKScene object:

```
let sprite = SKSpriteNode(color: SKColor.green,
                          size: CGSize(width: 64, height: 64))

sprite.position = CGPoint(x: 100, y: 100)

myScene.addChild(sprite)
```

Discussion

SKSpriteNode is a *node*: an object that can be put inside a scene. There are several different kinds of nodes, all of which are subclasses of the SKNode class.

SKSpriteNode is a type of node that can display either a colored rectangle, or an image. In this recipe, we're focusing on just colored rectangles; to show an image, see Recipe 6.10.

To create a colored rectangle sprite, you just need to provide the color you'd like to use, as well as the size of the rectangle:

```
let sprite = SKSpriteNode(color: SKColor.green,
                          size: CGSize(width: 64, height: 64))
```

The position of the sprite is controlled by the sprite's position property, which is a CGPoint. The position that you provide determines the location of the sprite's *anchor point*, which is the center point of the sprite:

```
sprite.position = CGPoint(x: 100, y: 100)
```

Sprites aren't visible unless they're inside an SKScene, which means you need to call the addChild method on the SKScene in which you want your sprite to appear:

```
myScene.addChild(sprite)
```

The position of a sprite—in fact, of any node—is determined relative to the position of the anchor point of the sprite's *parent*. This means that you can add sprites as children of *other sprites*. If you do this, the child sprites will move with their parents.

6.5 Adding a Text Sprite

Problem

You want to display some text in a SpriteKit scene.

Solution

Create an SKLabelNode, and add it to your scene:

```
let textNode = SKLabelNode(fontNamed: "Zapfino")
textNode.text = "Hello, world!"
textNode.fontSize = 42
textNode.position = CGPoint(x: myScene.frame.midX, y: myScene.frame.midY)

textNode.name = "helloNode"

myScene.addChild(textNode)
```

Discussion

An SKLabelNode is a node that displays text. Just like with other kinds of nodes, you add it to a scene to make it visible to the player (see Recipe 6.4).

Note also that we're specifying the *name* of the node here - we're setting it to "hello-Node". When you give a node a name, you can locate it by using the SKNode class's childNode(withName:) method.

To create an SKLabelNode, all you need to provide is the font that the label should use:

```
let textNode = SKLabelNode(fontNamed: "Zapfino")
```

The specific font name that you provide to the SKLabelNode(fontNamed:) method needs to be one of the fonts that's included in iOS, or a custom font included with your application. To learn what fonts are available for use in your game, see Recipe 6.6; to learn how you can include a custom font in your app, see Recipe 6.7.

Once you've got an SKLabelNode to use, you just need to provide it with the text that it needs to display, as well as the font size that it should use and its position on screen:

```
textNode.text = "Hello, world!"
textNode.fontSize = 42
textNode.position = CGPoint(x: myScene.frame.midX, y: myScene.frame.midY)
```

By default, the text is aligned so that it's centered horizontally on the *x* coordinate of the node's position and the baseline (i.e., the bottom part of the letters that don't have a descender—letter like *e*, *a*, and *b*) of the text is set to the *y* coordinate. However, you can change this: all you need to do is change the verticalAlignmentMode or horizontalAlignmentMode properties.

The `verticalAlignmentMode` property can be set to one of the following values:

`SKLabelVerticalAlignmentMode.baseline`
The baseline of the text is placed at the origin of the node (this is the default).

`SKLabelVerticalAlignmentMode.center`
The center of the text is placed at the origin.

`SKLabelVerticalAlignmentMode.top`
The top of the text is placed at the origin.

`SKLabelVerticalAlignmentMode.bottom`
The bottom of the text is placed at the origin.

Additionally, the `horizontalAlignmentMode` property can be set to one of the following values:

`SKLabelHorizontalAlignmentMode.center`
The text is center-aligned (this is the default).

`SKLabelHorizontalAlignmentMode.left`
The text is left-aligned.

`SKLabelHorizontalAlignmentMode.right`
The text is right-aligned.

6.6 Determining Available Fonts

Problem

You want to know which fonts are available for your game to use.

Solution

The following code logs the name of every font available for use in your game to the debugging console:

```
for fontFamilyName in UIFont.familyNames {
    for fontName in UIFont.fontNames(forFamilyName: fontFamilyName) {
        print("Available font: \(fontName)")
    }
}
```

Discussion

The `UIFont` class, which represents fonts on iOS, allows you to list all of the *font families* available to your code, using the `familyNames` method. This method returns an array of strings, each of which is the name of a font family.

However, a font family name isn't the same thing as the name of a usable font. For example, the font Helvetica is actually a *collection* of different fonts: it includes Helvetica Bold, Helvetica Light, Helvetica Light Oblique, and so on.

Therefore, to get a font name that you can use with an SKLabel (or, indeed, any other part of iOS that deals in font names), you pass a font family name to the font Names(forFamilyName:) method in UIFont. This returns *another* array of string objects, each of which is the name of a font you can use.

Alternatively, you can visit iOS Fonts (*http://iosfonts.com/*), which is a third-party site that lists all of the available fonts and includes additional information about which fonts are available on different versions of iOS.

6.7 Including Custom Fonts

Problem

You want to include a custom font in your game, so that you can show text using fancy letters.

Solution

First, you'll need a font file, in either TrueType or OpenType format—that is, a *.ttf* or *.otf* file.

Add the file to your project, making sure that your game's Target is selected in the Add To Targets list. Next, go to your project's Info tab, and add a new entry to the Custom Target Properties, called "Fonts provided by application." This is an array; for each of the fonts you want to add, create a new entry in this array.

For example, if you've added a font file called *MyFont.ttf*, add *MyFont.ttf* to the "Fonts provided by application" list.

Discussion

Any fonts you include in your application are available through UIFont (see Recipe 6.6); you don't have to do anything special to get access to them.

If you don't have a font, Dafont (*http://www.dafont.com*) is an excellent place to find free fonts—just be sure that any fonts you get are allowed to be used for commercial purposes.

6.8 Transitioning Between Scenes

Problem

You want to move from one scene to another.

Solution

Use the `presentScene:` method on an `SKView` to change which scene is being shown:

```
// newScene is an SKScene object that you want to switch to
self.view?.presentScene(newScene)
```

Using `presentScene:` immediately switches over to the new scene. If you want to use a transition, you create an `SKTransition`, and then call `presentScene(, transition:)`:

```
let crossFade = SKTransition.crossFade(withDuration: 0.5)
self.view?.presentScene(newScene, transition: crossFade)
```

Discussion

When an `SKScene` is presented, the `willMove(from:)` method is called on the scene that's about to be removed from the screen. This gives the scene a chance to tidy up, or to remove any sprites that might take up a lot of memory. The `SKScene` that's about to be shown in the `SKView` is sent the `didMove(to:)` message, which is its chance to prepare the scene's content.

If you call `presentScene`, the new scene will immediately appear. However, it's often good to use an animation to transition from one scene to another, such as a fade or push animation.

To do this, you use the `SKTransition` class, and provide that to the `SKView` through the `presentScene(_, transition:)` method.

You create an `SKTransition` through one of the factory methods, and provide any additional information that that type of transition needs. All transitions need to know how long the transition should run, and a few transitions need additional information, such as a direction. For example, you create a cross-fade transition like this:

```
let crossFade = SKTransition.crossFade(withDuration: 0.5)
```

There are a variety of transitions available for you to use, each with a corresponding method for creating it. Try them out! Options include:

Cross-fade (`crossFade(withDuration:)`*)*
    The current scene fades out while the new scene fades in.

Doors close horizontal (`doorsCloseHorizontal(withDuration:)`*)*
> The new scene comes in as a pair of horizontal closing "doors."

Doors close vertical (`doorsCloseVertical(withDuration:)`*)*
> The new scene comes in as a pair of vertical closing "doors."

Doors open horizontal (`doorsOpenHorizontal(withDuration:)`*)*
> The current scene splits apart, and moves off as a pair of horizontally opening "doors."

Doors open vertical (`doorsOpenVertical(withDuration:)`*)*
> The current scene splits apart, and moves off as a pair of vertically opening "doors."

Doorway (`doorway(withDuration:)`*)*
> The current scene splits apart, revealing the new scene in the background; the new scene approaches the camera, and eventually fills the scene by the time the transition is complete.

Fade with color (`fade(with:, duration:)`*)*
> The current scene fades out, revealing the color you specify; the new scene then fades in on top of this color.

Fade (`fade(withDuration:)`*)*
> The current scene fades to black, and then the new scene fades in.

Flip horizontal (`flipHorizontal(withDuration:)`*)*
> The current scene flips horizontally, revealing the new scene on the reverse side.

Flip vertical (`flipVertical(withDuration:)`*)*
> The current scene flips vertically, revealing the new scene on the reverse side.

Move in with direction (`moveIn(with:, duration:)`*)*
> The new scene comes in from off-screen, and moves in on top of the current scene.

Push in with direction (`push(with:, duration:)`*)*
> The new scene comes in from off-screen, pushing the current scene off the screen.

Reveal with direction(`reveal(with: , duration:)`*)*
> The current scene moves off-screen, revealing the new scene underneath it.

`CIFilter` *transition (*`SKTransition(ciFilter:, duration:)`*)*
> You can use a `CIFilter` object to create a custom transition.

6.9 Moving Sprites and Labels Around

Problem

You want your sprites and labels to move around your scene.

Solution

You can use SKAction objects to make any node in the scene perform an *action*. An action is something that changes the position, color, transparency, or size of any node in your scene.

The following code makes a node move up and to the right while fading away, then runs some code, and finally removes the node from the scene:

```
// In this example, 'node' is any SKNode

// Move 100 points up and 100 points to the right over 1 second
let moveUp = SKAction.move(by: CGVector(dx: 100, dy: 100), duration: 1.0)

// Fade out over 0.5 seconds
let fadeOut = SKAction.fadeOut(withDuration: 0.5)

// Run a block of code
let runBlock = SKAction.run {
    print("Hello!")
}

// Remove the node
let remove = SKAction.removeFromParent()

// Run the movement and fading blocks at the same time
let moveAndFade = SKAction.group([moveUp, fadeOut])

// Move and fade, then run the block, then remove the node
let sequence = SKAction.sequence([moveAndFade, runBlock, remove])

// Run these actions on the node
node.run(sequence)
```

Discussion

An SKAction is an object that represents an action that a node can perform. There are heaps of different kinds of actions available for you to use—too many for us to list here, so for full information, check out Apple's documentation for SKAction (*http://bit.ly/skaction*).

Generally, an action is something that changes some property of the node to which it applies. For example, the move(by:, duration:) action in the preceding example changes the position of the node by making it move by a certain distance along the x- and y-axes (represented by a `CGVector`). Some actions don't actually change the node, though; for example, you can create an action that simply waits for an amount of time, or one that runs some code.

To run an action, you first create an `SKAction` with one of the factory methods. Then, you call `runAction` on the `SKNode` that you'd like to have perform that action.

You can add an action to multiple nodes—if you want several nodes to all do the same thing, just create the `SKAction` once and then call `runAction:` on each of the `SKNodes` that you want to perform the action.

Most actions are things that take place over a period of time: for example, moving, rotating, fading, changing color, and so on. Some actions take place immediately, however, such as running code or removing a node from the scene.

An action can work on its own, or you can combine multiple actions with *sequences* and *groups*. A sequence is an `SKAction` that runs *other* actions, one after the other. The first action is run, and once it's complete the next is run, and so on until the end; at this point, the sequence action is considered done. To create a sequence, use the `sequence` method, which takes an array of `SKAction` objects:

```
let sequence = SKAction.sequence([action1, action2, action3])
```

A group, by contrast, runs a collection of actions simultaneously. A group action is considered complete when the longest-running of the actions it's been given has completed. Creating groups looks very similar to creating sequences. To create a group, you pass an array of `SKAction` objects to the `group` method:

```
let group = SKAction.group([action1, action2, action3])
```

You can combine groups and sequences. For example, you can make two sequences run at the same time by combining them into a group:

```
let sequence1 = SKAction.sequence([action1, action2])
let sequence2 = SKAction.sequence([action1, action2])

let groupedSequences = SKAction.group([sequence1, sequence2])
```

You can also create sequences that contain groups; if, for example, you have a sequence with two groups in it, the second group will not run until all actions in the first group have finished.

Some actions are able to be reversed. By sending the `reversed` message to these actions, you get back an `SKAction` that performs the opposite action to the original. Not all actions can be reversed; for details on which can and can't, check the documentation for `SKAction`.

As we've already mentioned, you start actions by calling `runAction` on an `SKNode`. You can also make SpriteKit run a block when the action that you've submitted finishes running, using the `run(_, completion:)` method:

```
let action = SKAction.fadeOut(withDuration: 1.0)

node.run(action) {
    print("Action's done!")
}
```

You can add multiple actions to a node, which will all run at the same time. If you do this, it's often useful to be able to keep track of the actions you add to a node. You can do this with the `run(_, withKey:)` method, which lets you associate actions you run on an `SKNode` with a name:

```
node.run(action, withKey: "My Action")
```

If you add two actions with the same name, the old action is removed before the new one is added.

Once you've added an action with a name, you can use the `action(forKey:)` method to get the action back:

```
let theAction = node.action(forKey: "My Action")
```

You can also remove actions by name, using the `removeAction(forKey:)` method:

```
node.removeAction(forKey: "My Action")
```

Finally, you can remove *all* actions from a node in one line of code using the `removeAllActions` method:

```
node.removeAllActions()
```

When you remove an action, the action stops whatever it was doing. However, any changes that the action had *already* made to the node remain.

For example, if you've added an action that moves the sprite, and you remove it before the action finishes running, the sprite will be left partway between its origin point and the destination.

6.10 Adding a Texture Sprite

Problem

You want to create a sprite that uses an image.

Solution

First, add the image that you want to use to your project (see Recipe 2.5).

Next, create an `SKSpriteNode` with the `SKSpriteNode(imageNamed:)` method:

```
let imageSprite = SKSpriteNode(imageNamed: "Spaceship")
```

Discussion

When you create a sprite with `SKSpriteNode(imageNamed:)`, the size of the sprite is based on the size of the image.

Once you've created the sprite, it works just like any other node: you can position it, add it to the scene, run actions on it, and so on.

6.11 Creating Texture Atlases

Problem

You want to use texture atlases, which save memory and make rendering more efficient.

Solution

Create a folder named *Textures.atlas* and put all of the textures that you want to group in it.

Add this folder to your project by dragging the folder into the Project Navigator.

Discussion

A *texture atlas* is a texture composed of other, smaller textures. Using a texture atlas means that instead of several smaller textures, you use one larger texture. This atlas uses slightly less memory than if you were to use lots of individual textures, and more importantly is more efficient for rendering. When a sprite needs to be drawn, a subregion of the texture atlas is used for drawing.

If your game involves lots of sprites that each use different images, the SpriteKit renderer needs to switch images every time it starts drawing a different sprite. Switching images has a small performance cost, which adds up if you're doing it multiple times. However, if multiple sprites share the same texture, SpriteKit doesn't have to switch images, making rendering faster.

When you put images in a folder whose name ends with *.atlas*, and turn on Texture Atlas Generation, Xcode will automatically create a texture atlas for you based on whatever images are in that folder. Your images will be automatically trimmed for transparency, reducing the number of wasted pixels, and images are packed together as efficiently as possible.

When you're using texture atlases, your SpriteKit code remains the same. The following code works regardless of whether or not you're using atlases:

```
let imageSprite = SKSpriteNode(imageNamed: "Spaceship")
```

6.12 Using Shape Nodes

Problem

You want to use shape nodes to draw vector shapes.

Solution

Use an SKShapeNode to draw shapes:

```
let path = UIBezierPath(roundedRect: CGRect(x: -100, y: -100,
                                            width: 200, height: 200),
                        cornerRadius: 20)

let shape = SKShapeNode(path: path.cgPath)

shape.strokeColor = SKColor.green
shape.fillColor = SKColor.red

shape.glowWidth = 4

shape.position = CGPoint(x: myScene.frame.midX,
                         y: myScene.frame.midY)

myScene.addChild(shape)
```

Discussion

SKSceneNode draws *paths*, which are objects that represent shapes. A path can be a rectangle, a circle, or any shape you can possibly think of. For more information on working with paths, see Recipe 6.15.

The coordinates of the path that you provide are positioned relative to your node's anchor point. For example, a shape that has a line that starts at (–10,–10) and moves to (10,10) starts above and to the left of the node's position, and ends below and to the right of the position.

You can use the fillColor and strokeColor properties to change the colors used to draw the shape. Use SKColor to define the colors you want to use. The *fill color* is the color used to fill the contents of the shape, and the *stroke color* is the color used to draw the line around the outside of the shape. By default, the fill color is clear (i.e., no color, just empty space), and the stroke color is white.

Finally, you can specify how thick the line is. By default, the thickness is 1 point; Apple notes that specifying a line thickness of more than 2 points may lead to rendering problems. In these cases, you're better off using an SKSpriteNode. In addition, you can make the stroke line glow by setting the glowWidth property to a value higher than 0.

6.13 Using Blending Modes

Problem

You want to use different blending modes to create visual effects.

Solution

Use the blendMode property to control how nodes are blended with the rest of the scene:

```
shape.blendMode = SKBlendMode.add
```

Discussion

When a node is drawn into the scene, the way that the final scene looks depends on the node's *blend mode*. When a node is blended into the scene, the SpriteKit renderer looks at the color of each pixel of the node, and the color underneath each pixel, and determines what the resulting color should be.

By default, all SKNodes use the same blending mode, SKBlendMode.Alpha, which uses the alpha channel of the image multiplied by the sprite's alpha property to determine how much the node's color should contribute to the scene. This is generally the blending mode you want to use most of the time.

However, it isn't the *only* blending mode that you can use. Other options exist:

SKBlendMode.add
    The colors of the node are added to the scene. This leads to a brightening, semi-transparent effect. (Good for lights, fires, laser beams, and explosions!)

SKBlendMode.subtract
    The colors of the node are subtracted from the scene. This creates a rather weird-looking darkening effect. (Not very realistic, but it can lead to some interesting effects.)

`SKBlendMode.multiply`

> The colors of the node are multiplied with the scene. This darkens the colors. (Very good for shadows, and for tinting parts of the scene.)

`SKBlendMode.multiplyX2`

> The same as `SKBlendMode.Multiply`, but the colors of the sprite are doubled after the first multiplication. This creates a brighter effect than plain multiply.

`SKBlendMode.screen`

> The colors of the node are added to the scene, multiplied by the inverse of the scene's color. This creates a more subtle brightening effect than `SKBlend Mode.add`. (Good for glosses and shiny areas.)

`SKBlendMode.replace`

> The colors of the node replace the scene and are not blended with any existing colors. This means that any `alpha` information is completely ignored. This mode is also the fastest possible drawing mode, because no blending calculations need to take place.

6.14 Using Image Effects to Change the Way That Sprites Are Drawn

Problem

You want to use image effects on your sprites to create different effects.

Solution

Use an `SKEffectNode` with a `CIFilter` to apply visual effects to nodes:

```
let effect = SKEffectNode()

guard let filter = CIFilter(name: "CIGaussianBlur") else {
    fatalError("Failed to get the filter!")
}
filter.setValue(20.0, forKey: "inputRadius")

effect.filter = filter;

myScene.addChild(effect)
effect.addChild(imageSprite)
```

Discussion

A `CIFilter` is an object that applies an effect to images. `CIFilters` are incredibly powerful, and are used all over iOS and OS X. One of the most popular examples of where they're used is in the Photo Booth app, where they power the visual effects that you can apply to photos.

To use a CIFilter with SpriteKit, you create an SKEffectNode and add any nodes that you want to have the effect apply to as children of that node. (Don't forget to add the SKEffectNode to your scene.)

Once you've done that, you get a CIFilter, configure it how you like, and provide it to the SKEffectNode. You get a CIFilter using the filterWithName method of the CIFilter class, which takes a string: the name of the filter you'd like to use.

Different filters have different properties, which you can configure using the CIFilter's setValue(_, forKey:) method.

There are dozens of CIFilters that you can use—lots more than we could sensibly list here. Here are a couple of especially cool ones:

CIGaussianBlur
Applies a Gaussian blur. The default blur radius is 10.0; change it by setting inputRadius to something different.

CIPixellate
Makes the image all blocky and pixelated. The default pixel size is 8.0; change it by setting inputScale to something different.

CIPhotoEffectNoir
Makes the image black and white, with an exaggerated contrast. This filter has no parameters you can change.

6.15 Using Bézier Paths

Problem

You want to draw shapes using Bézier paths (custom shapes and lines).

Solution

Use the UIBezierPath class to represent shapes:

```
let rectangle = UIBezierPath(rect:CGRect(x: 0, y: 0,
                                         width: 100, height: 200))


let roundedRect = UIBezierPath(roundedRect:CGRect(x: -100, y: -100,
                                                  width: 200, height: 200),
                               cornerRadius:20)


let oval = UIBezierPath(ovalIn:CGRect(x: 0, y: 0,
                                      width: 100, height: 200))
```

```
let customShape = UIBezierPath()
customShape.move(to: CGPoint(x: 0, y: 0))
customShape.addLine(to: CGPoint(x: 0, y: 100))
customShape.addCurve(to: CGPoint(x: 20, y: 50),
                             controlPoint1:CGPoint(x: 100, y: 100),
                             controlPoint2:CGPoint(x: 100, y: 0))

customShape.close()
```

Discussion

UIBezierPath objects represent shapes, which you can display on the screen with an SKShapeNode.

Creating a rectangle, rounded rectangle, or oval is pretty easy—there are built-in factory methods for these. There's no built-in method for creating circles, but it's easy to make one—just create an oval inside a square rectangle (i.e., a rectangle with an equal width and height).

In addition to these basic shapes, you can also create your own custom shapes. You do this by using the move(to:), addLine(to:), and addCurve(to:, controlPoint1: controlPoint2:) methods.

When you're drawing a custom shape, it helps to imagine a virtual pen poised over a sheet of paper. When you call move(to:), you're positioning your hand over a specific point. When you call addLine(to:), you place the pen down on the paper and draw a straight line from the pen's current location to the destination. You can call moveToPoint again to lift the virtual pen from the paper and reposition your hand somewhere else.

The addCurve(to:, controlPoint1:, controlPoint2:) method lets you draw a cubic Bézier curve. A Bézier curve is a curved line that starts at the pen's current location and moves toward the destination point you provide, bending toward the two control points. A Bézier curve is often useful for drawing smoothly curving things in games, such as roads.

When you're done creating a shape, you call close. Doing this draws a straight line from the pen's current position to the starting position.

To use a UIBezierPath with an SKShapeNode, you ask the UIBezierPath for its CGPath property, and give that to the SKShapeNode. For more information on how SKShapeNode works, see Recipe 6.12.

6.16 Creating Smoke, Fire, and Other Particle Effects

Problem

You want to create fire, smoke, snow, or other visual effects.

Solution

You can use particle effects to simulate these kinds of effects. To create a particle effect, follow these steps:

1. From the File menu, choose New→File. Select Resource, and then select SpriteKit Particle File.

2. You'll be asked to pick a template to start from. Pick whichever you like—Jon happens to like the Fire template.

3. Open the newly created file, and you'll enter the Emitter editor. This component of Xcode allows you to play with the various properties that define how the particle system looks, including how many particles are emitted, how they change over time, and how they're colored. Additionally, you can click and drag to see how the particle system looks when it's moving.

Once you're done configuring the particle system, you can add the effect to your scene with the following code (adjust the filenames to suit your needs):

```
guard let fireNode = SKEmitterNode(fileNamed: "Fire.sks") else {
    fatalError("Failed to load fire node!")
}

myScene.addChild(fireNode)
```

Discussion

Particle effects can be used for a variety of natural-looking effects that would be difficult to create with individual sprites. Individual particles in a particle system have much less overhead than creating the sprites yourself, so you can create rather complex-looking effects without dramatically affecting performance.

Because there are so many different parameters available to customize, creating a particle system that suits your needs is very much more an art than a science. Be prepared to spend some time playing with the available settings, and try the different built-in presets to get an idea of what's possible.

6.17 Shaking the Screen

Problem

You want the screen to shake—for example, an explosion has happened, and you want to emphasize the effect by rattling the player's view of the scene around.

Solution

Create an empty node, and call it `cameraNode`. Add it to the screen. Put all of the nodes that you'd normally put into the scene into this new node.

Add the following method to your scene's code:

```
func shakeNode(node: SKNode) {
    // Cancel any existing shake actions
    node.removeAction(forKey: "shake")

    // The number of individual movements that the shake will be made up of
    let shakeSteps = 15

    // How "big" the shake is
    let shakeDistance = 20.0

    // How long the shake should go on for
    let shakeDuration = 0.25

    // An array to store the individual movements in
    var shakeActions : [SKAction] = []

    // Loop 'shakeSteps' times
    for i in 0...shakeSteps  {

        // How long this specific shake movement will take
        let shakeMovementDuration : Double = shakeDuration / Double(shakeSteps)

        // This will be 1.0 at the start and gradually move down to 0.0
        let shakeAmount : Double = Double(shakeSteps - i) / Double(shakeSteps)

        // Take the current position - we'll then add an offset from that
        var shakePosition = node.position

        // Pick a random amount from -shakeDistance to shakeDistance
        let xPos = (Double(arc4random_uniform(UInt32(shakeDistance*2))) -
            Double(shakeDistance)) * shakeAmount
        let yPos = (Double(arc4random_uniform(UInt32(shakeDistance*2))) -
            Double(shakeDistance)) * shakeAmount
        shakePosition.x = shakePosition.x + CGFloat(xPos)
        shakePosition.y = shakePosition.y + CGFloat(yPos)

        // Create the action that moves the node to the new location, and
```

```
        // add it to the list
        let shakeMovementAction = SKAction.move(to: shakePosition,
                                          duration:shakeMovementDuration)
        shakeActions.append(shakeMovementAction)

    }

    // Run the shake!
    let shakeSequence = SKAction.sequence(shakeActions)
    node.run(shakeSequence, withKey:"shake")


}
```

When you want to shake the screen, just call `shakeNode` and pass in `cameraNode`:

```
    shakeNode(node: cameraNode)
```

Discussion

Shaking the screen is a really effective way to emphasize to the player that something big and impressive is happening. If something forceful enough to shake the *world* around you is going on, then you know it means business!

So, what does a shake actually mean in terms of constructing an animation? Well, a shake is when you start at a neutral resting point and begin moving large distances back and forth over that neutral point. An important element in realistic-looking shakes is that the shake gradually settles down, with the movements becoming less and less drastic as the shaking comes to an end.

To implement a shake, therefore, you need to construct several small movements. These can be implemented using `SKAction`s: each step in the shake is an `SKAction` that moves the node from its current location to another location.

During the `for` loop, to attenuate the shake—that is, to make the movements smaller and smaller—subtract the number of steps taken from the total number of steps, producing the number of steps remaining. This is divided by the total number of steps, which gives us a number from 0 to 1, by which the movement is multiplied. Eventually, the amount of movement is multiplied by 0—in other words, the movement settles back down to the neutral position.

6.18 Animating a Sprite

Problem

You want to make a SpriteKit animation using a collection of images. For example, you've got a "running" animation, and you want your sprite to play that animation.

Solution

In this solution, we're going to assume that you've already got all of your individual frames, and you've put them into a folder named *Animation.atlas*, which has been added to your project.

Use SKAction's animate(with:, timePerFrame:) method to animate a collection of sprites:

```
// Load the texture atlas that contains the frames
let atlas = SKTextureAtlas(named: "Animation")

// Get the list of texture names, and sort them
let textureNames = atlas.textureNames.sorted {
    (first, second) -> Bool in
    return first < second
}

// Load all textures
var allTextures : [SKTexture] = textureNames.map { (textureName) -> SKTexture in
    return atlas.textureNamed(textureName)
}

// Create the sprite, and give it the initial frame; position it
// in the middle of the screen
let animatedSprite = SKSpriteNode(texture:allTextures[0])
animatedSprite.position = CGPoint(x: self.frame.midX,
                                  y: self.frame.midY)
self.addChild(animatedSprite)

// Make the sprite animate using the loaded textures, at a rate of
// 30 frames per second
let animationAction = SKAction.animate(with: allTextures,
                                       timePerFrame:(1.0/30.0))

animatedSprite.run(SKAction.repeatForever(animationAction))
```

Discussion

The SKAction class is capable of changing the texture of a sprite over time. If you have a sequence of images that you want to use as an animation, all you need is an array containing each of the textures you want, with each one stored as an SKTexture.

When you create the animation action using animate(with:, timePerFrame:), you provide the array and the amount of time that each texture should be displayed. If you want to run your animation at 30 FPS, then each frame should be shown for 1/30 of a second (0.033 seconds per frame).

To get the SKTextures for display, you either need to load them using SKTexture's SKTexture(imageNamed:) initializer, or else get them from a texture atlas that contains them. Texture atlases were discussed in Recipe 6.11, and are an excellent way to group the frames for your animation together. They're also better for memory, and ensure that all necessary frames are present for your animation—the game won't pause halfway through your animation to load more frames.

6.19 Parallax Scrolling

Problem

Using SpriteKit, you want to show a 2D scene that appears to have depth, by making more *distant* objects move slower than *closer* objects when the *camera* moves.

Solution

The specific approach for implementing parallax scrolling will depend on the details of your game. In this solution, we're creating a scene where there are four components, listed in order of proximity:

- A dirt path
- Some nearby hills
- Some further distant hills
- The sky

You can see the final scene in Figure 6-5. (Unless you have magic paper, or possibly some kind of hyper-advanced *computer reader* technology that as yet to be invented, the following image will not be scrolling.)

Figure 6-5. The final parallax scrolling scene

In this scene, we've drawn the art so that each of these components is a separate image. Additionally, each of these images can tile horizontally without visible edges. The art has been put in a texture atlas (see Recipe 6.11 to learn how to use these). The names of the textures for each of the components are *Sky.png*, *DistantHills.png*, *Hills.png*, and *Path.png* (shown in Figure 6-6).

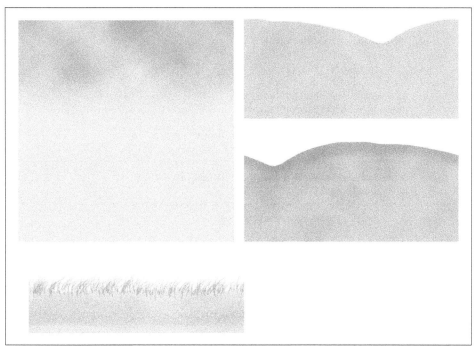

Figure 6-6. The components of the parallax scene. Note that all four components can tile horizontally.

With that out of the way, here's the source code for the SKScene that shows these four components scrolling horizontally at different speeds:

```
class ParallaxScene: SKScene {

    // Sky
    var skyNode : SKSpriteNode
    var skyNodeNext : SKSpriteNode

    // Foreground hills
    var hillsNode : SKSpriteNode
    var hillsNodeNext : SKSpriteNode

    // Background hills
    var distantHillsNode : SKSpriteNode
    var distantHillsNodeNext : SKSpriteNode

    // Path
    var pathNode : SKSpriteNode
    var pathNodeNext : SKSpriteNode

    // Time of last frame
    var lastFrameTime : TimeInterval = 0
```

```
// Time since last frame
var deltaTime : TimeInterval = 0

override init(size: CGSize) {

    // Prepare the sky sprites
    skyNode = SKSpriteNode(texture:
        SKTexture(imageNamed: "Sky"))
    skyNode.position = CGPoint(x: size.width / 2.0,
                              y: size.height / 2.0)

    skyNodeNext = skyNode.copy() as! SKSpriteNode
    skyNodeNext.position =
        CGPoint(x: skyNode.position.x + skyNode.size.width,
                y: skyNode.position.y)

    // Prepare the background hill sprites
    distantHillsNode = SKSpriteNode(texture:
        SKTexture(imageNamed: "DistantHills"))
    distantHillsNode.position =
        CGPoint(x: size.width / 2.0,
                y: size.height - 284)

    distantHillsNodeNext = distantHillsNode.copy() as! SKSpriteNode
    distantHillsNodeNext.position =
        CGPoint(x: distantHillsNode.position.x +
            distantHillsNode.size.width,
                y: distantHillsNode.position.y)

    // Prepare the foreground hill sprites
    hillsNode = SKSpriteNode(texture:
        SKTexture(imageNamed: "Hills"))
    hillsNode.position =
        CGPoint(x: size.width / 2.0,
                y: size.height - 384)

    hillsNodeNext = hillsNode.copy() as! SKSpriteNode
    hillsNodeNext.position =
        CGPoint(x: hillsNode.position.x + hillsNode.size.width,
                y: hillsNode.position.y)

    // Prepare the path sprites
    pathNode = SKSpriteNode(texture:
        SKTexture(imageNamed: "Path"))
    pathNode.position =
        CGPoint(x: size.width / 2.0,
                y: size.height - 424)

    pathNodeNext = pathNode.copy() as! SKSpriteNode
    pathNodeNext.position =
        CGPoint(x: pathNode.position.x +
```

```
                pathNode.size.width,
                    y: pathNode.position.y)

        super.init(size: size)


        // Add the sprites to the scene
        self.addChild(skyNode)
        self.addChild(skyNodeNext)

        self.addChild(distantHillsNode)
        self.addChild(distantHillsNodeNext)

        self.addChild(hillsNode)
        self.addChild(hillsNodeNext)

        self.addChild(pathNode)
        self.addChild(pathNodeNext)
    }

    required init?(coder aDecoder: NSCoder) {
        fatalError("Not implemented")
    }

    // Move a pair of sprites leftward based on a speed value;
    // when either of the sprites goes off-screen, move it to the
    // right so that it appears to be seamless movement
    func move(sprite : SKSpriteNode,
            nextSprite : SKSpriteNode, speed : Float) -> Void {
        var newPosition = CGPoint.zero

        // For both the sprite and its duplicate:
        for spriteToMove in [sprite, nextSprite] {

            // Shift the sprite leftward based on the speed
            newPosition = spriteToMove.position
            newPosition.x -= CGFloat(speed * Float(deltaTime))
            spriteToMove.position = newPosition

            // If this sprite is now offscreen (i.e., its rightmost edge is
            // farther left than the scene's leftmost edge):
            if spriteToMove.frame.maxX < self.frame.minX {

                // Shift it over so that it's now to the immediate right
                // of the other sprite.
                // This means that the two sprites are effectively
                // leap-frogging each other as they both move.
                spriteToMove.position =
                    CGPoint(x: spriteToMove.position.x +
                        spriteToMove.size.width * 2,
                            y: spriteToMove.position.y)
            }
```

```
        }
    }

    override func update(_ currentTime: TimeInterval) {
        // First, update the delta time values:

        // If we don't have a last frame time value, this is the first frame,
        // so delta time will be zero.
        if lastFrameTime <= 0 {
            lastFrameTime = currentTime
        }

        // Update delta time
        deltaTime = currentTime - lastFrameTime

        // Set last frame time to current time
        lastFrameTime = currentTime

        // Next, move each of the four pairs of sprites.
        // Objects that should appear move slower than foreground objects.
        self.move(sprite: skyNode, nextSprite:skyNodeNext, speed:25.0)
        self.move(sprite: distantHillsNode, nextSprite:distantHillsNodeNext,
                speed:50.0)
        self.move(sprite: hillsNode, nextSprite:hillsNodeNext, speed:100.0)
        self.move(sprite: pathNode, nextSprite:pathNodeNext, speed:150.0)
    }

}
```

Discussion

Parallax scrolling is no more complicated than moving some things quickly and other things slowly. In SpriteKit, the real trick is getting a sprite to appear to be continuously scrolling, showing no gaps.

In this solution, each of the four components in the scene—the sky, hills, distant hills, and path—are drawn with two sprites each: one shown onscreen, and one to its immediate right. For each pair of sprites, they both slide to the left until one of them has moved completely off the screen. At that point, it's repositioned so it's placed to the right of the other sprite.

In this manner, the two sprites are leap-frogging each other as they move. You can see the process illustrated in Figure 6-7.

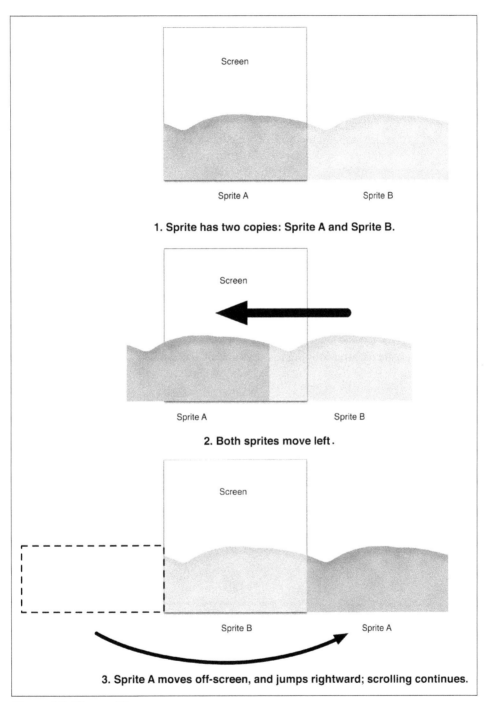

Figure 6-7. *The scrolling process*

Getting the speed values right for your scene is a matter of personal taste. However, it's important to make sure that the relationships between the speeds of the different layers make sense: if you have an object that's in the foreground and is moving much, much faster than a relatively close background, it won't look right.

 Simulating perspective using parallax scrolling is a great and simple technique, but be careful with it. Your fearless authors wrote this recipe while in the back of a car that was driving down a winding road, and we developed a little motion sickness while testing the source code.

Motion sickness in games, sometimes known as "simulation sickness," is a real thing that affects many game players around the world. If you're making a game that simulates perspective—either in a 3D game or a 2D game where you're faking perspective—make sure you test with as many people as you can find.

6.20 Creating Images Using Noise

Problem

You want to create organic-looking textures and effects using visual noise.

Solution

Noise is *incredibly useful* in games, and it's especially useful in textures when natural-looking patterns are sought. You can see an example of a noise texture in Figure 6-8.

To generate an SKTexture filled with noise, you use SKTexture(noiseWithSmoothness:, size, grayscale). You can then use this texture in a sprite, or combine it with other information:

```
let noiseTexture = SKTexture(noiseWithSmoothness: 0.2,
    size: CGSize(width: 200, height: 200), grayscale: true)
let noiseSprite = SKSpriteNode(texture: noiseTexture)
myScene.addChild(noiseSprite)
```

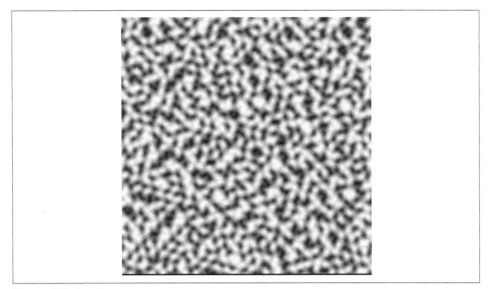

Figure 6-8. A noise texture

Discussion

Noise is an incredibly effective method for creating natural, organic-looking textures. You can use it for a number of things, including fire, fog, smoke, lightning—all you need to do is change the `smoothness` parameter. Noise works best when blended with other images.

A slightly more complex and better-looking type of noise is *Perlin* noise. Perlin was invented by Ken Perlin in 1985, and was based on earlier work done for the Disney film *Tron* (1982). Perlin himself later won an Academy Award for Technical Achievement in 1997 for his work on Perlin noise. You can see a full description, as well as links to implementations of the algorithm, at *http://en.wikipedia.org/wiki/Perlin_noise*.

CHAPTER 7

Physics

If, like us, you've visited a planet that has gravity, you'll be familiar with the fact that objects react to forces and collide with other objects. When you pick up an object and let go, it falls down until it hits something. When it hits something, it bounces (or shatters, depending on what you dropped). In games, we can make objects have this kind of behavior through *physics simulation*.

Physics simulation lets you do things like:

- Make objects have gravity and fall to the ground
- Give objects properties like weight, density, friction, and bounciness
- Apply forces to objects, and make them move around realistically
- Attach objects together in a variety of configurations

In short, adding physics simulation to your game often gives you a lot of realism for free.

SpriteKit has built-in support for simulating physics in two dimensions, and we'll mostly be talking about physics in SpriteKit in this chapter. (If you're not familiar with SpriteKit yet, go check out Chapter 6.) Before we get to the recipes, though, let's go over some terminology.

7.1 Reviewing Physics Terms and Definitions

Physics simulation has its basis in math, and math people tend to like giving everything its own name. These terms are used by the physics simulation system built into iOS, and it's important to know what's being referred to when you encounter, say, a *polygon collision body*.

In this section, before we get into the recipes themselves, we're going to present a list of definitions that you'll very likely run into when working with physics. Some of these are terms that you've probably heard in other contexts, and others are fairly specific to physics:

World

A physics world is the "universe" in which all of your objects exist. If an object isn't in the world, it isn't being physically simulated, and nothing will interact with it. A physics world contains settings that apply to all objects in the world, such as the direction and strength of gravity.

Mass

Mass is a measure of how much stuff is inside an object. The more mass there is, the heavier it is.

Velocity

Velocity is a measure of how quickly an object is moving, and in which direction. In 2D physics, velocity has two components: horizontal velocity, or "x-velocity," and vertical velocity, or "y-velocity."

Body

A body is an object in the physics simulation. Bodies react to forces, and can collide with other bodies. Bodies have mass and velocity. You can optionally make a body be *static*, which means that it never reacts to forces and never moves.

Force

A force is something that causes a body to move. For example, when you throw a ball, your arm is imposing a force on the ball; when your hand releases the ball, the ball's got a large amount of built-up velocity, and it flies out of your hand. Gravity is another force, and it applies to all objects in your physics world. The amount of force needed to make an object move depends on how much mass is in that object. If you apply the exact same force to a heavy object and to a light object, the light object will move farther.

Friction

When an object rubs against something else, it slows down. This is because of friction. In the real world, friction converts kinetic energy (i.e., movement) into heat, but in SpriteKit, the energy is just lost. You can configure how much friction an object has. For example, if you make an object have very low friction, it will be slippery.

Collider

A collider defines the shape of an object. Common shapes include squares, rectangles, circles, and polygons. In SpriteKit, all bodies have a collider, which you define when you create the body. (In some other physics engines, bodies and colliders are separate entities.)

Edge collider

An edge collider is a collider that is composed of one or more infinitely thin lines. Edge colliders are useful for creating walls and obstacles, because they're simple to create and very efficient to simulate. A body with an edge collider never moves; it's always static.

Collision

A collision is when two objects come into contact. Note that a *collision* is different from a *collider*—a collision is an event that happens, whereas a collider is a shape. When a collision happens, you can get information about it, such as which objects collided, where they collided, and so on.

Joint

A joint is a relationship between two objects. Several different kinds of joints exist. Some common ones include "pin" joints, in which one object is allowed to rotate freely but isn't allowed to move away from a certain point relative to another body, and "spring" joints, in which one object is allowed to move away from another but, if it moves beyond a threshold, begins to be pushed back toward the first object.

7.2 Adding Physics to Sprites

Problem

You want to make sprites be affected by gravity and other physical forces.

Solution

To make an SKSpriteNode be physically simulated, create an SKPhysicsBody and then set the sprite's physicsBody property to it:

```
// 'scene' is an SKScene

let sprite = SKSpriteNode(color:SKColor.white,
                          size:CGSize(width: 100, height: 50))
sprite.position = CGPoint(x: self.frame.midX, y: self.frame.midY)
sprite.physicsBody = SKPhysicsBody(rectangleOf:sprite.size)

scene.addChild(sprite)
```

Discussion

When you add an SKPhysicsBody to an SKSpriteNode, SpriteKit physically simulates the sprite's movement in the scene.

This has the following effects:

- The physics engine will start keeping track of physical forces that apply to the body, such as gravity.
- The position and rotation of the body will be updated every frame, based on these forces.
- The body will collide with other SKPhysicsBody objects.

When you run the sample code, you'll notice that the sprite falls off the bottom of the screen. This is because there's nothing for the sprite to land on—the physics body that you added to the sprite is the only physically simulated body in the entire scene. To learn how to create objects for your sprite's body to land on, see Recipe 7.3.

7.3 Creating Static and Dynamic Objects

Problem

You want to create an immobile object—one that never moves, but that other objects can collide with.

Solution

Set the dynamic property of your SKPhysicsBody to false:

```
let staticSprite = SKSpriteNode(color:SKColor.yellow,
                                size:CGSize(width: 200, height: 25))

staticSprite.position = CGPoint(x: self.frame.midX, y: self.frame.midY - 100)
staticSprite.physicsBody = SKPhysicsBody(rectangleOf:staticSprite.size)
staticSprite.physicsBody?.isDynamic = false


scene.addChild(staticSprite)
```

Discussion

There are two kinds of physics bodies used in SpriteKit:

- *Dynamic bodies* respond to physical forces, and move around the scene.
- *Static bodies* don't respond to physical forces—they're fixed in place, and dynamic bodies can collide with them.

When you set the dynamic property of an SKPhysicsBody to false, the body immediately stops responding to forces and stops moving and rotating. However, you can still reposition it by setting the sprite's position and rotation, or by using actions (see Recipe 6.9 to learn how to do this).

7.4 Defining Collider Shapes

Problem

You want to specify a custom shape for physics bodies.

Solution

To make your physics bodies use a shape other than a rectangle, you create them by using a different method, such as SKPhysicsBody(circleOfRadius:) or SKPhysics Body(polygonFromPath:), as shown here:

```
let circleSprite = SKShapeNode()
let circleRect: CGRect =
    CGRect(x: -50, y: -50, width: 100, height: 100)
circleSprite.path =
    UIBezierPath(ovalIn:circleRect).cgPath

circleSprite.lineWidth = 1
circleSprite.physicsBody = SKPhysicsBody(circleOfRadius:50)
circleSprite.position =
    CGPoint(x: self.frame.midX + 40, y: self.frame.midY + 100)

self.addChild(circleSprite)
```

Discussion

There are a number of different ways that you can create an SKPhysicsBody. When you create one, you specify what sort of *collider* the body is using—that is, the actual shape of the body (a circle, a rectangle, or some other shape).

The easiest way to create a body is with the SKPhysicsBody(rectangleOf:) method, which lets you (as you might expect, given the name), create a rectangle given a size (you don't set the position of the body—that's determined by the position of the node to which the body's attached).

 A circular collider is the simplest possible collider, and requires the least amount of computation to simulate. If you need to create a large number of colliders, consider making them circular where possible.

In addition to creating rectangular or circular colliders, you can define your own custom shapes by defining a path and creating an SKPhysicsBody with it:

```
let polygonSprite = SKShapeNode()

let path = UIBezierPath()
```

```
path.move(to: CGPoint(x: -25, y: -25))
path.addLine(to: CGPoint(x: 25, y: 0))
path.addLine(to: CGPoint(x: -25, y: 25))
path.close()

polygonSprite.physicsBody = SKPhysicsBody(polygonFrom:path.cgPath)
```

You can learn more about creating paths using UIBezierPath in Recipe 6.15.

 When you create a path for use as a polygon body, the points in the path need to be defined in clockwise order.

Additionally, the path you provide isn't allowed to contain any curves—it can only contain straight lines. (You won't get any crashes if you use curves, but the resulting shape will behave strangely.)

If you want to more easily visualize the custom shapes you're creating for use with physics bodies, you can attach the same path that you've created to an SKShapeNode, as illustrated in Figure 7-1. See Recipe 6.12 for more information about this.

Finally, you can define a physics body based on the transparent regions of a sprite's texture:

```
let texture = SKTexture(imageNamed: "Spaceship")

let texturedSpaceShip = SKSpriteNode(texture: texture)
texturedSpaceShip.physicsBody = SKPhysicsBody(
    texture: texture,
    size: CGSize(width: texturedSpaceShip.size.width,
                 height: texturedSpaceShip.size.height))

self.addChild(texturedSpaceShip)
```

 You can't change the shape of a body's collider after it's been created. If you want a sprite to have a different shape, you need to replace the sprite's SKPhysicsBody.

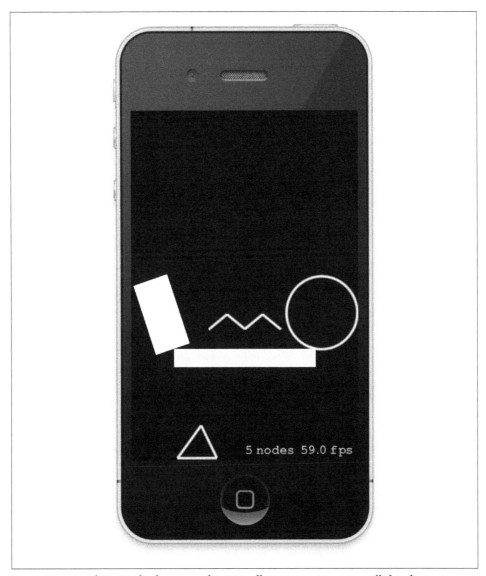

Figure 7-1. SKShapeNodes being used to visually represent custom collider shapes

7.5 Setting Velocities

Problem

You want to make an object start moving at a specific speed and in a specific direction.

Solution

To change the velocity of an object, you modify the `velocity` property:

```
// Start moving upwards at 500 units per second (quite fast!)
sprite.physicsBody?.velocity = CGVector(dx: 0, dy: 500)
```

Discussion

The simplest way to change the velocity of a physics body is to directly set the `veloc` `ity` property. This is a `CGVector` that represents the velocity, in pixels per second, at which the body is moving.

Note that directly setting the velocity tends to have the best-looking results when you use the technique to set the initial velocity of an object. For example, if you want to create rockets that come out of a rocket launcher, those rockets should start out moving quickly. In this case, you'd create the rocket sprite, and then immediately set the velocity of its physics body to make it start moving.

If you want things to *change* their movement in a realistic way, consider using forces on your bodies (see Recipe 7.14). Alternatively, if you want precise frame-by-frame control over how your objects move, make the physics bodies static (see Recipe 7.3), and manually set the position of the objects or use actions (see Recipe 6.9).

7.6 Working with Mass, Size, and Density

Problem

You want to control how heavy your objects are.

Solution

Set the `density` or `mass` properties of your physics bodies to control how heavy they are:

```
// Change density, and the mass will be updated (based on size)
sprite.physicsBody?.density = 2.0

// Alternatively, set the mass property (which will change density)
sprite.physicsBody?.mass = 4.0
```

Discussion

An object's *mass* is how much matter the object is composed of. Note that this is different from how much the object *weighs*, which is the amount of force applied to an object by gravity, dependent on the object's mass and how strong gravity is.

Objects with more mass require more force to move around. If you apply the same force to an object with low mass and one with high mass, the object with lower mass will move farther.

The mass of an object is calculated based on the volume of the object (i.e., its size) and the object's *density*. The mass of an object is automatically calculated when you create the body, based on the size of the body and a default density of 1; however, you can change an object's mass and density at any time you like.

The initial mass of an object is calculated like this:

```
Mass = Area x Density
```

The default density of an object is 1.0. The area depends on the shape of the body:

- The area of a rectangle is width × height.
- The area of a circle is $\pi \times r^2$ (where r is the radius).
- The area of a polygon depends on its shape; search the web for "irregular polygon area" for different kinds of formulae. A common strategy is to break the polygon into triangles, calculate the area for each one, and then add them together.

The actual units you use for density and mass don't matter—you can use pounds, kilograms, or grapnars (if you are from Venus). However, the values you choose should be consistent across the objects in your scene. For example, if you create two crates, both of the same size, and you set the mass of the first to 2 (kilograms) and the second to 4 (pounds), it won't be apparent to the user why one appears lighter than the other.

Because mass and density are linked, if you change an object's density, the mass will change (and vice versa).

7.7 Creating Walls in Your Scene

Problem

You want to create walls for your collision scene.

Solution

The most efficient way to create walls is to use edge colliders:

```
let wallsNode = SKNode()
wallsNode.position = CGPoint(x: self.frame.midX, y: self.frame.midY)

let rect = self.frame.offsetBy(
    dx: -self.frame.width / 2.0,
    dy: -self.frame.height / 2.0
)
wallsNode.physicsBody = SKPhysicsBody(edgeLoopFrom:rect)

scene.addChild(wallsNode)
```

Discussion

An *edge collider* is a collider that's just a single line, or a collection of connected lines. Edge colliders are different from other kinds of colliders in that they have no volume or mass, and are always treated as static colliders.

There are two different types of edge colliders: *edge loops* and *edge chains*. An edge chain is a linked collection of lines; an edge loop always links from the end point to the start point.

Edge colliders can have almost any shape you want. The easiest ways to create them are either to create a single line from one point to another:

```
let point1 = CGPoint(x: -50, y: 0)
let point2 = CGPoint(x: 50, y: 0)

let edgeBody = SKPhysicsBody(edgeFrom: point1, to: point2)
```

or with a rectangle, using `SKPhysicsBody(edgeLoopFromRect:)`, as seen in the preceding example.

In addition to lines and rectangles, you can create arbitrary shapes. These can be either edge chains or edge loops.

You create these shapes using a path, much like when you make polygon bodies (see Recipe 7.4). In this case, though, there's a difference: you don't have to close your paths, because edge chains don't have to form a closed polygon:

```
let path = UIBezierPath()
path.move(to: CGPoint(x: -50, y:-10))
path.addLine(to: CGPoint(x: -25, y:10))
path.addLine(to: CGPoint(x: 0, y:-10))
path.addLine(to: CGPoint(x: 25, y:10))
path.addLine(to: CGPoint(x: 50, y:-10))

let wallNode = SKShapeNode()
wallNode.path = path.cgPath
```

```
wallNode.physicsBody = SKPhysicsBody(edgeChainFrom: path.cgPath)
wallNode.position = CGPoint(x: self.frame.midX, y: self.frame.midY-50)
```

7.8 Controlling Gravity

Problem

You want to customize the gravity in your scene.

Solution

To change the gravity in your scene, you must first get access to your scene's `physics World`. Once you have that, you can change the physics world's `gravity` property:

```
// Half gravity
self.physicsWorld.gravity = CGVector(dx: 0.0, dy: -4.5)
```

Discussion

For the purposes of a physics simulation, *gravity* is a constant force that's applied to all bodies. (Gravity in the real universe is quite a bit more complex than that, but this simplification is more than adequate for most games.)

A game that deals with gravity in a much more realistic way than "gravity equals down" is Kerbal Space Program (*http://www.kerbal spaceprogram.com*), in which players launch rockets and use orbital mechanics to travel to other planets. In this kind of game, the force of gravity depends on how close you are to various planets, each of which has a different mass.

By default, the gravity in a scene is set to (0, –9.81). That is to say, all bodies have a constant force that's pushing them down (i.e., toward the bottom of the screen), at a rate of 9.81 pixels per second per second. By changing this property, you can make gravity nonexistent:

```
// Zero gravity
self.physicsWorld.gravity = CGVector(dx: 0.0, dy: 0.0)
```

Or, you can reverse gravity:

```
// Reverse gravity
self.physicsWorld.gravity = CGVector(dx: 0.0, dy: 9.81)
// note the lack of a minus symbol
```

You can also make an individual physics body be unaffected by gravity by changing the body's `affectedByGravity` property:

```
sprite.physicsBody?.affectedByGravity = false
```

Note that a body that isn't affected by gravity still has mass, and still responds to other forces. A really heavy object that's floating in the air will still require quite a bit of force to move.

 If you want to make an object fixed in midair, and never be affected by physical forces, you want a *static* physics body, and should go look at Recipe 7.3.

7.9 Keeping Objects from Falling Over

Problem

You want to prevent certain objects, such as the player character, from rotating.

Solution

Change the allowsRotation property of your body:

```
sprite.physicsBody?.allowsRotation = false
```

Discussion

In many games with 2D physics, it's useful to have some objects that move around, but never rotate. For example, if you're making a platform game, you almost never want the character to actually rotate.

Locking the rotation of a body means that it won't ever rotate, no matter how many forces are applied to it. However, you can still change the angle of the body by manually setting the zRotation of the node, or by using an action (see Recipe 6.9).

7.10 Controlling Time in Your Physics Simulation

Problem

You want to pause or speed up the physics simulation.

Solution

Change the speed property of your scene's SKPhysicsWorld to control how quickly time passes in your scene's physics simulation:

```
self.physicsWorld.speed = 2.0

self.physicsWorld.speed = 0.0
```

```
self.physicsWorld.speed = 1.0
```

Discussion

The `speed` property of your scene's `SKPhysicsWorld` controls the rate at which time passes in your physics simulation. For example, setting the speed to 2.0 makes things move twice as fast (note, however, that increasing the speed of the simulation can lead to some instability in your simulation).

You can also use this to create slow-motion effects: if you set the `speed` property to a value between 0 and 1, time will be slowed down, which you can use to highlight totally sweet stunts or explosions.

7.11 Detecting Collisions

Problem

You want to detect when objects collide.

Solution

First, make your `SKScene` subclass conform to the `SKPhysicsContactDelegate` protocol.

Next, implement the `didBeginContact` and `didEndContact` methods in your `SKScene`:

```
func didBegin(_ contact: SKPhysicsContact) {
    print("Contact started between \(contact.bodyA) and \(contact.bodyB)")
}

func didEnd(_ contact: SKPhysicsContact) {
    print("Contact ended between \(contact.bodyA) and \(contact.bodyB)")
}
```

When you're setting up your scene's contents, set the `contactDelegate` property of your scene's `physicsWorld` to the scene:

```
self.physicsWorld.contactDelegate = self
```

Next, make every physics body for which you want to get notifications about collisions set its `contactTestBitMask` to a nonzero value, like `0x01`. You'll probably want to store it in a variable, like so:

```
let myObjectBitMask : UInt32 = 0x00001
```

You can then apply it to your `SKPhysicsBody` objects:

```
physicsSprite.physicsBody?.contactTestBitMask = myObjectBitMask;
```

Now, every object collision that occurs will make your `didBeginContact` and `didEnd`
`Contact` methods get called.

Discussion

If you want an object to be notified about objects coming into contact with each
other, you make that object conform to the `SKPhysicsContactDelegate` protocol,
and then set the scene's `physicsWorld` to use the object as its `contactDelegate`.

The contact delegate methods, `didBeginContact` and `didEndContact`, will only be
called when two objects that have an intersecting `contactTestBitMask` come into
contact with each other.

The contact test bitmask lets you define categories of objects. By default, it's set to
zero, which means that objects aren't in any collision category.

The contact delegate methods receive an `SKPhysicsContact` object as their parameter, which contains information about which bodies collided, at which point they collided, and with how much force.

7.12 Finding Objects

Problem

You want to find physics objects in the scene.

Solution

Use the `enumerateBodies(in:, using:)`, `enumerateBodies(at:, using:)`, and `enu`
`merateBodies(alongRayStart:, end:, using:)` methods to find `SKPhysicsBody`
objects in your world:

```
let searchRect = CGRect(x: 10, y: 10, width: 200, height: 200)

self.physicsWorld.enumerateBodies(in: searchRect) { (body, stop) in
    print("Found a body: \(body)")
}

let searchPoint = CGPoint(x: 40, y: 100)

self.physicsWorld.enumerateBodies(at: searchPoint) { (body, stop) in
    print("Found a body: \(body)")
}

let searchRayStart = CGPoint(x: 0, y: 0)
let searchRayEnd = CGPoint(x: 320, y: 480)

self.physicsWorld.enumerateBodies(alongRayStart: searchRayStart,
```

```
      end: searchRayEnd) { (body, point, normal, stop) in
         print("Found a body: \(body) (point: \(point), normal: \(normal))")
   }
```

Discussion

You can use these methods to find SKPhysicsBody objects in a rectangle, at a certain point, or along a line. When you call them, you pass in the location you want to search, as well as a block; this block is called for each body that is found.

All of the result blocks used by these methods receive as parameters the body that was found and stop, which is a pointer to a Bool variable. If you set this variable to true, the search will stop. This means that if you're looking for a specific body, you can stop the search when you find it, which saves time:

```
// Stop when we've found two bodies
var count : Int = 0
self.physicsWorld.enumerateBodies(in: searchRect) { (body, stop) in
    count = count + 1

    if count >= 2 {
        stop.initialize(to: true)
    }
}
```

Note that when you call enumerateBodies(alongRayStart:, end:, using:), the results block takes *three* parameters: the block, a *normal*, and the stop variable. The normal is a vector that indicates the direction at which the line bounces off the body it hit. (This is useful for determining, for example, the directions in which sparks should fly when something hits a surface.)

If you're looking for a single body and don't care which one, you can use the body(at:), body(in:), and body(alongRayStart:, end:) methods, which just return the first body they find:

```
let firstBodyAtPoint = self.physicsWorld.body(at: searchPoint)

let firstBodyInRect = self.physicsWorld.body(in: searchRect)

let firstBodyAlongRay =
    self.physicsWorld.body(alongRayStart: searchRayStart, end: searchRayEnd)
```

These methods won't find nodes that don't have an SKPhysicsBody attached to them —they only check the physics simulation. If you're looking for nodes that have no physics body, use the nodes(at:), childNode(with:), or enumerateChildNo des(with:, using:) methods on your SKScene.

7.13 Working with Joints

Problem

You want to connect physics objects together.

Solution

Use one of the several SKPhysicsJoint classes available:

```
let anchor = SKSpriteNode(color:SKColor.white,
                          size:CGSize(width: 100, height: 100))
anchor.position = CGPoint(x: self.frame.midX, y: self.frame.midY)

let anchorBody = SKPhysicsBody(rectangleOf:anchor.size)
anchor.physicsBody = anchorBody
anchor.physicsBody?.isDynamic = false

scene.addChild(anchor)

let attachment = SKSpriteNode(color:SKColor.yellow,
                              size:CGSize(width: 100, height: 100))
attachment.position = CGPoint(x: self.frame.midX + 100,
                              y :self.frame.midY - 100)

let attachmentBody = SKPhysicsBody(rectangleOf:attachment.size)
attachment.physicsBody = attachmentBody

scene.addChild(attachment)

let pinJoint = SKPhysicsJointPin.joint(withBodyA: anchorBody,
                                       bodyB:attachmentBody,
                                       anchor:anchor.position)

scene.physicsWorld.add(pinJoint)
```

Discussion

A *joint* is an object that constrains the movement of one or more objects. Joints are pretty straightforward to work with: you create your joint object, configure it, and then give it to your scene's SKPhysicsWorld.

In this example, we're using a pin joint, which pins two bodies together at a point, and lets them rotate around that point. There are several different types of joints available:

- *Pin joints*, as we've just mentioned, let you pin two objects together. The objects can rotate around that pin point. Pin joints are sometimes called *hinge* joints in other physics systems.

- *Fixed joints* fuse two objects together. Once they're joined, they're not allowed to move relative to each other, and they're not allowed to rotate relative to each other. This is very useful for creating larger objects that you want to break apart later.

- *Slider joints* let you create objects that can move away from or closer to each other, but only along a certain line.

- *Limit joints* make it so that the two objects can move freely relative to each other, but aren't allowed to move past a certain radius. This makes them act as if they're tethered with a rope.

Once you've created your joint, you add it to the physics simulation by using the `add Joint` method:

```
scene.physicsWorld.add(pinJoint)
```

You can remove a joint from an `SKPhysicsWorld` by using the `removeJoint` method. Once you remove a joint, the bodies that it affected are able to move freely once again:

```
scene.physicsWorld.removeJoint(pinJoint)
```

A body can have multiple joints acting on it at once. Try connecting several bodies together with joints, and see what you come up with!

7.14 Working with Forces

Problem

You want to apply a force to an object.

Solution

Use the `applyForce` or `applyTorque` methods:

```
node.physicsBody?.applyForce(CGVector(dx: 0, dy: 100))
node.physicsBody?.applyTorque(0.01)
```

Discussion

When you apply a force, you change the movement of a body. When you're using the SpriteKit physics engine, there's a constant gravitational force being applied to all bodies in the scene, which makes them move downward.

You can apply your own forces to bodies using the `applyForce` method, which takes a `CGVector` that describes the amount of force you'd like to apply. Forces get applied immediately.

When you call `applyForce`, the force is evenly applied across the entire body. If you need to apply the force to a specific point on the body, you can use `applyForce(_, at:)`:

```
// Apply a force just to the right of the center of the body
let position = CGPoint(x: 10, y: 0)
node.physicsBody?.applyForce(CGVector(dx: 0, dy: 100), atPoint: position)
```

The point that you provide to `applyForce(_, at:)` is defined in scene coordinates.

In addition to force, which changes the position of a body, you can also apply *torque*, which is a change to the angular movement (i.e., the spin) of a body.

 The units that you use with `applyForce` and `applyTorque` don't really matter as long as they're consistent. Technically, they're measured in newtons and newton-meters, respectively.

7.15 Adding Thrusters to Objects

Problem

You want to make an object move continuously in a certain direction.

Solution

First, add this property to your SKScene subclass:

```
var lastTime = 0.0
```

Then, in your scene's `update` method, apply whatever forces and torque you need:

```
override func update(_ currentTime: TimeInterval) {

    if self.lastTime == 0 {
        self.lastTime = currentTime
    }


    let deltaTime = currentTime - self.lastTime

    if let node = self.childNode(withName: "Box") {

        node.physicsBody?.applyForce(CGVector(dx: 0 * deltaTime,
                                              dy: 10 * deltaTime))
        node.physicsBody?.applyTorque(CGFloat(0.5 * deltaTime))

    }
}
```

Discussion

The `update` method is called on your `SKScene` subclass every frame, immediately before physics simulation and rendering. This is your opportunity to apply any continuous forces to your objects.

The `update` method receives one parameter: a float named `currentTime`. This variable contains the current system time, measured in seconds. To apply an even amount of force per second, you need to know how long each frame takes to render. You can calculate this by subtracting the system time at the last frame from the system time at the current frame (you can learn more about this in Recipe 1.5):

```
deltaTime = time at start of current frame - time at start of last frame
```

Once you have that, you can multiply forces by that number.

7.16 Creating Explosions

Problem

You want to apply an explosion force to some objects.

Solution

Add this method to your `SKScene`:

```swift
func applyExplosion(at point: CGPoint,
    radius:CGFloat, power:CGFloat) {

    // Work out which bodies are in range of the explosion
    // by creating a rectangle
    let explosionRect = CGRect(x: point.x - radius,
        y: point.y - radius,
        width: radius*2, height: radius*2)

    // For each body, apply an explosion force
    self.physicsWorld.enumerateBodies(in: explosionRect,
                                    using:{ (body, stop) in

        // Work out if the body has a node that we can use
        if let bodyPosition = body.node?.position {

            // Work out the direction that we should apply
            // the force in for this body
            let explosionOffset =
                CGVector(dx: bodyPosition.x - point.x,
                    dy: bodyPosition.y - point.y)

            // Work out the distance from the explosion point
            let explosionDistance =
```

```
                    sqrt(explosionOffset.dx * explosionOffset.dx +
                        explosionOffset.dy * explosionOffset.dy)

            // Normalize the explosion force
            var explosionForce = explosionOffset
            explosionForce.dx /= explosionDistance
            explosionForce.dy /= explosionDistance

            // Multiply by explosion power
            explosionForce.dx *= power
            explosionForce.dy *= power

            // Finally, apply the force
            body.applyForce(explosionForce)
        }
    })

}
```

When you want an explosion to happen, call this method like so:

```
// 'point' is a CGPoint in world space
self.applyExplosion(at: point, radius:150, power:10)
```

Discussion

An explosion is simply a force that's applied to a group of nearby bodies, which pushes those bodies away from a point.

So, to make an explosion, you need to do the following:

1. Determine which bodies are affected by the explosion.

2. Decide in which direction each body should be sent.

3. Calculate how much force should be applied.

4. Apply that force to each body!

Simple, right?

You can determine which bodies are affected by the explosion by using the enumerate Bodies(in:, using:) method on your scene's SKPhysicsWorld. This calls a block for each body that it finds, which gives you your opportunity to calculate the forces for each body.

To calculate the amount of force you need to apply to each body, you do the following:

1. Subtract the body's position from the explosion's position. This is the *explosion offset*, calculated as follows:

```
let explosionOffset =
    CGVector(dx: bodyPosition.x - point.x,
    dy: bodyPosition.y - point.y)
```

2. Determine the distance from the body's position by *normalizing* the explosion offset. This means calculating the length (or *magnitude*) of the vector, and then dividing the vector by that magnitude.

To calculate the magnitude of the vector, you take the square root of the sums of the squares of the components of the offset vector:

```
let explosionDistance =
    sqrt(explosionOffset.dx * explosionOffset.dx +
        explosionOffset.dy * explosionOffset.dy)
```

Once you have that, you divide the offset by this length, and then multiply it by the power. This ensures that all affected objects get the same total amount of power, regardless of their position:

```
let explosionDistance =
    sqrt(explosionOffset.dx * explosionOffset.dx +
        explosionOffset.dy * explosionOffset.dy)
```

3. Finally, you apply this calculated force vector to the body:

```
body.applyForce(explosionForce)
```

7.17 Using Device Orientation to Control Gravity

Problem

You want the direction of gravity to change when the player rotates her device.

Solution

First, make your application only use the portrait orientation by selecting the project at the top of the Project Navigator, selecting the General tab, scrolling down to Device Orientation, and turning off everything except Portrait. This will keep your app from rotating its interface as you rotate the device.

Next, open your SKScene subclass. Import the Core Motion module:

```
import CoreMotion
```

and add a new instance variable to your class:

```
let motionManager = CMMotionManager()
```

Finally, when your scene is being set up, add the following code:

```
motionManager.startDeviceMotionUpdates(
    to: OperationQueue.main, withHandler: { (motion, error) -> Void in
        if let motion = motion {
            let gravityMagnitude = 9.91
            let gravityVector = CGVector(
                dx: motion.gravity.x * gravityMagnitude,
                dy: motion.gravity.y * gravityMagnitude)

            self.physicsWorld.gravity = gravityVector
        } else if let error = error {
            print("Error getting motion data: \(error)")
        } else {
            fatalError("Failed to get motion data OR error?")
        }
})
```

Discussion

When you create a `CMMotionManager` and call `startDeviceMotionUpdates(to:` , `withHandler:)`, the motion system will call a block that you provide and give it information on how the player's device is moving.

To get the direction of gravity, you ask the `motion` object that gets passed in as a parameter for its `gravity` property. Gravity has three components: x, y, and z. These correspond to how much gravity is pulling on the sides of the device, the top and bottom edges of the device, and the front and back of the device.

In a 2D game, there are only two dimensions we care about: x and y. That means that we can just discard the z component of gravity, and build a `CGVector` out of the x and y information stored in the `motion` object.

However, the values contained in the `gravity` property are measured in *gravities*—that is, if you lay your phone perfectly flat with the back of the phone pointed down, there will be precisely one gravity of force on the z-axis. In SpriteKit, however, gravity is measured in meters per second (by default). So, you need to convert between the two units.

The conversion is very easy: one gravity is equal to 9.81 meters per second. So, all you need to do is multiply both the x and y components of the gravity vector by 9.81.

Finally, this updated gravity vector is given to the scene's `physicsWorld`, which in turn affects the physics objects in the scene.

7.18 Dragging Objects Around

Problem

You want the player of your game to be able to drag physics objects on the screen.

Solution

First, create two new instance variables: an SKNode object called dragNode and an SKPhsyicsJointPin called dragJoint.

In the code for your SKScene, add the following methods:

```
override func touchesBegan(_ touches: Set<UITouch>,
                          with event: UIEvent?) {

    // We only care about one touch at a time

    // Ensure we have a touch to work with
    guard let touch = touches.first else {
        return
    }

    // Work out what node got touched
    let touchPosition = touch.location(in: self)
    let touchedNode = self.atPoint(touchPosition)

    // Make sure that we're touching something that _can_ be dragged
    guard let touchedPhysicsBody = touchedNode.physicsBody else {
            return
    }

    // Create the invisible drag node, with a small static body
    let newDragNode = SKNode()
    newDragNode.position = touchPosition

    let dragPhysicsBody = SKPhysicsBody(rectangleOf:CGSize(width: 10,
                                                    height: 10))
    dragPhysicsBody.isDynamic = false
    newDragNode.physicsBody = dragPhysicsBody

    self.addChild(newDragNode)

    // Link this new node to the object that got touched
    let newDragJoint = SKPhysicsJointPin.joint(
        withBodyA: touchedPhysicsBody,
        bodyB:dragPhysicsBody,
        anchor:touchPosition)

    self.physicsWorld.add(newDragJoint)

    // Store the reference to the joint and the node
    self.dragNode = newDragNode
    self.dragJoint = newDragJoint


}
```

```
override func touchesMoved(_ touches: Set<UITouch>, with event: UIEvent?) {

    guard let touch = touches.first else {
        return
    }
    // When the touch moves, move the static drag node.
    // The joint will drag the connected
    // object with it.
    let touchPosition = touch.location(in: self)

    dragNode?.position = touchPosition

}

override func touchesEnded(_ touches: Set<UITouch>, with event: UIEvent?) {

    stopDragging()
}

override func touchesCancelled(_ touches: Set<UITouch>, with event: UIEvent?) {

    stopDragging()
}

func stopDragging() {

    guard dragJoint != nil else {
        return
    }

    // Remove the joint and the drag node.
    self.physicsWorld.remove(dragJoint!)
    dragJoint = nil

    dragNode?.removeFromParent()
    dragNode = nil
}
```

Discussion

The first thing that often comes into people's heads when they start thinking about how to do this is something like this: "When a touch begins, store a reference to the object that got touched. Then, when the touch moves, update the position property, and it'll move with it!"

This has a couple of problems, though. First, if you're only setting the position of the object that the user is dragging when the touch updates, gravity's going to be dragging the object down. This will have the effect of making the object's position flicker quite noticeably as it's moved around.

Second, if you're directly setting the position of an object, it becomes possible to make an object move through walls or through other objects, which may not be what you want.

A better solution, which is what we're doing in this recipe, is to create a static, invisible object, and connect it to the object that you want to actually let the user drag around. When the touch moves, you change the position of this static object, not the object you want dragged—as a result, the joint will move the object around. Because we're not overriding the physics system, the object being dragged around won't do impossible things like intersect with other objects. Additionally, by attaching the dragged body via a pin joint, the object will swing slightly as you move it, which looks really nice.

You'll notice that in both the touchesEnded and touchesCancelled methods, a new method called stopDragging is called. It's important to call stopDragging in both the ended and cancelled phases of the touch—a touch can get cancelled while the user's dragging the object around (such as when a gesture recognizer claims the touch), in which case you'll need to act as if the finger has been deliberately lifted up.

7.19 Creating a Car

Problem

You want to create a vehicle that has wheels attached to it.

Solution

A vehicle is composed of at least two main parts: the body of the vehicle and one or more wheels. In the case of a car (at least, a 2D car) we can model this with a box and two wheels—in other words, a rectangular SKSpriteNode and two SKShapeNodes that are set up to draw circles (see Figure 7-2).

In addition to creating the nodes, we need to link the wheels to the body with two SKPhysicsJointPin objects:

```
func createWheel(radius: CGFloat) -> SKShapeNode {
    let wheelRect = CGRect(x: -radius, y: -radius,
        width: radius*2, height: radius*2)

    let wheelNode = SKShapeNode()
    wheelNode.path = UIBezierPath(ovalIn: wheelRect).cgPath

    return wheelNode
}

func createCar() -> SKNode {
```

```
// Create the car
let carNode = SKSpriteNode(color:SKColor.yellow,
    size:CGSize(width: 150, height: 50))
let carPhysicsBody = SKPhysicsBody(rectangleOf:carNode.size)
carNode.physicsBody = carPhysicsBody

carNode.position = CGPoint(x: self.frame.midX, y: self.frame.midY);
self.addChild(carNode)

// Create the left wheel
let leftWheelNode = self.createWheel(radius: 30)
let leftWheelPhysicsBody = SKPhysicsBody(circleOfRadius:30)
leftWheelNode.physicsBody = leftWheelPhysicsBody
leftWheelNode.position = CGPoint(x: carNode.position.x-80,
    y: carNode.position.y)
self.addChild(leftWheelNode)

// Create the right wheel
let rightWheelNode = self.createWheel(radius: 30)
let rightWheelPhysicsBody = SKPhysicsBody(circleOfRadius:30)
rightWheelNode.physicsBody = rightWheelPhysicsBody
rightWheelNode.position = CGPoint(x: carNode.position.x+80,
    y: carNode.position.y)
self.addChild(rightWheelNode)

// Attach the wheels to the body
let leftWheelPosition = leftWheelNode.position
let rightWheelPosition = rightWheelNode.position

let leftPinJoint = SKPhysicsJointPin.joint(withBodyA: carPhysicsBody,
    bodyB:leftWheelPhysicsBody, anchor:leftWheelPosition)
let rightPinJoint = SKPhysicsJointPin.joint(withBodyA: carPhysicsBody,
    bodyB:rightWheelPhysicsBody, anchor:rightWheelPosition)

self.physicsWorld.add(leftPinJoint)
self.physicsWorld.add(rightPinJoint)

return carNode
}
```

Discussion

When you create an SKPhysicsJointPin, you define the anchor point in scene coordinates, not relative to any other body. In this recipe, the pin anchors are set at the center of each wheel, which makes them rotate around their axes; if you set the anchor to be somewhere else, you'll end up with bumpy wheels (which may actually be what you want!).

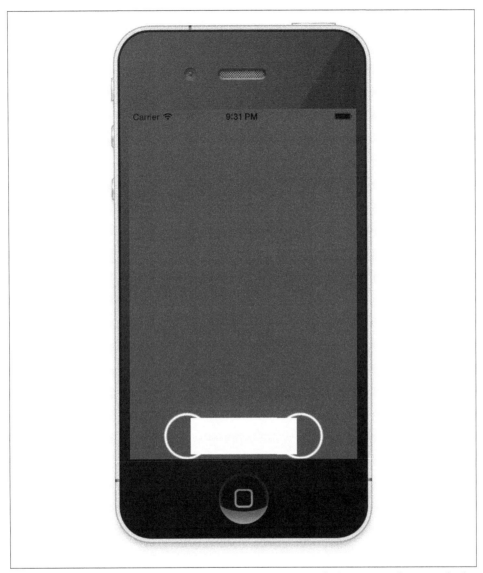

Figure 7-2. The car object described in this recipe, composed of a rectangular main body, two circles for wheels, and two pin joints to connect the wheels to the main body

CHAPTER 8

SceneKit

SceneKit is a simple framework for creating, configuring, and rendering a 3D scene in real time. SceneKit's designed for all kinds of 3D rendering situations, ranging from visualization of data to games. If you want to make a 3D game but don't want to spend ages learning how to deal with low-level OpenGL or Metal code, SceneKit's a great way to get started.

8.1 Setting Up for SceneKit

Problem

You want to set up your game to use SceneKit for rendering graphics.

Solution

Open your application's storyboard, and locate the view controller that you want to use to present the 3D content in your game.

Select the view, and go to the Identity inspector. Change the class to SCNView.

Next, go to your view controller's source code. At the top of the file, you need to import the SceneKit module:

```
import SpriteKit
```

The simplest way to ensure that SceneKit is working properly is to make your SCNView show a background color. In the implementation of viewDidLoad, add the following code:

```
let sceneView = self.view as! SCNView
sceneView.backgroundColor = UIColor(white: 0.6, alpha: 1.0)
```

Discussion

An `SCNView` is responsible for drawing 3D content in your game. While you don't often work directly with the view, it's a necessary first step to make sure that you've got a view and that it's working. Once you have it, you can move on to bigger and brighter things.

8.2 Creating a SceneKit Scene

Problem

You want to manage your 3D objects by grouping them into scenes.

Solution

Once you have an `SCNView` to render content, you need to create an `SCNScene`, and tell the `SCNView` to present it, like so:

```
let scene = SCNScene()
sceneView.scene = scene
```

Discussion

In SceneKit, your 3D content is grouped into collections called *scenes*. Each scene contains a number of *nodes*, which contain the 3D objects that you want to show the user.

It's good practice to divide up your game into multiple scenes. For example, a simple game might have a main menu scene, a settings scene, a credits scene, and a scene for each of the game's levels.

> In a game that uses SceneKit, you can often have just a single view controller, and manage all of the game's contents using scenes.

8.3 Showing a 3D Object

Problem

You want to render a 3D object on the screen.

Solution

First, define a geometry object, which describes to SceneKit what the visual shape of the object is:

```
let capsule = SCNCapsule(capRadius: 2.5, height: 6)
```

Then, create an SCNNode with that geometry, position it, and add it to the scene:

```
let capsuleNode = SCNNode(geometry: capsule)
capsuleNode.position = SCNVector3(x: 0, y: 0, z: 0)
scene.rootNode.addChildNode(capsuleNode)
```

Discussion

Nodes are invisible objects that simply occupy a position in space. On their own, they do nothing at all; to make them influence the scene that the user sees, you attach various objects to them, including geometry, cameras, lights, and more. We'll be looking at these kinds of objects in other recipes in this chapter.

Nodes can also have *other nodes* attached to them. This allows you to pair objects together: if you move a node, all of the nodes attached to it will move with it. This allows you to create quite complex scenes while still being able to manage them in a simple way.

The scene contains a node called the *root node*. If you want an object to be in the scene, you need to add it to the scene by calling addChildNode on the scene's root node, or on another node that's already part of the scene.

8.4 Working with SceneKit Cameras

Problem

You want to control how the player views your 3D scene using a camera.

Solution

First, create an SCNCamera object and configure it, by specifying how wide of a field of view it should have.

```
let camera = SCNCamera()
camera.fieldOfView = 75
```

Next, attach it to a node, position it, and add that node to the scene:

```
let cameraNode = SCNNode()
cameraNode.camera = camera

cameraNode.position = SCNVector3(x: 0, y: 0, z: 20)
```

```
scene.rootNode.addChildNode(cameraNode)
```

Discussion

A camera object controls how SceneKit renders the contents of the scene. There are two main kinds of cameras: *perspective* cameras and *orthographic* cameras.

When you're using a perspective camera, objects get smaller as they move away from the camera, just like in real life. With an orthographic camera, objects don't get smaller when they move away from the camera.

Perspective cameras are used when you want to present a scene as though the user is moving around in 3D space. An orthographic camera is better for when you aren't going for a realistic look in your game, such as in a side-scrolling or isometric game.

8.5 Creating Lights

Problem

You want to set up and control the lighting of your scene.

Solution

To use lights, you create a light object and attach it to an SCNNode.

To start, it's often best to create an *ambient light* object, which applies an even light from all directions:

```
let ambientLight = SCNLight()
ambientLight.type = SCNLight.LightType.ambient
ambientLight.color = UIColor(white: 0.25, alpha: 1.0)

let ambientLightNode = SCNNode()
ambientLightNode.light = ambientLight

scene.rootNode.addChildNode(ambientLightNode)
```

Next, add a *point light* (also called an *omni light*), which emits light in all directions from a single point:

```
let omniLight = SCNLight()
omniLight.type = SCNLight.LightType.omni
omniLight.color = UIColor(white: 1.0, alpha: 1.0)

let omniLightNode = SCNNode()
omniLightNode.light = omniLight
omniLightNode.position = SCNVector3(x: -5, y: 8, z: 5)

scene.rootNode.addChildNode(omniLightNode)
```

Discussion

There are four different types of light:

Omni lights
> Omni lights emit light from a single point, in all directions.

Directional lights
> Directional lights emit light in a single direction, and have no position. The sun is generally approximated through the use of a directional light.

Spot lights
> Spot lights emit light from a single position, in a single direction. You can also control the angle at which light is emitted, to make the light cone smaller or wider.

Ambient lights
> Ambient lights have no position or direction, and apply light from all directions.

8.6 Animating Objects

Problem

You want your objects to move around the scene.

Solution

To animate objects in SceneKit, you use the animation classes from Core Animation. To create an animation, you first define what property you want to animate. Use that to create an animation object, such as a `CABasicAnimation`:

```
// This animation changes the 'position' property
let moveUpDownAnimation = CABasicAnimation(keyPath: "position")

// Move 5 units on the y-axis (i.e., up)
moveUpDownAnimation.byValue = SCNVector3(x: 0, y: 3, z: 0)
// Accelerate and decelerate at the ends, instead of
// mechanically bouncing
moveUpDownAnimation.timingFunction =
    CAMediaTimingFunction(name: CAMediaTimingFunctionName.easeInEaseOut)

// Animation automatically moves back at the end
moveUpDownAnimation.autoreverses = true

// Animation repeats an infinite number of times (i.e., loops forever)
moveUpDownAnimation.repeatCount = Float.infinity

// The animation takes 2 seconds to run
moveUpDownAnimation.duration = 2.0
```

Once you have created the animation, you then apply it to the node that should animate:

```
capsuleNode.addAnimation(moveUpDownAnimation, forKey: "updown")
```

Discussion

You use the same class (`CAAnimation` and its subclasses) for animating SceneKit content as you do UIKit content. This means that you can use both `CABasicAnimation` and `CAKeyframeAnimation` to control your animations, and you have the same level of control over the animations as you do for animating `CALayer`s.

Only certain properties can be animated. To work out whether you can animate a property, look at the documentation for `SCNNode` and `SCNMaterial`; the properties that you can animate have *Animatable* in their description.

8.7 Working with Text Nodes

Problem

You want to render 3D text in your scene.

Solution

3D text is a kind of geometry, which you attach to a node. To create a 3D text geometry object, use the `SCNText` class, and attach it to a node:

```
let text = SCNText(string: "Text!", extrusionDepth: 0.2)

// text will be 2 units (meters) high
text.font = UIFont.systemFont(ofSize: 2)
let textNode = SCNNode(geometry: text)
// Positioned slightly to the left, and above the
// capsule (which is 10 units high)
textNode.position = SCNVector3(x: -2, y: 6, z: 0)

// Add the text node to the capsule node (not the scene's root node!)
capsuleNode.addChildNode(textNode)
```

Discussion

When you create an `SCNText` object, you provide it with a `UIFont`, in order to specify what font to use and its size. Keep in mind that the font size you provide is in SceneKit units in 3D space, not screen points in 2D space.

8.8 Customizing Materials

Problem

You want to control the way your objects react to light.

Solution

To control the appearance of your objects, you create a *material*. Materials in Scene-Kit are represented by the SCNMaterial class:

```
// Make the material be green and shiny
let greenMaterial = SCNMaterial()
greenMaterial.diffuse.contents = UIColor.green
greenMaterial.specular.contents = UIColor.white
greenMaterial.shininess = 1.0
```

Once you have a material, you apply it to a geometry object, which should be attached to a node:

```
// 'capsule' is an SCNGeometry
capsule.materials = [greenMaterial]
```

 The materials property is an array, because more complex meshes —especially meshes created in a 3D authoring tool—can use multiple materials.

Discussion

Materials are composed of a number of elements that control the color of the surface. The most important ones are:

diffuse
: This property controls the *base* color of the material.

specular
: This property applies a shiny effect to the material, and controls the brightness and color of this effect.

emissive
: This property makes the material appear to glow, regardless of what light is reflecting off it.

transparent
: This property controls which areas of the material are transparent, and the amount of transparency for them.

`normal`
> This property modifies the slope of the material, which affects how light bounces off it.

You can set `diffuse` and `specular` to be a color, an image, a `CALayer`, a path to a file (as a string or URL), a SpriteKit scene, or an `SKTexture`. If you set a material's property to a color, it can be animated.

8.9 Texturing Objects

Problem

You want your objects to have a texture applied to them.

Solution

To apply a texture to an object, you first need to get that texture from somewhere. Usually, you'll be loading this texture from a file:

```
let loadedTexture = SKTexture(imageNamed: "Ball")
```

Once you have your image, set it to the `diffuse` component of the material you want to use:

```
let textureMaterial = SCNMaterial()
textureMaterial.diffuse.contents = loadedTexture

text.materials = [textureMaterial]
```

Discussion

In addition to loading images from files, you can also use SpriteKit's ability to generate noise textures:

```
let noiseTexture = SKTexture(noiseWithSmoothness: 0.25,
    size: CGSize(width: 512, height: 512), grayscale: true)
let noiseMaterial = SCNMaterial()
noiseMaterial.diffuse.contents = noiseTexture
// We can now attach noiseMaterial to an object
```

8.10 Normal Mapping

Problem

You want to give your objects a bumpy texture.

Solution

To make the surface of your objects appear roughened, apply a *normal map* to your material. You can load a normal map from a texture, or you can generate one using SpriteKit:

```
let noiseNormalMapTexture =
    noiseTexture.generatingNormalMap(withSmoothness: 0.1,
                                     contrast: 1.0)
```

Once you have your normal map texture, apply it to the `normal` property of your geometry's material:

```
greenMaterial.normal.contents = noiseNormalMapTexture
```

Discussion

When determining the color of an object that's receiving light, the 3D renderer works out how bright each pixel of the object is based on the direction of the light and the angle at which the light hits the object. This angle is called the *normal*. Under ordinary circumstances, the normal of any location on an object is perpendicular to the surface; that is, if you lay your phone flat on a table, the normal of the phone's top surface is pointing straight up.

When you apply a *normal map* to a material, you override the normal and tell the 3D renderer to make light bounce in a slightly different way. Because your eye uses variations in shading to get information about the surface it's looking at, the surface will appear to be roughened. The end result is that when you add a single texture to your material, the object will appear to have a lot more geometric detail, and can often look a lot better.

8.11 Constraining Objects

Problem

You want the position or rotation of objects to be tied to other objects.

Solution

First, create an object that should be constrained:

```
let pointer = SCNPyramid(width: 0.5, height: 0.9, length: 4.0)
let pointerNode = SCNNode(geometry: pointer)
pointerNode.position = SCNVector3(x: -5, y: 0, z: 0)

scene.rootNode.addChildNode(pointerNode)
```

Next, create a constraint object and add it to the object you want to constrain:

```
let lookAtConstraint = SCNLookAtConstraint(target: capsuleNode)

// When enabled, the constraint will try to rotate
// around only a single axis
lookAtConstraint.isGimbalLockEnabled = true
pointerNode.constraints = [lookAtConstraint]
```

Discussion

A *constraint* is an object that indicates to SceneKit that some part of an object's position or rotation should be based on other objects. For example, you can constrain a shadow square so that its *x* and *z* positions are always the same as the player's, which would mean that the shadow would be positioned underneath the object, but wouldn't move upward if the player jumped.

There are several different constraints you can use:

- *Look-at* constraints make one object point toward another object.
- *Transform* constraints allow you to attach a code block that updates the position and rotation of an object every frame.
- *Inverse kinematics (IK)* constraints allow you to chain together a collection of objects—such as a hand, forearm, and upper arm—that can reach toward a point while obeying the limits of how far each joint can rotate.

8.12 Loading COLLADA Files

Problem

You have an object that you've designed using 3D editing software, and you want to add it to your SceneKit scene.

Solution

You can load 3D objects using the COLLADA file format. To use COLLADA, you first load the file from disk:

```
let critterDataURL =
    Bundle.main.url(forResource: "Critter",
                                    withExtension: "dae")
let critterData = SCNSceneSource(url: critterDataURL!, options: nil)
```

Once it's loaded, you can retrieve objects from it, such as nodes and geometry objects:

```
// Find the node called 'Critter'; if it exists, add it
let critterNode = critterData?.entryWithIdentifier("Critter",
                                                withClass: SCNNode.self)
if critterNode != nil {
```

```
        critterNode?.position = SCNVector3(x: 5, y: 0, z: 0)
        scene.rootNode.addChildNode(critterNode!)
    }
```

Discussion

Most 3D editing tools can export into the COLLADA format, including 3D Studio Max, Maya, and Blender. COLLADA files don't contain just a single object—they're entire libraries, and they can contain a bunch of stuff. You can define an entire scene, with node hierarchies, materials, and lights, in your 3D editor and load them into the scene.

In addition, if you click a COLLADA file in the Project Inspector, you can view the contents of the file directly inside Xcode.

8.13 Using 3D Physics

Problem

You want your 3D objects to have physical behavior.

Solution

To add physics to your objects, you need to provide two pieces of information: the collision *shape*, and the object's *physics body*.

First, you define the shape:

```
var critterPhysicsShape : SCNPhysicsShape?
if let geometry = critterNode?.geometry {
    critterPhysicsShape =
        SCNPhysicsShape(geometry: geometry,
                        options: nil)
}
```

Next, you create a physics body and provide it with a shape:

```
let critterPhysicsBody =
    SCNPhysicsBody(type: SCNPhysicsBodyType.dynamic,
                   shape: critterPhysicsShape)
```

Finally, you add the body to a node. Once a node has a physics body, it will begin to react to collisions and to physical forces like gravity:

```
critterNode?.physicsBody = critterPhysicsBody
```

Discussion

When you create a physics shape, you need to provide it with a geometry object that SceneKit can use to build the shape from. Different geometries will result in different shapes. Keep in mind that SceneKit will simplify the collision shape in order to make the physics system run smoothly, so the collision shape will be slightly different from the geometry that you see on screen.

When you create the body, you specify whether it is static, dynamic, or kinematic. Dynamic bodies respond to gravity, and can move around the scene. Static bodies are fixed in place, and while things can collide with them, they are themselves unaffected by collisions. Kinematic bodies are halfway between the two: they aren't affected by physical bodies or collisions, but they can move (when their node's position is changed) and can generate collisions when they do.

8.14 Adding Reflections

Problem

You want to add a reflective floor to your scene.

Solution

Use an SCNFloor object:

```
let floor = SCNFloor()
let floorNode = SCNNode(geometry: floor)
floorNode.position = SCNVector3(x: 0, y: -5, z: 0)
scene.rootNode.addChildNode(floorNode)
```

Discussion

A floor is a great way to visually ground the scene, and give a sense of where objects are in 3D space.

You can also add physics to your SCNFloor object, to provide a surface for objects to fall onto:

```
let floorPhysicsBody =
    SCNPhysicsBody(type: SCNPhysicsBodyType.static,
                   shape: SCNPhysicsShape(geometry: floor, options: nil))
floorNode.physicsBody = floorPhysicsBody
```

8.15 Hit-Testing the Scene

Problem

You want to tap on the screen, and receive information about what object is under the user's finger.

Solution

Use the `SCNView`'s `hitTest` function:

```
// locationToQuery is a CGPoint in view-space

// Find the object that was tapped
let sceneView = self.view as! SCNView
let hits = sceneView.hitTest(locationToQuery,
                             options: nil)

for hit in hits {
    print("Found a node: \(hit.node)")
}
```

Discussion

Hit tests return every object at a point. This can return a lot of nodes; pass the dictionary [SCNHitTestFirstFoundOnlyKey: true] for the options parameter to return only the first one.

8.16 Loading a Scene File

Problem

You want to load a preprepared SceneKit scene from a file.

Solution

Create a SceneKit scene file by opening the File menu, and choosing New → File. Select "SceneKit Scene File," and click Next. Save the new file somewhere in the project.

Once the file has been created, you can open it through the Project Navigator, and you'll be taken to the SceneKit editor. From here, you can visually create your SceneKit scenes.

To demonstrate this, create a simple scene using the editor. In the Object Library, scroll down to the Sphere, and drag it into the scene.

To use this scene, you can load it from disk. Use the SCNScene(named:) initializer, and pass in the name of the scene file you want to load:

```
if let loadedScene = SCNScene(named: "SceneFile.scn") {

    // Get a copy of the root node of this scene
    let newSceneContents = loadedScene.rootNode.clone()

    // Add it to this scene
```

```
        scene.rootNode.addChildNode(newSceneContents)
    }
```

Discussion

You can use the SceneKit editor to build up your game's scenes, rather than having to do everything through code. This can be a much faster and easier method of building things like game levels.

8.17 Particle Systems

Problem

You want to use a particle system to create visual effects.

Solution

First, you'll need to define the particle system itself.

Open the File menu, and choose New → File. Choose "SceneKit Particle System File." Click Next, and choose one of the templates.

To load a particle system, you create an instance of the SCNParticleSystem class, and specify the file you want to load from:

```
if let particleSystem = SCNParticleSystem(
    named: "Fire.scnp", inDirectory: nil) {
    let particlesNode = SCNNode()
    particlesNode.position = SCNVector3(2, 5, 5)

    particlesNode.addParticleSystem(particleSystem)

    scene.rootNode.addChildNode(particlesNode)
}
```

 Particle systems aren't nodes themselves; instead, you get a particle system, and attach it to another node.

Discussion

Particle systems create large numbers of individual *particles*, which are simple textured shapes that move according to patterns defined by the artist who designed the system.

Particle systems are very good at mimicking objects and phenomena that don't have a rigidly defined shape, like clouds of steam or rainfall. Play around with the properties in the SceneKit editor, and see how it changes the appearance of your particle system.

8.18 Using Metal

Problem

You want to learn more about Metal, the lower-level rendering engine that powers SceneKit.

Solution

Download and play with the Metal Fundamental Lessons examples (*https://apple.co/ 2NEIFye*). These lessons also come with detailed discussions about *why* the code is doing what it's doing.

Discussion

Metal is Apple's low-level graphics interface that drives the GPU. While SceneKit provides you with a high-level API, in which you work with things like nodes, geometry, and materials, Metal deals in terms of command buffers and shaders. Metal requires more work from you as a programmer, but can be significantly more efficient.

Learning how to use Metal is by no means a requirement for making games on iOS, but if you're interested (or feel like you're at the point where technologies like SceneKit and SpriteKit are holding you back), then it's definitely worth checking out.

CHAPTER 9

Artificial Intelligence and Behavior

Games are often at their best when they're challenging for players. There are a number of ways to make your game challenging, including creating complex puzzles; however, one of the most satisfying challenges that a player can enjoy is defeating something that's trying to outthink or outmaneuver her.

In this chapter, you'll learn how to create movement behavior, how to pursue and flee from targets, how to find the shortest path between two locations, and how to design an AI system that thinks ahead.

9.1 Making Vector Math Nicer in Swift

Problem

You have a collection of CGPoint values, and you want to be able to use the +, -, *, and / operators with them. You also want to treat CGPoints like vectors, and get information like their length or a normalized version of that vector.

Solution

Use Swift's operator overloading feature to add support for working with two CGPoints, and for working with a CGPoint and a scalar (like a CGFloat):

```
/* Adding points together */
func + (left: CGPoint, right : CGPoint) -> CGPoint {
    return CGPoint(x: left.x + right.x, y: left.y + right.y)
}

func - (left: CGPoint, right : CGPoint) -> CGPoint {
    return CGPoint(x: left.x - right.x, y: left.y - right.y)
}
```

```
func += ( left: inout CGPoint, right: CGPoint) {
    left = left + right
}

func -= ( left: inout CGPoint, right: CGPoint) {
    left = left + right
}

/* Working with scalars */

func + (left: CGPoint, right: CGFloat) -> CGPoint {
    return CGPoint(x: left.x + right, y: left.y + right)
}

func - (left: CGPoint, right: CGFloat) -> CGPoint {
    return left + (-right)
}

func * (left: CGPoint, right: CGFloat) -> CGPoint {
    return CGPoint(x: left.x * right, y: left.y * right)
}

func / (left: CGPoint, right: CGFloat) -> CGPoint {
    return CGPoint(x: left.x / right, y: left.y / right)
}

func += ( left: inout CGPoint, right: CGFloat) {
    left = left + right
}

func -= ( left: inout CGPoint, right: CGFloat) {
    left = left - right
}

func *= ( left: inout CGPoint, right: CGFloat) {
    left = left * right
}

func /= ( left: inout CGPoint, right: CGFloat) {
    left = left / right
}
```

Additionally, you can extend the CGPoint type to add properties like length and normalized:

```
extension CGPoint {
    var length :  CGFloat {
        return sqrt(self.x * self.x + self.y * self.y)
    }

    var normalized : CGPoint {
        return self / length
```

```
    }

    func rotatedBy(radians : CGFloat) -> CGPoint {
        var rotatedPoint = CGPoint(x: 0, y: 0)
        rotatedPoint.x = self.x * cos(radians) - self.y * sin(radians)
        rotatedPoint.y = self.y * cos(radians) + self.x * sin(radians)

        return rotatedPoint
    }

    func dot(other : CGPoint) -> CGFloat {
        return self.x * other.x + self.y * other.y
    }

    init (angleRadians : CGFloat) {
        self.init() // Necessary because 'CGPoint' is actually a C structure,
        // so it has to call its own base 'init' method

        self.x = sin(angleRadians)
        self.y = cos(angleRadians)
    }

}
```

Discussion

When you override an operator, you're defining exactly what it means for an operator to be applied to a value. It's extremely convenient to be able to type vector1 += vector2 instead of vector1.x += vector2.x; vector1.y += vector2.y, and operator overloading lets you do just that.

Note that the first parameters of += and related operators are an inout parameter. This is because += assigns the value of the operator and stores the result in the left-hand operand, rather than returning a brand new value (like + and its related operators do).

 The rest of the recipes in this chapter make use of these operators and helper functions. If you just copy another recipe's code without also including a file that includes this recipe's code in your project, you'll get errors.

9.2 Making an Object Move Toward a Position

Problem

You want an object to move toward another object.

Solution

Subtract the target position from the object's current position, normalize the result, and then multiply it by the speed at which you want to move toward the target. Then, add the result to the current position:

```
// Work out the direction to this position
var offset = self.position - targetPosition

// Reduce this vector to be the same length as our movement speed
offset = offset.normalized
offset *= CGFloat(self.movementSpeed) * deltaTime

// Add this to our current position
let newPosition = self.position + offset

self.position = newPosition;
```

Discussion

To move toward an object, you need to know the direction of your destination. To get this, you take your destination's position minus your current position, which results in a vector.

Let's say that you're located at [0, 5], and you want to move toward [1, 8] at a rate of 1 unit per second. The destination position minus your current location is:

```
My Location    = [0, 5]
Target Location = [1, 8]

Offset         = Target Location - My Location
               = [1, 8] - [0, 5]
               = [1, 3]
```

However, the length (or magnitude) of this vector will vary depending on how far away the destination is. If you want to move toward the destination at a fixed speed, you need to ensure that the length of the vector is 1, and then multiply the result by the speed at which you want to move.

Remember, when you normalize a vector, you get a vector that points in the same direction but has a length of 1. If you multiply this normalized vector with another number, such as your speed, you get a vector with that length.

So, to calculate how far you need to move, you take your offset, normalize it, and multiply the result by your movement speed.

To get smooth movement, you're likely going to run this code every time a new frame is drawn. Every time this happens, it's useful to know how many seconds have elapsed between the last frame and the current frame (see Recipe 1.5).

To calculate how far an object should move, given a speed in units per second and an amount of time measured in seconds, you just use the time-honored equation:

```
Speed = Distance ÷ Time
```

Rearranging, you get:

```
Distance = Speed × Time
```

You can now substitute, assuming a delta time of 1/30 of a second (i.e., 0.033 seconds):

```
Movement speed = 5
Delta time     = 0.033
Distance       = Movement Speed * Delta Time
               = 5 * 0.333
               = 1.666
```

Having worked out how much farther you must travel, and the direction in which you need to travel, you normalize the direction vector and multiply it by distance:

```
Normalized offset = Normalize(Offset) * Distance
                  = [0.124, 0.992]
Muliplied offset  = Normalized offset * Distance
                  = [0.206, 1.652]
```

You can then add this multiplied offset to your current position to get your new position. Then, you do the whole thing over again on the next frame.

This method of moving from a current location to another over time is fundamental to all movement behaviors, because everything else relies on being able to move.

9.3 Making Things Follow a Path

Problem

You want to make an object follow a path from point to point, turning to face the next destination.

Solution

When you have a path, keep a list of points. Move to the target (see Recipe 9.2). When you reach it, remove the first item from the list; then move to the new first item in the list.

Here's an example that uses SpriteKit (discussed in Chapter 6):

```
func moveAlongPath(points: [CGPoint]) {

    // If we've been given an empty path, do nothing
    if points.count == 0 {
```

```
        return
    }

    // Go through the list, and add an SKAction that moves from the previous
    // point to the current point
    var currentPoint = self.position
    var actions : [SKAction] = []

    for point in points {
        // Work out how long the movement should take, based on how
        // far away this point is and our movement speed
        let distance = (currentPoint - point).length
        let time = distance / CGFloat(self.movementSpeed)

        // Create a move-to action
        let moveToPoint = SKAction.move(to: point, duration: TimeInterval(time))
        actions.append(moveToPoint)

        // Use this current point as the 'previous point' for the next step
        currentPoint = point
    }

    // Run all of these actions in sequence
    let sequence = SKAction.sequence(actions)
    self.run(sequence)
}
```

Discussion

This recipe shows you how to make an object move along a path, but in order to have a path to follow, you need to either produce one yourself, or calculate one using a pathing algorithm, such as the one discussed in Recipe 9.9.

9.4 Making an Object Intercept a Moving Target

Problem

You want an object to move toward another object, intercepting it.

Solution

Calculate where the target is going to move to based on its velocity, and use the "move to" algorithm from Recipe 9.2 to head toward that position:

```
let toTarget = target.position - self.position

let lookAheadTime = toTarget.length / CGFloat(self.movementSpeed
    + target.movementSpeed)

let destination = target.position
```

```
    + (CGFloat(target.movementSpeed) * lookAheadTime)

self.moveToPosition(targetPosition: destination, deltaTime:deltaTime)
```

Figure 9-1 illustrates the result.

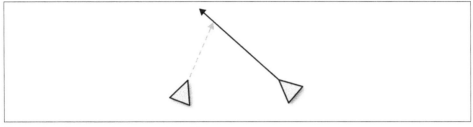

Figure 9-1. Intercepting a moving object

Discussion

When you want to intercept a moving object, your goal should be to move to where the target is going to be, rather than where it is right now. If you just move to where the target currently is, you'll end up always chasing it.

Instead, what you want to do is calculate where the target is going to be when you arrive by taking the target's current position and its speed, determining how fast you can get there, and then seeking toward that.

9.5 Making an Object Flee When It's in Trouble

Problem

You want an object to flee from something that's chasing it.

Solution

Use the "move to" method, but use the reverse of the force it gives you:

```
var offset = target.position - self.position

// Reduce this vector to be the same length as our movement speed
offset = offset.normalized

// Note the minus sign - we're multiplying by the reverse of our
// movement speed, which means we're moving away from it
offset *= CGFloat(-self.movementSpeed) * deltaTime

// Add this to our current position
let newPosition = self.position + offset

self.position = newPosition
```

Discussion

Moving away from a point is very similar to moving toward a point. All you need to do is use the inverse of your current movement speed. This will give you a vector that's pointing in the opposite direction of the point you want to move away from.

9.6 Making an Object Decide on a Target

Problem

You want to determine which of several targets is the best target for an object to pursue.

Solution

The general algorithm for deciding on the best target looks like this:

1. Set `bestScoreSoFar` to the worst possible score (either zero or infinity, depending on what you're looking for).

2. Set `bestTargetSoFar` to nothing.

3. Loop over each possible target:

   a. Check the score of the possible target.

   b. If the score is better than `bestScoreSoFar`:

      i. Set `bestTargetSoFar` to the possible target.

      ii. Set `bestScoreSoFar` to the possible target's score.

4. After the loop is done, `bestTargetSoFar` will either be the best target, or it will be nothing.

This algorithm is shown in code form in the following example. The `bestScoreSoFar` variable is called `nearestTargetDistance`; it stores the distance to the closest target found so far, and begins as the highest possible distance (i.e., infinity). You then loop through the array of possible targets, resetting it every time you find a new target nearer than the previous ones:

```
var nearestNodeDistance = CGFloat.infinity
var nearestNode : Critter? = nil

// Find the nearest critter
scene?.enumerateChildNodes(withName: "Critter") { (node, stop) -> Void in
    if let otherCritter = node as? Critter {

        if otherCritter == self {
            return
```

```
        }

        let distanceToTarget = (otherCritter.position - self.position).length

        if distanceToTarget < nearestNodeDistance {
            nearestNode = otherCritter
            nearestNodeDistance = distanceToTarget
        }

    }
}

self.target = nearestNode
```

Discussion

It's worth keeping in mind that there's no general solution to this problem because it can vary a lot depending on what your definition of "best" is. You should think about what the best target is in your game. Is it:

- Closest?
- Most dangerous?
- Weakest?
- Worth the most points?

Additionally, it depends on what information you can access regarding the nearby targets. Something that's worth keeping in mind is that doing a search like this can take some time if there are many potential targets. Try to minimize the number of loops that you end up doing.

9.7 Making an Object Steer Toward a Point

Problem

You want an object to steer toward a certain point, while maintaining a constant speed.

Solution

You can steer toward an object by figuring out the angle between the direction in which you're currently heading and the direction to the destination. Once you have this, you can limit this angle to your maximum turn rate:

```
// Work out the vector from our position to the target
let toTarget = target - self.position
```

```
// Work out our forward direction)
let forward = CGPoint(x: 0, y: 1).rotatedBy(radians: self.zRotation)

// Get the angle needed to turn towards this position
var angle = toTarget.dot(other: forward)
angle /= acos(toTarget.length * forward.length)

// Clamp the angle to our turning speed
angle = min(angle, CGFloat(self.turningSpeed))
angle = max(angle, CGFloat(-self.turningSpeed))

// Apply the rotation
self.zRotation += angle * deltaTime
```

Discussion

You can calculate the angle between two vectors by taking the dot product of the two vectors, dividing it by the lengths of both, and then taking the arc cosine of the result.

To gradually turn over time, you then limit the result to your maximum turning rate (to stop your object from turning instantaneously), and then multiply *that* by how long you want the turning action to take, in seconds.

9.8 Making an Object Know Where to Take Cover

Problem

You want to find a location where an object can move to, where it can't be seen by another object.

Solution

First, draw up a list of nearby points that your object (the "prey") can move to.

Then, draw lines from the position of the other object (the "predator") to each of these points. Check to see if any of these lines intersect an object. If they do, this is a potential cover point.

Then, devise paths from your object to each of these potential cover points (see Recipe 9.9). Pick the point that has the shortest path, and start moving toward it (see Recipe 9.3).

If you're using SpriteKit with physics bodies, you can use the body(alongRayStart:, end) method to find out whether you can draw an uninterrupted line from your current position to the potential cover position:

```
func findPotentialCover(steps : Int, distance : CGFloat) -> [CGPoint] {

    // Start with an empty list
```

```
    var coverPoints : [CGPoint] = []

    // Step around the circle 'steps' times
    for coverPoint in 0..<steps {

        // Work out the angle at which we're considering
        let angle = Float(.pi * 2.0) * (Float(coverPoint) / Float(steps))

        // Use that to create a point to check for cover
        let potentialPoint = CGPoint(angleRadians: CGFloat(angle)) * distance

        // Check to see if there's something between there and here
        if self.scene?.physicsWorld.body(alongRayStart: self.position,
                                    end: potentialPoint) != nil {
            // There's something between where we are and where we're
            // considering, so add this to the list
            coverPoints.append(potentialPoint)
        }
    }

    // Return the list of points that we found
    return coverPoints
}
```

Discussion

A useful addition to this algorithm is to make some cover "better" than others. For example, chest-high cover in a shooting game may be worth less than full cover, and cover that's closer to other, nearby cover may be worth more than an isolated piece of cover.

In these cases, your algorithm needs to take into account both the distance to the cover and the "score" for the cover.

9.9 Calculating a Path for an Object to Take

Problem

You want to determine a path from one point to another, avoiding obstacles.

Solution

There are several path-calculation algorithms for you to choose from; one of the most popular is called A* (pronounced "A star").

To use the A* algorithm, you give it the list of all of the possible waypoints at which an object can be ahead of time, and determine which points can be directly reached from other points. Later, you run the algorithm to find a path from one waypoint to another.

You can create a single data type that represents a collection of traversable points, and use Swift's ability to extend types to write a pretty compact implementation of the A* algorithm:

```
// Add support for storing CGPoints inside dictionaries, so that
// our code can be nice and elegant
extension CGPoint : Hashable {
    public var hashValue : Int {
        // Derive the hash by using hash values of
        // the x and y components
        return self.x.hashValue << 32 ^ self.y.hashValue
    }

    // Also add a convenience function that calculates
    // how far away this point is from another
    public func distanceTo(_ other : CGPoint) -> CGFloat {
        return (self - other).length
    }
}

struct NavigationGrid {

    // The points that this structure knows about
    var points : [CGPoint]

    // For each point in self.points, a list of points
    // that are one 'hop' away
    var neighbors : [CGPoint : [CGPoint]]

    // When starting up, store the points we're given,
    // plus a list of neighbors for each node
    init (points:[CGPoint], maximumDistance: CGFloat) {

        self.points = points
        self.neighbors = [:]

        // Make a list of neighbors for each node and store that
        for point in self.points {

            // Start with an empty list
            self.neighbors[point] = []

            // Check all other points..
            for otherPoint in self.points {

                // (..except this current one)
                if point == otherPoint {
                    continue
                }
```

```
            // Add this point as a neighbor if it's within range
            if point.distanceTo(otherPoint) <= maximumDistance {
                self.neighbors[point]?.append(otherPoint)
            }
        }
    }
}


// Find the nearest point in our collection of points
func nearestPoint(to point : CGPoint) -> CGPoint {
    var nearestPointSoFar : CGPoint = self.points[0]
    var nearestDistanceSoFar = CGFloat.infinity

    for node in self.points {
        let distance = node.distanceTo(point)
        if distance < nearestDistanceSoFar {
            nearestDistanceSoFar = distance
            nearestPointSoFar = node
        }
    }

    return nearestPointSoFar
}

func pathTo(start: CGPoint, end:CGPoint) -> [CGPoint]? {

    // g-score of a node: the known length of the path
    // that reaches this node
    var gScores : [CGPoint : CGFloat] = [:]

    // f-score of a node: how important it is that we
    // check this node (= g-score + distance from this
    // point to goal); lower value means higher priority
    var fScores : [CGPoint : CGFloat] = [:]


    // Find the points in our collection that are closest
    // to where we've been asked to search from and to
    let startPoint = self.nearestPoint(to: start)
    let goalPoint = self.nearestPoint(to: end)

    // Closed nodes are nodes that we've checked
    var closedNodes = Set<CGPoint>()

    // Open nodes are nodes that we should check; the node
    // with the lowest f-score will be checked next
    var openNodes = Set<CGPoint>()

    // We begin the search at the start point
    openNodes.insert(startPoint)
```

```
// Stores how we got from one node to another; used
// to generate the final list of points once search
// reaches the goal
var cameFromMap : [CGPoint : CGPoint] = [:]

// Keep searching for as long as we have points to check
while openNodes.count > 0 {

    // Find the point with the lowest f-score
    // We do this by turning the set into an array,
    // then sorting it based on the f-score of each
    // item in the array, then taking the first item
    // in the resulting array
    let currentNode = Array(openNodes).sorted{
        (first, second) -> Bool in
        return fScores[first, default: 0] < fScores[second, default: 0]
    }.first!

    // If we are now looking at the goal point, we're
    // done! Call reconstructPath to work backwards
    // from the goal point, following the came-from
    // map to get back to the start.
    if currentNode == goalPoint {
        var path : [CGPoint] = []
        path += [start]
        path += reconstructPath(cameFromMap: cameFromMap,
                                currentNode: currentNode)

        path += [end]

        return path
    }

    // Move this point from the open set to the closed set
    openNodes.remove(currentNode)
    closedNodes.insert(currentNode)

    let nodeNeighbors = self.neighbors[currentNode] ?? []

    // Examine each neighbor for this point
    for neighbor in nodeNeighbors {

        // Work out the scores for this node if it's
        // used in the path
        let tentativeGScore =
            (gScores[currentNode] ?? 0.0)
            + currentNode.distanceTo(neighbor)

        let tentativeFScore = tentativeGScore
            + currentNode.distanceTo(goalPoint)

        // If this neighbor is in the closed set,
```

```swift
                    // and using it would result in a worse
                    // path, don't use it
                    if closedNodes.contains(neighbor)
                        && tentativeFScore >=
                            (fScores[neighbor] ?? 0.0) {
                            continue
                    }

                    // If this neighbor is in the open set, OR
                    // using it would result in a better path,
                    // consider using it (by adding it to the
                    // open set, so we possibly consider it next
                    // iteration)
                    if openNodes.contains(neighbor)
                        || tentativeFScore <
                            (fScores[neighbor] ?? CGFloat.infinity) {

                            // Mark this neighbor on the path
                            // (indicating how we got to it)
                            cameFromMap[neighbor] = currentNode

                            // Give this neighbor its score
                            fScores[neighbor] = tentativeFScore
                            gScores[neighbor] = tentativeGScore

                            // Add this neighbor to the open set -
                            // depending on its f-score, it might
                            // be the next node we check!
                            openNodes.insert(neighbor)
                    }
                }
            }

            // If we've run through the entire open set and
            // still haven't found a path to the goal, it's
            // unreachable; return nil to indicate that we
            // found no path
            return nil

    }

    // Given a node and the came-from map, start working
    // backwards until we reach the only node that has no
    // came-from node (which is the start node)
    func reconstructPath(cameFromMap: [CGPoint:CGPoint],
        currentNode:CGPoint) -> [CGPoint] {

        if let nextNode = cameFromMap[currentNode] {
            return reconstructPath(cameFromMap: cameFromMap,
                currentNode: nextNode) + [currentNode]
        } else {
            return [currentNode]
        }
```

```
        }
    }


}
```

Discussion

The A* algorithm is a reasonably efficient algorithm for computing a path from one point to another. It works by incrementally building up a path; every time it looks at a new point, it checks to see if the total distance traveled is lower than that traveled using any of the other potential points, and if that's the case, it adds it to the path. If it ever gets stuck, it backtracks and tries again. If it can't find *any* path from the start to the destination, it returns an empty path.

9.10 Pathfinding on a Grid

Problem

You want to find the shortest path between two points on a GameplayKit grid (discussed in Recipe 1.19).

Solution

Use the GKGridGraph class's findPath(from:, to:) method:

```
import GameplayKit

// Define an 8x8 grid
let grid = GKGridGraph(fromGridStartingAt: [0,0],
                       width: 8, height: 8,
                       diagonalsAllowed: false)

// Remove a chunk of nodes from the middle of the grid,
// so that our path is a little more interesting
let nodesToRemove = (1...7).map {
    return grid.node(atGridPosition: [3, $0])!
}
grid.remove(nodesToRemove)

// Find a path from the top-left corner to the bottom-right
let startNode = grid.node(atGridPosition: [0,0])!
let destinationNode = grid.node(atGridPosition: [7,7])!

let path = grid.findPath(
    from: startNode,
    to: destinationNode
    ) as! [GKGridGraphNode]
```

```
// Print out the path
print("Path found:")
for point in path {
    print(point.gridPosition)
}
```

Discussion

While it's useful to know how the A* algorithm works, it's also useful to take advantage of library code that solves problems for you.

Don't forget that if `findPath` can't find a path, the array that it returns will be nil. Additionally, the array that it returns is of the type `GKGraphNode`, not `GKGridGraph Node`, so you'll need to cast it (as we have done in this recipe).

9.11 Finding the Next Best Move for a Puzzle Game

Problem

In a turn-based game, you want to determine the next best move to make.

Solution

The exact details here will vary from game to game, so in this solution, we'll talk about the general approach to this kind of problem.

Let's assume that the entire state of your game—the location of units, the number of points, the various states of every game object—is being kept in memory.

Starting from this current state, you figure out all possible moves that the next player can make. For each possible move, create a copy of the state where this move has been made.

Next, determine a score for each of the states that you've made. The method for determining the score will vary depending on the kind of game; some examples include:

- Number of enemy units destroyed minus number of my units destroyed
- Amount of money I have minus amount of money the enemy has
- Total number of points I have, ignoring how many points the enemy has

Once you have a score for each possible next state, take the top-scoring state, and have your computer player make that next move.

Discussion

The algorithm in this solution is often referred to as a *brute force* approach. This can get very complicated for complex games. Strategy games may need to worry about economy, unit movement, and so on—if each unit has 3 possible actions, and you have 10 units, you could end up in more than 59,000 possible states. To address this problem, you need to reduce the number of states that you calculate.

It helps to break up the problem into simpler, less-precise states for your AI to consider. Consider a strategy game in which you can, in general terms, spend points on attacking other players, researching technologies, or building defenses. Each turn, your AI just needs to calculate an estimate for the benefit that each general strategy will bring. Once it's decided on that, you can then have dedicated attacking, researching, or defense-building AI modules take care of the details.

9.12 Determining If an Object Can See Another Object

Problem

You want to find out if an object (the *hunter*) can see another object (the *prey*), given the direction the hunter is facing, the hunter's field of view, and the positions of both the hunter and the prey.

Solution

First, you need to define how far the hunter can see, as well as the field of view of the hunter. You also need to know what direction the hunter is currently facing. Finally, you need the positions of both the hunter and the prey.

The first test is to calculate how far away the prey is from the hunter. If the prey is farther away than `distance` units, the hunter won't be able to see it at all:

```
// Target is an SKNode,
// fieldOfView is a CGFloat,
// distance is a CGFloat

if (target.position - self.position).length > distance {
    return false
}
```

If the prey is within seeing distance, you then need to determine if the prey is standing within the hunter's field of view:

```
let facingDirection = CGPoint(x:0, y:1).rotatedBy(radians: self.zRotation)

let vectorToTarget = (target.position - self.position).normalized
let angleToTarget = acos(facingDirection.dot(other: vectorToTarget))
```

```
return abs(angleToTarget) < fieldOfView / 2.0
```

Discussion

Figuring out if one object can see another is a common problem. If you're making a stealth game, for example, where the player needs to sneak behind guards but is in trouble if she's ever seen, you need to be able to determine what objects the guard can actually see. Objects that are within the field of view are visible, whereas those that are outside of it are not, as shown in Figure 9-2.

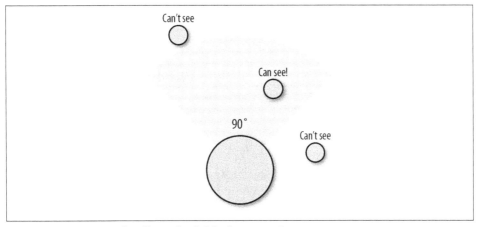

Figure 9-2. An example of how the field of view works

Calculating the distance between objects is very straightforward—you just need to have their positions, and use the length function to calculate how far each point is from the other. If the prey is too far away from the hunter, it isn't visible.

Figuring out whether or not the prey is within the angle of view of the hunter requires more math. What you need to do is to determine the angle between the direction the hunter is facing and the direction that the hunter would need to face in order to be directly facing the prey.

To do this, you create two vectors. The first is the vector representing the direction the hunter is facing:

```
let facingDirection = CGPoint(x:0, y:1).rotatedBy(radians: self.zRotation)
```

The second vector represents the direction from the hunter to the prey, which you calculate by subtracting the hunter's position from the prey's position, and then normalizing:

```
let vectorToTarget = (target.position - self.position).normalized
```

Once you have these vectors, you can figure out the angle between them by first taking the dot product of the two vectors, and then taking the arc cosine of the result:

```
let angleToTarget = acos(facingDirection.dot(other: vectorToTarget))
```

You now know the angle from the hunter to the prey. If this angle is less than half of the field-of-view angle, the hunter can see the prey; otherwise, the prey is outside the hunter's field of view.

9.13 Tagging Parts of Speech with NSLinguisticTagger

Problem

You want to identify where important parts of a sentence are in a string.

Solution

Use the `NSLinguisticTagger` class to identify the parts of speech:

```
// Define the string we want to analyse
let input = "You'll need to destroy the Ring, Mr Frodo"

// Specify some options for how the linguistic tagger should operate
let options: NSLinguisticTagger.Options = [
    .omitWhitespace,
    .omitPunctuation,
    .joinNames
]

// Define what labels we're looking for in the input
let schemes = [
    NSLinguisticTagScheme.nameTypeOrLexicalClass,
    NSLinguisticTagScheme.lemma
]

// Create the tagger
let tagger = NSLinguisticTagger(tagSchemes: schemes,
                                options: Int(options.rawValue))
tagger.string = input

// Define a range that matches the entire input.
let range = NSRange(0..<input.count)

for scheme in schemes {
    print("Evaluating for scheme \(scheme.rawValue)")

    // For each word in the input, tag it with the current scheme and
    // run a closure.
    tagger.enumerateTags(in: range, scheme: scheme, options: options) {
```

```
            (tag, tokenRange, _, _) in

            // Get the part of the string that contains this word
            let token = (input as NSString).substring(with: tokenRange)

            // Print the information we found
            if let tag = tag {
                print("\(token): \(tag.rawValue)")
            } else {
                print("(no \(scheme.rawValue) tag for \"\(token)\")")
            }
        }
    }
```

This code results in the following:

```
Evaluating for scheme NameTypeOrLexicalClass
You: Pronoun
'll: Verb
need: Verb
to: Particle
destroy: Verb
the: Determiner
Ring: Noun
Mr Frodo: PersonalName

Evaluating for scheme Lemma
You: you
'll: will
need: need
to: to
destroy: destroy
the: the
Ring: ring
Mr Frodo: Mr
```

Discussion

Linguistic tagging can be useful for text-based games, where, for instance, you can identify the verb in a command string the user has typed in (such as "open the door").

There are multiple tagging schemes available, depending on what language you're analyzing. To find out which schemes are available, you can use the NSLinguistic Tagger class's availableTagSchemes method:

```
// Find all tag schemes for English
NSLinguisticTagger.availableTagSchemes(forLanguage: "en")
```

9.14 Using AVFoundation to Access the Camera

Problem

You want direct access to the camera, so that you can present a live view.

Solution

Use the AVFoundation framework to create an AVCaptureSession, which you set up
to use the camera as an input source:

1. First, create a new project, using the single-view template.

2. Open the *Main.storyboard* file. Locate the *Tap Gesture Recognizer* in the Object
   Library, and drag it onto the view controller's view.

3. Locate the *Tap Gesture Recognizer* you just added in the Outliner. If you don't
   have the Outliner open, click the icon at the lower-left corner of the canvas.

4. Open the Assistant pane to reveal the source code to the ViewController class.

5. Hold down the Control key, and drag from the Tap Gesture Recognizer into the
   ViewController's code. When the connection pop-up appears, set the connection type to Action, and the name of the connection to "capturePhoto."

6. Next, in *ViewController.swift*, import the AVFoundation framework:

   ```
   import AVFoundation
   ```

7. Update your ViewController's code to look like the following:

   ```
   class ViewController: UIViewController {



       // An output that's used to capture still images.
       let photoOutput = AVCapturePhotoOutput()

       override func viewDidLoad() {
           super.viewDidLoad()

           let captureSession = AVCaptureSession()

           // Search for available capture devices that are
           // 1. on the rear of the device
           // 2. are a wide angle camera (not a telephoto)
           // 3. can capture video

           let availableDevices = AVCaptureDevice.DiscoverySession(
               deviceTypes: [.builtInWideAngleCamera],
               mediaType: AVMediaType.video,
   ```

```
            position: .back).devices

        // Find the first one
        guard let rearCamera = availableDevices.first else {
            fatalError("No suitable capture device found!")
        }

        // Set up the capture device and add it to the capture session
        do {

            let captureDeviceInput = try AVCaptureDeviceInput(device: rearCamera)
            captureSession.addInput(captureDeviceInput)

        } catch {
            print("Failed to create the device input! \(error)")
        }

        // Add the photo capture output to the session.
        captureSession.addOutput(photoOutput)


        // Create a preview layer for the session
        let previewLayer = AVCaptureVideoPreviewLayer(session: captureSession)

        // Add it to the view, underneath everything
        previewLayer.frame = view.frame
        view.layer.insertSublayer(previewLayer, at: 0)

        // Start the session
        captureSession.startRunning()
    }

    // Called when the user taps on the view.
    @IBAction func capturePhoto(_ sender: Any) {

        // Specify that we want to capture a JPEG
        // image from the camera.
        let settings = AVCapturePhotoSettings(format: [
            AVVideoCodecKey: AVVideoCodecType.jpeg
            ])

        // Signal that we want to capture a photo, and it
        // should notify this object when done
        photoOutput.capturePhoto(
            with: settings,
            delegate: self
        )
    }
}

// Contains methods that respond to a photo being captured.
extension ViewController : AVCapturePhotoCaptureDelegate {
```

```
// Called after a requested photo has finished being
// captured.
func photoOutput(
    _ output: AVCapturePhotoOutput,
    didFinishProcessingPhoto photo: AVCapturePhoto,
    error: Error?) {

    if let error = error {
        print("Error processing photo: \(error)")
    } else if let jpegData = photo.fileDataRepresentation() {

        // jpegData now contains an encoded JPEG image
        // that we can use

        let photoSizeKilobytes = jpegData.count / 1024

        print("Captured a photo! It was " +
            "\(photoSizeKilobytes)kb in size.")
    }
  }
}
```

8. Finally, open your project's *Info.plist* file, and add a new entry. Set the key to NSCa meraUsageDescription, and set the text to something like "We'll use the camera to show you what you're looking at."

9. Test the app on a device. You should see the view through the camera; when you tap the screen, the console will log the size of the captured JPEG image.

Discussion

The AVCaptureSession class allows you to have low-level access to the media capture hardware present on iOS devices. AVCaptureSession is incredibly powerful—you can capture video, still images, and audio from the variety of systems built into the device, and make use of the data coming out of them in just about any way you wish.

AVCaptureSession works as a connector between AVCaptureInputs and AVCaptur eOutputs. In this example, the input is specifically the rear wide-angle camera, and the output is a still photo handler, but others exist, such as video outputs and video encoders.

The AVCaptureVideoPreviewLayer class allows you to display a preview of the input coming in from the camera. It's not a UIView, but rather a CALayer—a lower-level component that you can add to a UIView to display content.

9.15 Importing a Core ML Model

Problem

You want to import a trained Core ML machine learning model, so that you can use it to make predictions.

Solution

First, you'll need a Core ML model that you want to use. If you don't already have one, Apple hosts a number of popular models on their CoreML site, at *https://devel oper.apple.com/machine-learning/*.

 Another source of Core ML models is *http://coreml.store*, which hosts several interesting models for analyzing text and images.

Once you've downloaded the model, add it to your project by dragging and dropping it into the Project Navigator. Xcode will identify the model, and prepare it for use in your code (see Recipe 9.16 for an example of using it in practice).

Discussion

Core ML is the framework that uses trained machine learning models to make predictions. These models can take a variety of inputs, such as text, numbers, or images, and compute predictions based on how they were trained.

Core ML can only make use of models that are in the `.mlmodel` format, but Apple provides a tool that can convert models produced by a wide variety of machine learning systems, including Keras, Theano, Torch, and TensorFlow.

For more information about Core ML, see Apple's documentation: *https://devel oper.apple.com/documentation/coreml*.

9.16 Identifying Objects in Images

Problem

You want to use the Core ML and Vision frameworks to identify the contents of images.

Solution

In this recipe, we'll use the Inceptionv3 model, which is designed to "detect the dominant objects present in an image from a set of 1000 categories such as trees, animals, food, vehicles, people, and more," according to the researchers. We'll also be building on top of Recipe 9.14.

Specifically, we'll add an `AVCaptureOutput` that continuously captures frames from the camera and passes them to a method that runs the frame data through the Core ML model. This will result in a string that describes what the model thinks is present in the image, which will be used to update a text label.

Because raw frames of video that come out of an `AVSession` are in a fairly low-level format, we'll make use of the `Vision` framework, which provides some classes that can handle the conversion between formats for us:

1. Download the Inceptionv3 *.mlmodel* file from Apple's Core ML site (*https:// apple.co/2zw9snS*).
2. Add the *.mlmodel* file to your project.
3. Build the project, to ensure that Xcode has processed the Core ML model.

Next, we'll add the label:

1. Open the *Main.storyboard* file, and drag a label onto the view.
2. Open the Assistant pane, revealing the source code to the `ViewController` class.
3. Hold down the Control key, and drag from the label into the `ViewController`'s code. When the pop-up appears, set the type of the connection to Outlet, and the name to `outputLabel`.
4. Import the `Vision` framework by adding the following code near the top of *ViewController.swift*:

```
import Vision
```

5. Add the following property to the `ViewController` class:

```
// Produces a Vision wrapper for a CoreML model.
lazy var model : VNCoreMLModel = {
    let coreMLModel = Inceptionv3().model

    do {
        return try VNCoreMLModel(for: coreMLModel)

    } catch let error {
        fatalError("Failed to create model! \(error)")
```

```
        }
    }()
```

6. Add the following code to the `viewDidLoad` method, after the line in which the `photoOutput` is added to the session:

```
let captureOutput = AVCaptureVideoDataOutput()
// Set up the video output, and add it to the capture session
// Tell the capture output to notify us every time it captures a frame of video

captureOutput.setSampleBufferDelegate(self,
    queue: DispatchQueue(label: "videoQueue"))
captureSession.addOutput(captureOutput)
```

7. Add the following code to the end of the file:

```
extension ViewController : AVCaptureVideoDataOutputSampleBufferDelegate {

    // Called every time a frame is captured
    func captureOutput(_ output: AVCaptureOutput,
        didOutput sampleBuffer: CMSampleBuffer,
        from connection: AVCaptureConnection) {

        // Create a request that uses the model

        let request = VNCoreMLRequest(model: model) { (finishedRequest, error) in

            // Ensure that we have an array of results
            guard let results = finishedRequest.results
                as? [VNClassificationObservation] else {
                    return
            }

            // Ensure that we have at least one result
            guard let observation = results.first else {
                return
            }

            // This whole queue runs on a background
            // queue, so we need to be sure we update
            // the UI on the main queue
            OperationQueue.main.addOperation {
                self.outputLabel.text =
                "\(observation.identifier)"
            }
        }

        // Convert the frame into a CVPixelBuffer, which
        // Vision can use
        guard let pixelBuffer: CVPixelBuffer =
            CMSampleBufferGetImageBuffer(sampleBuffer) else {
                return
```

```
    }

    // Create and execute a handler that uses this request
    let handler = VNImageRequestHandler(
        cvPixelBuffer: pixelBuffer,
        options: [:]
    )

    try? handler.perform([request])
}

}
```

8. Test the application. When you aim the camera at different objects, the label will update to show what the model thinks it's looking at (an example can be seen in Figure 9-3).

Figure 9-3. The image detection system, seen here correctly identifying a cat

Discussion

Core ML models that process images typically require the image to be resized to a certain size. By using the classes found in the Vision framework, most of this work is handled for you.

It's worth noting that a machine learning model is only as good as the data it's trained on. The Inceptionv3 model that's used in this recipe is quite good, but it only knows about a certain range of objects.

If you want to train your own models, Apple provides a tool called Turi Create, which allows you to create models without having to be an expert in machine learning. For more information, see Turi Create's project page on GitHub: *https://github.com/apple/turicreate*.

9.17 Using AI to Enhance Your Game Design

Problem

You want to make sure your game uses AI and behavior effectively to create a fun and engaging experience.

Solution

The fun in games comes from a number of places (see *http://8kindsoffun.com* for a discussion). In our opinion, one of the most important kinds of fun is challenge. Games that provoke a challenge for the player are often the most enjoyable.

Judicious and careful use of AI and behavior in your games can help them stand a cut above the rest in a sea of iOS games. You want to create an increasingly difficult series of challenges for your players, slowly getting more complex and introducing more pieces the longer they play.

Revealing the different components of gameplay as they play is an important way to stagger the difficulty, and it's important that any AI or behavior you implement isn't using tools that the player doesn't have access to.

Reveal the pieces of your game slowly and surely, and make sure the AI is only one step, if at all, ahead of the player.

Discussion

It's hard to make a game genuinely challenging without killing the fun factor by making it too difficult. The best way to do this is to slowly peel back the layers of your game, providing individual components one by one until the player has access to the full arsenal of things he can do in your game. The AI or behavior code of your game should get access to this arsenal at approximately the same rate as the player, or it will feel too difficult and stop being fun.

CHAPTER 10

Working with the Outside World

iOS devices can interact with a wide range of other devices. Some of these devices, such as external screens and game controllers, are particularly useful when you're building games!

iOS has supported multiple screens since iOS 2, and has supported game controllers since iOS 7. Game controllers are handheld devices that provide physical buttons for your players to use, and have both advantages and disadvantages when compared with touchscreens. Because a game controller has physical buttons, the player's hands can feel where the controls are, which makes it a lot easier to keep attention focused on the action in the game. Additionally, game controllers can have *analog inputs*: a controller can measure how hard a button is being held down, and the game can respond accordingly. However, game controllers have fixed buttons that can't change their position, or look and feel, which means that you can't change your controls on the fly.

Game controllers that work with iOS devices must obey a set of design constraints specified by Apple; these constraints mean that you can rely on game controllers built by different manufacturers to all behave in a consistent way and provide the same set of controls for your games. To make matters more complex, there are several different *profiles* of game controller. The simplest (and usually cheapest) is the *standard* game controller (see Figure 10-1), which features two shoulder buttons, four face buttons, a pause button, and a d-pad. The next step up is the *extended* gamepad (see Figure 10-2), which includes everything in the standard profile, and adds two thumb-sticks and two triggers. Your game doesn't need to make use of every single button that's available, but it helps.

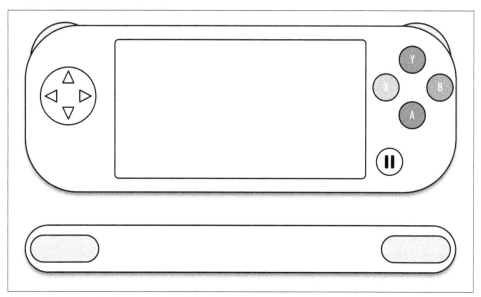

Figure 10-1. The basic game controller

Figure 10-2. The extended game controller (note the thumbsticks and additional shoulder buttons)

In addition to game controllers, iOS games can make use of external screens. These can be directly connected to your device via a cable, or they can be wirelessly connected via AirPlay. Using external screens, you can do a number of things: for example, you can make your game appear on a larger screen than the one that's built in, or even turn the iPhone into a game controller and put the game itself on a television screen (effectively turning the device into a portable games console).

Like controllers, external screens should never be required by your game. External screens are useful for displaying supplementary components of your game, or providing the main game view while the iOS device itself is used as a controller and secondary view.

In this chapter, you'll learn how to connect to and use game controllers, how to use multiple screens via cables and wireless AirPlay, and how to design and build games that play well on the iPhone/iPod touch and iPad, or both. We'll also discuss how to use the Taptic Engine for tactile feedback, how to record the user's screen, how to make use of ARKit for augmented reality, and how to make use of TestFlight for beta testing and Fastlane for build automation.

10.1 Detecting Controllers

Problem

You want to determine whether the user is using a game controller. You also want to know when the user connects and disconnects the controller.

Solution

Game controllers are represented by instances of the GCController class. Each GCController lets you get information about the controller itself and the state all of its buttons and controls.

To access the GCController class, you first need to import the GameController framework:

```
import GameController
```

To get a GCGameController, you ask the GCController class for the controllers property, which is the list of all currently connected controllers:

```
for controller in GCController.controllers() {
    NSLog("Found a controller: \(controller)")
}
```

The controllers array updates whenever controllers are connected or disconnected. If the user plugs in a controller or disconnects one, the system sends a GCController

DidConnect notification or a GCControllerDidDisconnect notification, respectively. You can register to receive these notifications like this:

```
let connectedSelector = #selector(self.controllerConnected(notification:))
let disconnectedSelector = #selector(self.controllerDisconnected(notification:))

NotificationCenter.default.addObserver(self,
                                        selector: connectedSelector,
                                        name: .GCControllerDidConnect,
                                        object: nil)

NotificationCenter.default.addObserver(self,
                                        selector: disconnectedSelector,
                                        name: .GCControllerDidDisconnect,
                                        object: nil)
```

When a controller is connected, you can find out whether it's a standard gamepad or an extended gamepad by using the gamepad and extendedGamepad properties:

```
if controller.extendedGamepad != nil {
    // It's an extended gamepad
    NSLog("This is an extended gamepad")
} else if controller.gamepad != nil {
    // It's a standard gamepad
    NSLog("This is a standard gamepad")
} else {
    // It's something else entirely, and probably can't be used by your game\
    NSLog("I don't know what kind of gamepad this is")
}
```

You can also check to find out whether the controller is physically attached to the device, by checking the isAttachedToDevice property:

```
if controller.isAttachedToDevice {
    NSLog("This gamepad is physically attached")
} else {
    NSLog("This gamepad is wireless")
}
```

Discussion

The GCController class updates automatically when a controller is plugged in to the device. However, your user might have a wireless controller that uses Bluetooth to connect to the iPhone, and it might not be connected when your game launches.

Your player can leave the game and enter the Settings application to connect the device, but you might prefer to let the player connect the controller while still in your game. To do this, you use the startWirelessControllerDiscovery(completionHandler:) method. When you call this, the system starts looking for nearby game controllers, and sends you a GCControllerDidConnect notification for each one that it finds. Once the search process is complete, regardless of whether or not any controllers were found, the method calls a completion handler block:

```
// Once called, you'll receive
// GCControllerDidConnectNotification and
// GCControllerDidDisconnectNotification for
// wireless devices
GCController.startWirelessControllerDiscovery { () -> Void in
    NSLog("Finished searching for wireless controllers")
}
```

It's important to note that the system won't show any built-in UI when you're searching for wireless controllers. It's up to you to show the UI that indicates to the player that you're searching for controllers.

Once a wireless controller is connected, your game treats it just like a wired one—there's no difference in the way you talk to it.

Once you have a GCController, you can set the playerIndex property. When you set this property, an LED on the controller lights up to let the player know which player he is. This property is actually remembered by the controller and is the same across *all games*, so that the player can move from game to game and not have to relearn which player number he is in multiplayer games:

```
controller.playerIndex = GCControllerPlayerIndex.index1
```

At the time of writing, there are four possible player indices; one each for the first, second, third and fourth player.

10.2 Getting Input from a Game Controller

Problem

You would like people to be able to control your game using their external controllers.

Solution

Each controller provides access to its buttons through various properties:

```
// Pressed (true/false)
let isButtonAPressed = controller.gamepad?.buttonA.isPressed

// Pressed amount (0.0 .. 1.0)
let buttonAPressAmount = controller.gamepad?.buttonA.value
```

You use the same technique to get information about the gamepad's directional pads. The d-pad and the thumbsticks are both represented as GCControllerDirectionPad classes, which lets you treat them as a pair of axes (i.e., the x-axis and the y-axis), or as four separate buttons (up, down, left, and right):

```
let horizontalAxis = controller.gamepad?.dpad.xAxis

// Alternatively, just ask if the left button is pressed
let isLeftDirectionPressed = controller.gamepad?.dpad.left.isPressed
```

Discussion

There are two different types of inputs available in a game controller:

Button inputs
A *button input* tells you whether a button is being pressed, as a Boolean true or false. Alternatively, you can find out *how much* a button is being pressed down, as a floating-point value that goes from 0 (not pressed down at all) to 1 (completely pressed down).

Axis inputs
An *axis input* provides 2D information on how far left, right, up, and down the d-pad or thumbstick is being pressed by the user.

The face and shoulder buttons are all represented as GCControllerButtonInput objects, which let you get their value either as a simple bool or as a float. The d-pad and the thumbsticks are both represented as GCControllerAxisInput objects.

Both button inputs and axis inputs also let you provide *value changed handlers*, which are blocks that the system calls when an input changes value. You can use these to make your game run code when the user interacts with the controller, as opposed to continuously polling the controller to see its current state.

For example, if you want to get a notification every time the A button on the controller is interacted with, you can do this:

```
controller.gamepad?.buttonA.valueChangedHandler
    = { (input: GCControllerButtonInput!, value:Float, pressed:Bool) in

        NSLog("Button A pressed: \(pressed)")

}
```

This applies to both button inputs and axis inputs, so you can attach handlers to the thumbsticks and d-pad as well. Note that the value changed handler will be called multiple times while a button is pressed, because the value property will change continuously as the button is being pressed down and released.

In addition to adding handlers to the inputs, you can also add a handler block to the controller's pause button:

```
controller.controllerPausedHandler =
    { (controller: GCController!) in

        NSLog("Pause button pressed")

}
```

 The controller itself doesn't store any information about whether or not the game is paused—it's up to your game to keep track of the pause state. All the controller will do is tell you when the button is pressed.

10.3 Showing Content via AirPlay

Problem

You would like to use AirPlay to wirelessly display elements of your game on a high-definition screen via an Apple TV.

Solution

Use an MPVolumeView to provide a picker, which lets the user select an AirPlay device.

Because you can only add an MPVolumeView through code, positioning it isn't quite as simple as adding it in the Interface Builder. Instead, use code like the following:

```
let volumeView = MPVolumeView()
volumeView.showsRouteButton = true
volumeView.showsVolumeSlider = false

volumeView.sizeToFit()

self.volumeControlContainerView.addSubview(volumeView)
```

This creates a button that, when tapped, lets the user select an AirPlay device to connect to the existing device. When the user selects a screen, a UIScreenDidConnect notification is sent, and your game can use the AirPlay device using the UIScreen class (see Recipe 10.4).

The MPVolumeView will only show the AirPlay picker if there are AirPlay devices available. If no AirPlay device is nearby, nothing will appear.

Additionally, you'll only receive a UIScreenDidConnect notification if mirroring is turned on in the AirPlay options (accessible via Control Center). If mirroring is turned off, AirPlay will route any audio your app plays to the device the user has selected, but won't send any video.

Discussion

When the user has selected an AirPlay display, iOS treats it as if a screen is attached. You can then treat it as a UIScreen (there's no distinction made between wireless screens and plugged-in screens).

Just like with a plugged-in screen, the contents of the primary screen will be mirrored onto the additional screen. If you give the screen to a UIWindow object, mirroring will be turned off and the screen will start showing the UIWindow. If you remove the UIScreen from the UIWindow, the screen will return to mirroring mode.

If there are more than two screens attached, only one screen will mirror the main display. The other screens will be blank until you give them to a UIWindow.

10.4 Using External Screens

Problem

You would like to display elements of your game on a screen external to the iOS device.

Solution

To be notified of when a screen is connected or disconnected, use the Notification Center to register for screen connections and disconnections.

In your view controller, add the following methods:

```
@objc func screenConnected(_ notification: Notification) {
    NSLog("Screen connected: \(notification.object as! UIScreen)")
}

@objc func screenDisconnected(_ notification: Notification) {
```

```
    NSLog("Screen disconnected: \(notification.object as! UIScreen)")
}
```

Next, in your `viewDidLoad` method, you can register to be notified:

```
NotificationCenter.default.addObserver(self,
    selector: #selector(ViewController.screenConnected(_:)),
    name: UIScreen.didConnectNotification, object: nil)
NotificationCenter.default.addObserver(self,
    selector: #selector(ViewController.screenDisconnected(_:)),
    name: UIScreen.didDisconnectNotification, object: nil)
```

To get the list of currently available screens, you use the `UIScreen` class:

```
for connectedScreen in UIScreen.screens {
    if connectedScreen == UIScreen.main {
        NSLog("Main screen: \(connectedScreen)")
    } else {
        NSLog("External screen: \(connectedScreen)")
    }
}
```

On iPhones, iPod touches, and iPads, there's always at least one `UIScreen` available—the built-in touchscreen. You can get access to it through the `UIScreen`'s `main` property:

```
let mainScreen = UIScreen.main
```

When you have a `UIScreen`, you can display content on it by creating a `UIWindow` and giving it to the `UIScreen`. `UIWindows` are the top-level containers for all views—in fact, they're views themselves, which means you add views to a screen using the `addSubview` method:

```
if UIScreen.screens.count >= 2 {

    // This next step requires that there's a view controller
    // in the storyboard with the Identifier "ExternalScreen"
    let viewController = self.storyboard?
        .instantiateViewController(withIdentifier: "ExternalScreen")

    // Try and get the last screen..
    if let connectedScreen = UIScreen.screens.last {

        // Create a window, and put the view controller in it
        let window = UIWindow(frame: connectedScreen.bounds)
        window.rootViewController = viewController
        window.makeKeyAndVisible()

        // Put the window on the screen.
        window.screen = connectedScreen
    }
}
```

Discussion

You can detect when a screen is connected by subscribing to the `UIScreenDidConnect` and `UIScreenDidDisconnect` notifications. These are sent when a new screen becomes available to the system—either because it's been plugged in to the device, or because it's become available over AirPlay—and when a screen becomes unavailable.

If you want to test external screens on the iOS Simulator, you can select one by choosing Hardware→TV Out and choosing one of the available sizes of window (see Figure 10-3). Note that selecting an external display through this menu will restart the entire simulator, which will quit your game in the process. This means that while you can test *having* a screen connected, you can't test the `UIScreenDidConnect` and `UIScreenDidDisconnect` notifications.

Figure 10-3. Choosing the size of the external screen in the iOS Simulator

10.5 Designing Effective Graphics for Different Screens

Problem

You want your game to play well on different kinds of screens and devices, including iPhones, iPads, and large-scale televisions.

Solution

When you design your game's interface, you need to consider several factors that differ between iPhones, iPads, and connected displays. Keep the following things in mind when considering how the player is going to interact with your game.

Designing for iPhones

An iPhone:

Is very portable

People can whip out an iPhone in two seconds, and start playing a game within five. Because they can launch games very quickly, they won't want to wait around for your game to load.

Additionally, the iPhone is a very light device. Users can comfortably hold it in a single hand.

Has a very small screen

The amount of screen space available for you to put game content on is very small. Because the iPhone has a touchscreen, you can put controls on the screen. However, to use them, players will have to cover up the screen with their big, opaque fingers and thumbs. Keep the controls small—but not too small, because fingers are very imprecise.

Will be used in various locations, and with various degrees of attention

People play games on their iPhones in a variety of places: in bed, waiting for a train, on the toilet, at the dinner table, and more. Each place varies in the amount of privacy the user has, the amount of ambient noise, and the amount of distraction. If you're making a game for the iPhone, your players will thank you if the game doesn't punish them for looking away from the screen for a moment.

Additionally, you should assume that the players can't hear a single thing coming from the speaker. They could be sitting in a quiet room, but they could just as easily be in a crowded subway station. They could also be playing in bed and trying not to wake their partners, or they could be hard of hearing or deaf.

Your game's audio should be designed so that it enhances the game but isn't necessary for the game to work. (Obviously, this won't be achievable for all games; if you've got a game based heavily on sound, that's still a totally OK thing to make!)

Designing for iPads

An iPad:

Is portable, but less spontaneous

Nobody quickly pulls out an iPad to play a 30-second puzzle game, and then puts it back in his pocket. Generally, people use iPads less frequently than smartphones but for longer periods. This means that "bigger" games tend to do very well on the iPad, because the users start playing them with the intent to play for at least a few minutes rather than (potentially) a few seconds.

Has a comparatively large screen

There are two different types of iPad screens: the one present on the iPad mini, and the one present on larger-size iPads (such as the iPad Pro devices). The mini's screen is smaller, but still considerably larger than that on the iPhone. This gives you more room to place your controls, and gives the player a bigger view of the game's action.

However, the flipside is that the iPad is heavier than the iPhone. iPads generally need to be held in both hands, or placed on some kind of support (like a table or the player's lap). This contributes to the fact that iPads are used less often but for longer sessions: it takes a moment to get an iPad positioned just how the user wants it.

Will be used in calmer conditions

For the same reason, an iPad tends to be used when the user is sitting rather than walking around, and in less hectic and public environments. The user will also be more likely to give more of her attention to the device.

May be more often used by children

iPads are popular devices for children, because they're portable, relatively difficult to break, and have a wide library of games and software specifically designed for children. Consider making your next children's game with the iPad as the primary target platform.

Designing for larger screens

When players have connected a larger screen:

They're not moving around

An external screen tends to be fixed in place, and doesn't move around. If the screen is plugged directly into the iPad, this will also restrict movement. This means that players are likely to play for a longer period of time; because they've invested the energy in setting up the device with their TV, they'll be in for the (relatively) long haul.

The player has two screens to look at

A player who's connected an external screen to his iOS device will still be holding the device in his hands, but he's more likely to not be looking at it. This means that he's not looking at where your controls are. If he's not using a controller, which is likely, he won't be able to feel where one button ends and another begins. This means that your device should show *very large* controls on the screen, so that your users can focus on their wonderfully huge televisions and not have to constantly look down at the device.

Having two devices can be a tremendous advantage for your game, for example, if you want to display secondary information to your user—*Real Racing 2* does this very well, in that it shows the game itself on the external screen, and additional info like the current speed and the map on the device.

More than one person can comfortably look at the big screen

Large displays typically have a couch in front of them, and more than one person can sit on a couch. This means that you can have multiple people playing a game, though you need to keep in mind that only one device can actually send content to the screen.

Discussion

Generally, you'll get more sales if your game works on both the iPhone and the iPad. Players have their own preferences, and many will probably have either an iPhone or an iPad—it's rare to have both, because Apple products are expensive.

When it comes to supporting large screens, it's generally a cool feature to have, but it's not very commonplace to have access to one. You probably shouldn't consider external screen support to be a critical feature of your game unless you're deliberately designing a game to be played by multiple people in the same room.

10.6 Dragging and Dropping

Problem

You want to drag and drop objects into specific locations. If an object is dropped somewhere it can't go, it should return to its origin. (This is particularly useful in card games.)

Solution

This recipe shows you how you'd create your own drag-and-drop effect. However, there's also a built-in drag-and-drop system in iOS, which is primarily designed for apps that want to share content between different applications, or within different parts of a single application, and its API is mostly designed around packaging up data for transfer.

If you're interested in learning about it, Apple's documentation on the subject (*https://apple.co/2Ihvu0k*) is extremely informative.

Use gesture recognizers to implement the dragging itself. When the gesture recognizer ends, check to see whether the drag is over a view that you consider to be a valid *destination*. If it is, position the view over the destination; if not, move it back to its original location.

The following code provides an example of how you can do this. In this example, CardSlot objects create Cards when tapped; these Card objects can be dragged and dropped only onto other CardSlots, and only if those CardSlot objects don't already have a card on them, as shown in Figure 10-4.

Figure 10-4. The drag-and-drop example in this recipe

Additionally, card slots can be configured so they delete any cards that are dropped on them.

Create a new class called CardSlot, which is a subclass of UIImageView. Put the following code in *CardSlot.swift*:

```
@IBDesignable
class CardSlot: UIImageView {

    // @IBInspectable and @IBDesignable makes the deleteOnDrop
    // property appear in the interface builder
```

```
@IBInspectable
var deleteOnDrop : Bool = false

var currentCard : Card? {
    // If we're given a new card, and this card slot is
    // 'delete on drop', delete that card instead
    didSet {
        if self.deleteOnDrop == true {

            currentCard?.delete()
            self.currentCard = nil
            return
        }
    }
}


private var tap : UITapGestureRecognizer?

override func awakeFromNib() {
    let tappedSelector: Selector
        = #selector(CardSlot.tapped(recognizer:))

    self.tap = UITapGestureRecognizer(target: self,
                                      action: tappedSelector)
    self.addGestureRecognizer(self.tap!)

    self.isUserInteractionEnabled = true
}

@objc func tapped(recognizer: UITapGestureRecognizer) {

    if recognizer.state == .ended {
        // Only card slots that aren't "delete when cards
        // are dropped on them" can create cards
        if self.deleteOnDrop == false {
            let card = Card(cardSlot: self)

            self.superview?.addSubview(card)

            self.currentCard = card
        }
    }

}

}
```

Then, create another UIImageView subclass called Card. Put the following code in
Card.swift:

```
import UIKit

class Card: UIImageView {
```

```
// The CardSlot that this card is in.
var currentSlot : CardSlot?

// Detects when the user drags this card.
var dragGesture : UIPanGestureRecognizer?

// Prepares the card to be add
init(cardSlot: CardSlot) {
    currentSlot = cardSlot

    super.init(image: UIImage(named: "Card"))

    let draggedSelector = #selector(Card.dragged(dragGesture:))

    dragGesture = UIPanGestureRecognizer(target: self,
                                         action: draggedSelector)

    self.center = cardSlot.center

    self.addGestureRecognizer(self.dragGesture!)
    self.isUserInteractionEnabled = true
}

// Called when the drag gesture recognizer changes state
@objc func dragged(dragGesture: UIPanGestureRecognizer) {
    switch dragGesture.state {

    // The user started dragging
    case .began:

        // Work out where the touch currently is...
        var translation =
            dragGesture.translation(in: self.superview!)
        translation.x += self.center.x
        translation.y += self.center.y

        // Then animate to it.
        UIView.animate(withDuration: 0.1) { () -> Void in
            self.center = translation

            // Also, rotate the card slightly.
            self.transform =
                CGAffineTransform(rotationAngle: .pi / 16.0)
        }

        // Reset the gesture recognizer in preparation
        // for the next time this method is called.

        dragGesture.setTranslation(CGPoint.zero, in: self.superview)

        // If we aren't already at the front, bring ourselves
```

```
        // forward
        self.superview?.bringSubviewToFront(self)

    // The drag has changed position
    case .changed:

        // Update our location to where the touch is now
        var translation = dragGesture.translation(in: self.superview!)
        translation.x += self.center.x
        translation.y += self.center.y

        self.center = translation

        dragGesture.setTranslation(CGPoint.zero,
                                   in: self)

    // The drag ended
    case .ended:

        // Find out if we were dragging over a location
        var destinationSlot : CardSlot?

        // For each view in the superview..
        for view in self.superview!.subviews {

            // If it's a CardSlot..
            if let cardSlot = view as? CardSlot {

                // And if the touch is inside that view
                // AND that card slot doesn't have a card
                if cardSlot.point(
                    inside: dragGesture.location(in: cardSlot),
                    with: nil) == true
                    && cardSlot.currentCard == nil {

                        // ..Then this is our destination
                        destinationSlot = cardSlot
                        break;
                }
            }
        }

        // If we have a new card slot, remove ourselves
        // from the old one and add to the new one
        if destinationSlot != nil {

            self.currentSlot?.currentCard = nil
            self.currentSlot = destinationSlot
            self.currentSlot?.currentCard = self

        }
```

```
        UIView.animate(withDuration: 0.1) { () -> Void in
            self.center = self.currentSlot!.center
        }

    // The gesture was interrupted.
    case .cancelled:

        UIView.animate(withDuration: 0.1) { () -> Void in
            self.center = self.currentSlot!.center
        }

    default:
        () // do nothing

    }

    // If the drag has ended or was cancelled, remove the
    // rotation applied above
    if dragGesture.state == .ended ||
        dragGesture.state == .cancelled {
        UIView.animate(withDuration: 0.1) { () -> Void in
            self.transform = CGAffineTransform.identity
        }
    }

}

// Fade out the view, and then remove it
func delete() {

    UIView.animate(withDuration: 0.1, animations: { () -> Void in
        self.alpha = 0.0
    }) { (completed) -> Void in
        self.removeFromSuperview()
    }

}

// This initializer is required because we're a
// subclass of UIImageView
required init?(coder aDecoder: NSCoder) {
    super.init(coder: aDecoder)
}

}
```

Add two images to your asset catalog: one called *CardSlot* and another called *Card*.

Then, open your app's storyboard and drag in a `UIImageView`. Make it use the *CardSlot* image, and set its class to `CardSlot`. Repeat this process a couple of times, until you have several card slots. When you run your app, you can tap the card slots to make cards appear. Cards can be dragged and dropped between card slots; if you try to drop a card onto a card slot that already has a card, or try to drop it outside of a card slot, it will return to its original location.

You can also make a card slot delete any card that is dropped on it. To do this, select a card slot in the Interface Builder, go to the Attributes Inspector, and change Delete On Drop to On.

Discussion

Limiting where an object can be dragged and dropped provides constraints to your game's interface, which can improve the user experience of your game. If anything can be dropped anywhere, the game feels loose and without direction. If the game takes control and keeps objects tidy, the whole thing feels a lot snappier.

In this example, the *dragging* effect is enhanced by the fact that when dragging begins, the card is rotated slightly; when the drag ends or is cancelled, the card rotates back. Adding small touches like this can dramatically improve how your game feels.

The CardSlot class is marked with the keyword @IBDesignable at the start of the class definition. This indicates to Xcode that certain properties, which are marked with @IBInspectable in the class, should appear in the Attributes Inspector.

Note that if you want a property to appear in the inspector, you need to specify the property's type. For example, this won't work:

```
// a Bool, but won't appear in the inspector
@IBInspectable var someProperty = true
```

This, however, will:

```
// Explicitly giving the type will make it appear
@IBInspectable var someProperty : Bool = true
```

10.7 Providing Haptic Feedback with UIFeedbackGenerator

Problem

You want to provide tactile feedback to the user, through the Taptic Engine present in several models of iPhones.

Solution

Use the UIImpactFeedbackGenerator, UISelectionFeedbackGenerator, and UINotificationFeedbackGenerator classes to provide tactile feedback to the player.

To create an *impact* feedback effect, use the UIImpactFeedbackGenerator class, and specify either light feedback, medium feedback, or heavy feedback. When you want to deliver the feedback, call the impactOccurred method:

```
// Prepare 'impact' feedback generators with the
// style of feedback you want
let lightImpact = UIImpactFeedbackGenerator(style: .light)
let mediumImpact = UIImpactFeedbackGenerator(style: .medium)
let heavyImpact = UIImpactFeedbackGenerator(style: .heavy)

// Play a 'light impact' notification
lightImpact.impactOccurred()

// Play a 'medium impact' notification
mediumImpact.impactOccurred()

// Play a 'heavy impact' notification
heavyImpact.impactOccurred()
```

To create tactile feedback to indicate that a selection has changed, use the UISelectionFeedbackGenerator class:

```
// Prepare a 'selection changed' feedback generator
let selection = UISelectionFeedbackGenerator()

selection.selectionChanged()
```

To provide tactile feedback that notifies the user that something has succeeded or failed, or to deliver a warning to the user, use the UINotificationFeedbackGenerator, and call notificationOccurred with the notification type you want to deliver:

```
// Prepare a 'notification' feedback generator
let notification = UINotificationFeedbackGenerator()

notification.notificationOccurred(.warning)

notification.notificationOccurred(.success)

notification.notificationOccurred(.error)
```

Discussion

If timing is important, you can prepare a generator ahead of time and deliver the feedback when you need it. To do this, call the prepare method on the feedback generator ahead of time:

```
heavyImpact.prepare()
```

When you next call the method that delivers feedback on that generator, the feedback will happen more rapidly, because the Taptic Engine is already ready to deliver it:

```
// Note that we aren't calling a special method,
// just the regular one.  However, the notification
// will be delivered more quickly if the Taptic Engine
// was already in the prepared state.
heavyImpact.impactOccurred()
```

 The Taptic Engine will only stay in a prepared state for a few seconds, to save power.

 It's important to remember that not all devices have a Taptic Engine; in the devices that don't, the feedback simply won't be played. This means that you mustn't rely on tactile feedback for your games—it should be used to underline effects that are already visually or aurally present.

You should also choose the feedback generator based on its intended purpose, not on the specifics of how the feedback feels—they might change between different versions of iOS.

10.8 Recording the Screen with ReplayKit

Problem

You want to record the contents of the screen, so that users can share their gameplay with others or save it in their photo library.

Solution

Use the ReplayKit framework to record the screen.

To begin using ReplayKit, you first need to import the framework:

```
import ReplayKit
```

Recording the screen using ReplayKit is done through the RPScreenRecorder class. You don't create one yourself; rather, you use the RPScreenRecorder.shared() singleton:

```
let recorder = RPScreenRecorder.shared()
```

When you want to start recording, call the startRecording method. This will begin the recording process, and call a closure you supply when recording starts (or fails to start). If recording fails to start, the closure receives an error object:

```
recorder.startRecording { (error) in
    // handle error

    if let error = error {
        print("Error starting recording: \(error)")
    } else {
        print("Recording started successfully")


    }

}
```

After recording starts, anything that happens in the app will be captured by the recording.

When you're done recording, call the `stopRecording` method. When you call this method, you supply a closure, which takes as its parameters a view controller and an error.

 Both of these parameters are optional. If the view controller is nil, the error won't be, and vice versa.

The view controller that the closure receives is intended to be presented by your app, and allows users to review the video they recorded, trim it, and decide what to do with it:

```
recorder.stopRecording { (viewController, error) in

    if let error = error {
        print("Error finishing recording: \(error)")
    } else if let viewController = viewController {
        viewController.previewControllerDelegate = self
        self.present(viewController, animated: true, completion: nil)
    } else {
        fatalError("Didn't get an error or a view controller?")
    }

}
```

The view controller has a property called `previewControllerDelegate`, which can be set to any object that conforms to the `RPPreviewViewControllerDelegate` protocol. The most important method in this protocol is `previewControllerDidFinish`, which is called when the user dismisses the preview view controller:

```
extension GameViewController : RPPreviewViewControllerDelegate {
```

```
func previewControllerDidFinish(
    _ previewController: RPPreviewViewController) {
    self.dismiss(animated: true, completion: nil)
}

}
```

The preview view controller won't dismiss itself when the user taps its Done button. That's up to the RPPreviewViewControllerDelegate to do.

This means that, when your stopRecording closure receives the preview view controller, it needs to arrange for the view controller to be presented, and for its previewControllerDelegate to be set.

Recording only works on real devices. It won't work in the Simulator.

Discussion

When you begin recording, ReplayKit will ask the user for permission to record the screen. The user can choose to decline this, in which case the closure you provide to startRecording will receive an error.

ReplayKit won't ask for permission if the user has previously granted it within the last 8 minutes.

Because ReplayKit uses the video codec hardware that's built into the device, you can't record movies or anything played through AVKit, and AirPlay won't work while recording.

You can also configure the recorder object to capture the microphone and camera:

```
recorder.isMicrophoneEnabled = true

// Requires "Privacy - Camera Usage Description"
// in Info.plist to be set
recorder.isCameraEnabled = true
```

10.9 Displaying Augmented Reality with ARKit

Problem

You want to display *augmented reality*—that is, drawing 3D objects on top of the player's view of the real world through the camera, which appear to be virtually present.

Solution

ARKit is Apple's framework for displaying augmented reality scenes. By combining a view through the camera with the 3D movement sensors present in iOS devices, ARKit can calculate where your game's camera should be in virtual space in order to match the position of the device in the real world.

> ARKit doesn't work on iOS Simulators, because it needs access to the device's cameras and motion sensors. You'll need to use a real device to use the framework.

ARKit can be combined with a number of other frameworks to perform the 3D graphics, and in this recipe, we'll use SceneKit.

> Xcode comes with a template for ARKit that implements much of the steps shown in this recipe for you. In the interest of learning how the pieces fit together, we'll build it up from scratch in this recipe.

1. To begin, create a new single-view application from the Xcode template chooser. Once the project has been created, open the File menu, and choose New → File. Choose "SceneKit Scene" and click Next. Name the new file "Cube."

> Be sure not to accidentally choose "SpriteKit Scene." They're different, and it's easy to confuse the two.

2. Open the scene, and you'll be taken to the Scene Editor (Figure 10-5). Newly created scenes contain a single object—a camera. We don't need that, since ARKit will handle the camera for us.

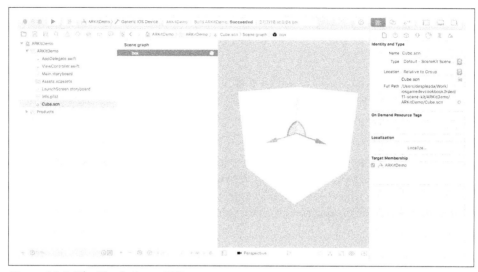

Figure 10-5. The Xcode Scene Editor

3. In the Object Library at the lower-right corner of the Xcode window, scroll down and find the Box node, and drag it into the scene.

4. Using the drag handles, position it in the middle of the world, or set its position in the Node inspector to 0, 0, 0. Save the scene.

5. Open the *Main.storyboard* file. In the Object Library, scroll down until you find the ARKit SceneKit View, or search for "ARSCNView." Drag one of these into the main view controller's view, and resize it to fill the view (Figure 10-6).

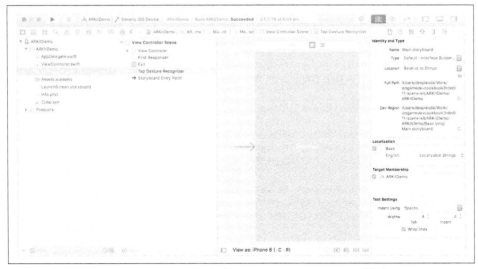

Figure 10-6. The main storyboard, with the ARKit SceneKit view added

6. Open the Assistant pane, and hold down the Control key and drag from the ARSCNView into the source code for the ViewController class. Xcode will ask you what kind of connection you want to make; set the connection type to Outlet, and the name of the connection to sceneView. Click Connect.

7. Update the ViewController class to look like the following code:

```
import ARKit

class ViewController: UIViewController, ARSCNViewDelegate {

    // The reference to the SceneKit view.
    @IBOutlet weak var sceneView: ARSCNView!

    override func viewDidLoad() {
        super.viewDidLoad()

        // Load the scene file.
        guard let scene = SCNScene(named: "Cube.scn") else {
            fatalError("Failed to load scene!")
        }

        // Provide the scene to the ARKit view.
        sceneView.scene = scene

        // This view controller is the delegate
        // for the ARSCNView. (This requires that
        // we conform to the ARSCNViewDelegate
        // protocol, seen above.
```

```
        sceneView.delegate = self


    }

    override func viewWillAppear(_ animated: Bool) {

        super.viewWillAppear(animated)

        // Create an ARKit configuration for
        // tracking movement through the world.
        let configuration = ARWorldTrackingConfiguration()

        // Tell the ARSCNView to start running
        // augmented reality with this configuration.
        sceneView.session.run(configuration)
    }


    override func viewWillDisappear(_ animated: Bool) {
        super.viewWillDisappear(animated)

        // Pause the ARKit view when this view controller goes away.
        sceneView.session.pause()
    }


}
```

8. Run the app on your device; after it's installed and launches, disconnect your device and relaunch the app. Walk around, and look through your phone. As you move around, you'll see a virtual cube in space (Figure 10-7).

Figure 10-7. An ARKit application

The cube is positioned at (0,0,0), which is also where your device starts. If you can't see the cube, move your device a little further, because it'll start *inside* the cube.

Discussion

ARKit, in addition to computing the camera position based on user movement, also figures out the ambient lighting conditions observed through the camera, and applies that lighting to the SceneKit scene.

ARKit can be used with just about any SceneKit scene. Because integrating the two frameworks is relatively simple, ARKit opens up a number of possibilities for new kinds of gameplay.

10.10 Hit-Testing the AR Scene

Problem

You want to detect when the user taps on a part of the real world via the ARKit view, and create an object where they tapped.

Solution

To detect where in the real world the user has tapped, you first need a way to detect that the user has tapped on the screen. Then, once you know where on the screen that tap landed, you can pass that position to ARKit, which will attempt to determine the location of that tap in the real world.

To begin, you'll first need to add a Tap Gesture Recognizer to your ARSCNView.

 This recipe follows on from Recipe 10.9.

1. Go to your *Main.storyboard*, and, in the Object Library, search for "tap gesture recognizer." Drag one onto your ARSCNView.

2. Locate the *Tap Gesture Recognizer* in the Outliner. (If you don't see the Outliner, click the button at the bottom-left corner of the canvas.)

3. Open the Assistant pane.

4. Hold down the Control key, and drag from the Tap Gesture Recognizer into the source code of the ViewController class. When the connection pop-up appears, set the type of the connection to Action, and name it sceneTapped. Click Connect, and the method will be added to the code.

When you add an action, it generates a method that takes the object that triggered the action as a parameter. However, the type of that parameter is set to Any, which means you can't get information out of it. That won't do for this case, because we want to ask the Tap Gesture Recognizer to give us information about where the tap landed. To fix that, you'll need to update the method:

1. Update the first line of the sceneTapped method to use the following code:

```
@IBAction func sceneTapped(_ sender: UITapGestureRecognizer) {
```

2. Update the method to include the following code:

```
@IBAction func sceneTapped(_ sender: UITapGestureRecognizer) {

    // This method is run when the tap gesture recognizer fires.

    // Get the location of the touch in the view.
    let touchLocation = sender.location(ofTouch: 0, in: sceneView)

    print("Tapped at \(touchLocation)")

    // Find all horizontal planes at this touch location
    let hitLocations = sceneView.hitTest(touchLocation,
                                  types: [.estimatedHorizontalPlane,
                                          .estimatedVerticalPlane])

    // Get the first location, if one was found
    guard let firstLocation = hitLocations.first else {
        print("Didn't find a hit location")
        return
    }

    // We'll now duplicate the 'box' object that was
    // already present in the scene.

    // Find the first node named 'box'; we'll make a copy of it
    guard let cube = sceneView.scene.rootNode
        .childNode(withName: "box", recursively: false) else {

        print("Error: couldn't find the box?")
        return
    }

    // Create a copy of that cube and add it to the scene
    let newCube = cube.clone()
    sceneView.scene.rootNode.addChildNode(newCube)

    // Convert the position and orientation of the plane to a
    // type that SceneKit can use
    let newCubeTransform = SCNMatrix4(firstLocation.worldTransform)
```

```
// Set this position and orientation
newCube.setWorldTransform(newCubeTransform)
```

}

3. Run the application, and aim the camera at the floor, or any other surface. Tap on the surface, and a cube will appear (Figure 10-8).

Figure 10-8. An ARKit scene, with several cubes placed on the table (and a pile on the floor)

Discussion

`ARKit` relies on estimating where flat surfaces are based on the information coming from the camera. This means that it won't always be able to detect a flat surface; for best results, use it in a well-lit environment, and on surfaces with a well defined texture. For example, a glossy, white table is difficult for `ARKit` to track.

10.11 Using TestFlight to Test Your App

Problem

You want to distribute copies of your game to beta testers.

Solution

Use TestFlight, Apple's beta-testing service, to distribute test builds to both people on your team and to certain members of the public who you want to test.

Because TestFlight is a service that's run by Apple via the iTunes Connect website, it's subject to change at any time. For the most current information on how to use it, see Apple's documentation on iTunes Connect, at *http://help.apple.com/itunes-connect/ developer/*.

Discussion

TestFlight allows you to upload builds of your app to iTunes Connect, and from there distribute them to users whom you can invite to a testing group. You can invite up to 10,000 people to test.

It's worth noting that it's a new app, or the version number has changed, the build has to be reviewed by Apple before it can be sent out. This review can take up to a few days, but is generally 24 hours or less. Don't promise people super fast turnaround times on beta builds!

10.12 Using Fastlane to Build and Release Your App

Problem

You want to automate the building and delivery of your game.

Solution

Use Fastlane, a set of tools for automating your build process.

Fastlane includes a number of command-line utilities that can, among other things:

- Perform a build of your game
- Upload your game to the App Store
- Distribute your game to your TestFlight testers (see Recipe 10.11)
- Take screenshots of your game

You can install Fastlane by following the steps at *https://fastlane.tools*.

Discussion

Fastlane supports both iOS and Android, though more features are available for iOS developers.

CHAPTER 11

Performance and Debugging

At some point during its development, every game will have performance issues, and every game will crash. Fortunately, iOS has some of the best tools around for squeezing as much performance as possible out of your games and finding bugs and other issues.

In this chapter, you'll learn about how to use these tools, how to fix problems, and how to get information about how your game's behaving.

11.1 Improving Your Frame Rate

Problem

You need to coax a better frame rate out of your game so that it plays smoothly.

Solution

To improve your frame rate, you first need to determine where the majority of the work is being done. In Xcode:

1. From the Scheme menu, select your device, so that the application will be installed to the device when you build.

2. Open the Product menu and choose Profile (or press Command-I).

   The application will build and install onto the device, and Instruments will open and show the template picker (see Figure 11-1).

3. Select the Time Profiler instrument, and click Choose. You'll see the main Instruments interface (Figure 11-2). Click the Run button, and the app will launch, and

you'll start seeing information about how much CPU time your game is taking up.

4. Click the Call Tree button at the bottom of the screen, and turn on Invert Call Tree, Hide Missing Symbols, and Hide System Libraries, and turn off everything else in the list, as shown in Figure 11-3.

5. Take note of the name of the functions that are at the top of the list:

   a. If the top functions are the method you use to call OpenGL, the game is spending most of its time rendering graphics. To improve your frame rate, reduce the number of objects on the screen, and make fewer calls to `glDra weElements` and its related functions.

   b. If not, the game is spending most of its time running code on the CPU. The function at the top of the list is your code, which the game is spending most of its time processing.

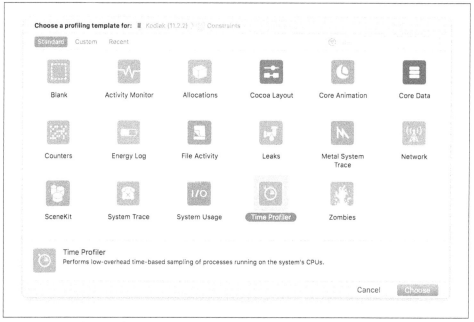

Figure 11-1. Selecting the Instruments template

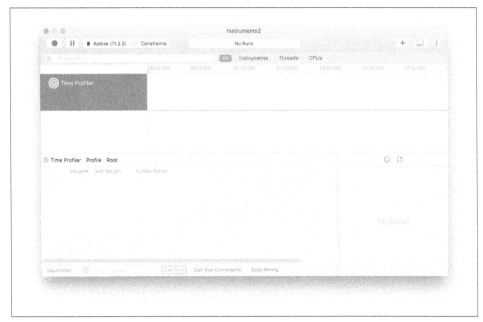

Figure 11-2. The main Instruments interface

If your game is spending most of its time rendering graphics, you can improve the speed by drawing fewer sprites (if you're using SpriteKit) or drawing fewer objects (if you're using OpenGL). If most of the time is spent running code on the CPU, it's less straightforward, because different games do different things. In this case, you'll need to look for ways to optimize your code. For example, if a long-running function is calculating a value that doesn't change very often, store the result in a variable instead of recalculating it.

Figure 11-3. Instruments in action

Discussion

You improve frame rates by taking less time to do the work you need to do per frame. This means either reducing the total amount of work you need to do, or not making the rendering of frames wait for work to complete.

 You should only profile using a real device, because the simulator performs differently than the real thing. The simulator has a faster CPU, but a slower GPU.

11.2 Making Levels Load Quickly

Problem

You want to make your levels load as quickly as possible, so that the player can get into the game immediately.

Solution

There are three main techniques for making a level load faster:

Load smaller or fewer resources
> Make the images and sounds that you load smaller. Reduce the dimensions of textures, use compressed textures, and use lower-quality audio. Alternatively, load fewer resources.

Show progress indicators
> When you begin loading resources for a new level, first count the number of resources you need to load; every time one gets loaded, show progress to the user, either using a progress indicator (such as a `UILabel` or `UIProgressView`) or a text field.

Stream textures
> When level loading begins, load very small resources, such as very small textures. Once the game has begun, begin loading full-size textures in the background; once each high-resolution texture has loaded, replace the small texture with the large one.

Discussion

Half the battle is making the game *look* like it's fast. The other half is actually *being* fast.

Loading smaller resources means that less data needs to be sent. An iOS device is really a collection of small, interconnected pieces, and it takes time to transfer data from the flash chips to the CPU and the GPU. In almost all cases, "faster loading" just means "loading less stuff."

If you can't increase the speed beyond a certain point, showing progress indicators at least means the user sees some kind of progress. If you just show a static "loading" screen, the player will get bored, and it will *feel* like it's taking longer. You can see this technique outside of games, too: when you launch an iOS application, the system first shows a placeholder image while the app launches in the background. Apple encourages developers to make this placeholder image look like part of the application, but without any text or actual data to show, and the result is that the app feels like it's launching faster.

Finally, it's often the case that you just want to get *something* on the screen so that the player can start playing, and it's OK if parts of the game don't look their best for the first few seconds. This is called *texture streaming*, and the idea is that you load a deliberately small texture during the normal loading process, let the player get into the game, and then start slowly loading a better texture in the background.

Texture streaming means that your game's loading process is faster because there's less data that needs to be transferred before the game can start. However, it can lead to visual problems: when the larger, higher-quality texture is loaded, a visible "pop" can happen. Additionally, loading two versions of the same texture at the same time means that more memory is being consumed, which can lead to memory pressure problems on iOS devices.

11.3 Dealing with Low-Memory Issues

Problem

Your app is randomly crashing when images or other resources are loaded into memory.

Solution

There are several ways you can reduce the amount of memory that your application is using. For example:

Use fewer textures
> If you can reuse an image for more than one sprite or texture, it's better than having multiple images that vary only slightly.

Trim your textures

If you have a texture that's got some transparent area around the edges, trim them. When a texture is loaded, every pixel counts toward memory usage, including ones that are entirely transparent.

Use texture atlases

If you're using SpriteKit, Xcode makes it pretty easy to create texture atlases. Texture atlases group multiple textures together, which is more efficient because per-texture overhead is minimized. Xcode also automatically trims your textures for you. To create a texture atlas, create a folder with a name ending in *.atlas*, and put your images into that. Once that's done, your textures will be combined into a single image, saving a little memory.

Memory-map large files

If you need to read a large file—for example, a level file, a large collection of data, or a large sound file—you'll often load it in as a `Data` object. However, the usual method of doing this, with `Data(contentsOf:)`, copies the data into memory. If you're reading from a file that you know won't change, you can instead *memory-map* it, which means instructing iOS to pretend that the entire file has been copied into memory, but to only actually read the file when parts of it are accessed. To do this, load your files using `Data(contentsOf:,options:)` and use the `.mappedIfSafe` option:

```
do {
    // 'url' is a URL object pointing to a file path
    let data = try Data(contentsOf: url, options: .mappedIfSafe)
} catch let error {
    // handle the error
}
```

Use compressed textures

Compressed textures can dramatically reduce the amount of memory that your game's textures take up. For more information, see Recipe 11.5.

Discussion

iOS has a very limited amount of memory, compared to OS X. The main reason for this is that iOS doesn't use a *swap file*, which is a file that operating systems use to extend the amount of RAM available by using the storage medium. On OS X, if you run out of physical RAM (i.e., space to fit stuff in the RAM chips), the operating system moves some of the information in RAM to the swap file, freeing up some room. On iOS, there's no swap file for it to move information into, so when you're out of memory, you're completely out of memory.

The reason for this is that writing information to flash memory chips, such as those used in iOS devices, causes them to degrade very slightly. If the system is constantly swapping information out of RAM and into flash memory, the flash memory gradually gets slower and slower. From Apple's perspective, it's a better deal for the user to have a faster device and for developers to deal with memory constraints.

Because there's a fixed amount of memory available, iOS terminates applications when they run out of memory. When the system runs low on memory, all applications are sent a low memory warning, which is their one and only notification that they're running low.

The amount of memory available to apps depends on the device; generally, an app can safely use around 60% of the memory that's built into a device (e.g., if a device has 2 GB of memory, it can generally use up to 1.2 GB without trouble). If an app ever goes above this limit, it will be immediately terminated by the operating system.

11.4 Tracking Down a Crash

Problem

You want to understand why an application is crashing, and how to fix it.

Solution

First, determine what kind of crash it is. The most common kinds of crashes are:

Exceptions
These occur when your code does something that Apple's code doesn't expect, such as trying to insert nil into an array. When an exception occurs, you'll see a backtrace appear in the debugging console.

Memory pressure terminations
As we saw in the previous recipe, iOS will terminate any application that exceeds its memory limit. This isn't strictly a crash, but from the user's perspective, it looks identical to one. When a memory pressure termination occurs, Xcode displays a notification.

Once you know what kind of crash you're looking at, you can take steps to fix it.

Discussion

The approach you take will depend on the kind of issue you're experiencing.

Fixing exceptions

To fix an exception, you need to know where the exception is being thrown from. The easiest way to do this is to add a breakpoint on Objective-C exceptions, which will stop the program at the moment the exception is thrown (instead of the moment that the exception causes the app to crash).

To add this breakpoint:

1. Open the Breakpoints navigator, and click the + button at the bottom-left of the window (see Figure 11-4).

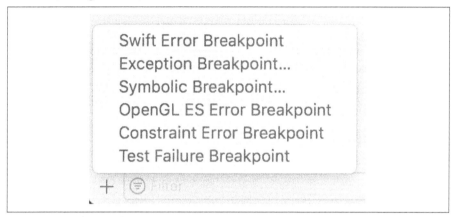

Figure 11-4. The Breakpoints menu

2. Click Exception Breakpoint.
3. Run the application again; when the exception is thrown, Xcode will stop inside your code.

Fixing memory pressure issues

There are lots of different approaches you can take to reduce the amount of memory being consumed by your application; see Recipe 11.3 for some pointers.

11.5 Working with Compressed Textures

Problem

You want to use compressed textures to save memory and loading time.

Solution

To work with compressed textures, you need to have compressed textures to load. Xcode comes with a texture compression tool, but it's sometimes tricky to use. It's better to write a simple script that handles many of the details of using the compression tool for you:

1. Create a new, empty file called *compress.sh*. Place this file anywhere you like.
2. Put the following text in it (note that the path must all appear on one line; it's broken here only to fit the page margins):

    ```
    PARAMS="-e PVRTC --channel-weighting-perceptual --bits-per-pixel-4"

    /Applications/Xcode.app/Contents/Developer/Platforms/iPhoneOS.platform/
      Developer/usr/bin/texturetool $PARAMS
        -o "$1.pvrtc" -p "$1-Preview.png" "$1"
    ```

3. Open the Terminal, and navigate to the folder where you put *compress.sh*.
4. Type the following commands:

    ```
    chmod +x ./compress.sh
    ./compress.sh MyImage.png
    ```

After a moment, you'll have two new images: *MyImage.png.pvrtc* and *MyImage.png-Preview.png*. The preview PNG file shows you what the compressed version of your image looks like, and the PVRTC file is the file that you should copy into your project.

Once you have your compressed texture, you load it like any other texture. If you're using SpriteKit, you load a texture using the `SKTexture(imageNamed:)` method, providing it with the name of your PVRTC file:

```
let texture = SKTexture(imageNamed: "MyCompressedTexture.pvrtc")
```

 Unfortunately, it's not possible to load a *.pvrtc* file using the `UIImage` class's methods. This means that you can't use compressed textures in `UIImageViews`, which is annoying. The only places you can use compressed textures are in OpenGL, Metal, `SceneKit`, and `SpriteKit`.

Discussion

Compressed textures use much less memory, and take less time to load (because there's less data to transfer to the graphics chip), but they look worse. How much "worse" depends on the type of image you want to compress:

- Photos and similar-looking textures do quite well with compression.

- Line art tends to get fuzzy fringes around the edges of lines.

- Images with transparent areas look particularly bad, because the transparent edges of the image get fuzzy.

On iOS, compressed textures are available as 2 bits per pixel (bpp; not bytes, *bits*) and 4 bits per pixel. Whereas a full-color 512-by-512 image would take up 1 MB of graphics memory, a 4 bpp version of the same image would take up only 128 kb of graphics memory.

The compression system used is called PVRTC, which stands for PowerVR Texture Compression (PowerVR provides the graphics architecture for iOS devices).

An image can only be compressed when it fits all of the following requirements:

- The image is square (i.e., the width is the same as the height).

- The image is at least 8 pixels high and wide.

- The image's width and height are a power of 2 (i.e., 8, 16, 32, 64, 128, 512, 1024, 2048, 4096).

Use compressed textures with care. While they can dramatically improve performance, reduce memory usage, and speed up loading times, if they're used without care they can make your game look very ugly, as in the zoomed-in images in Figure 11-5. The image on the left is the compressed version; PVRTC introduces compression artifacts, which creates a slight "noisy" pattern along the edge of the circle. There's also a subtle color difference between the image on the left and on the right, which is an additional consequence of compression. (If you're reading the print version of this book, Figure 11-5 is black and white, and the difference might be too subtle to see. The main difference is that the colors in the PVRTC-compressed image are slightly paler.) Experiment, and see what looks best in your game.

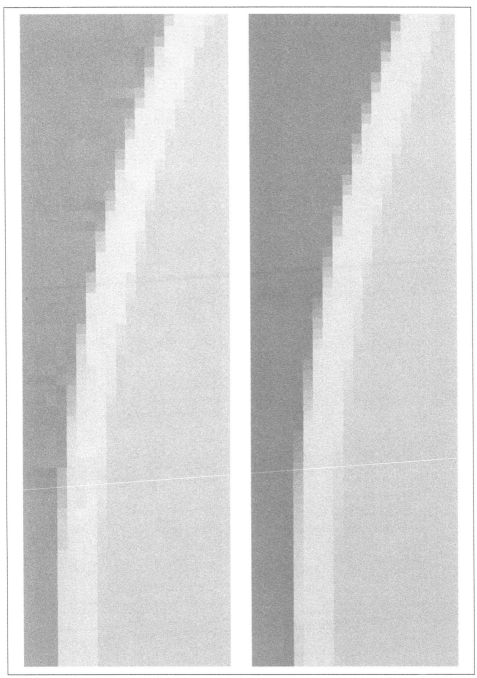

Figure 11-5. Compressed image (left) and original image (right)

11.6 Working with Watchpoints

Problem

You want to know when a specific variable changes.

Solution

To make Xcode stop your program when a variable changes from one value to another, you use a watchpoint. To set a watchpoint on a variable:

1. First, stop your program using a breakpoint.

   When the program stops, the list of visible variables appears in the debugging console.

2. Add the watchpoint for the variable you want to watch.

   Find the variable you want to watch, right-click it, and choose "Watch *name of your variable*," as shown in Figure 11-6.

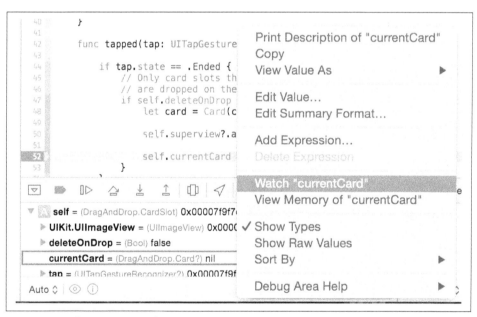

Figure 11-6. Creating a watchpoint

3. Continue the application.

   The application will stop when the variable you've watched changes value.

Discussion

Watchpoints are breakpoints that "watch" a location in memory and stop the program the moment the value stored in that location changes.

Keep in mind that when you stop and relaunch a program, the locations of the variables you were watching last time will have changed, and you'll need to add the watchpoints again.

11.7 Logging Effectively

Problem

You want to log additional information about what your application is doing when information is logged to the console.

Solution

You can write methods that know about the file name, line number and function name from which they were called.

Add the following function to one of your Swift files. Don't put it in a class—this is a global function, so put it outside any class definitions:

```
func Log(message: String,
    file: String = __FILE__,
    line : Int = __LINE__,
    function: String = __FUNCTION__) {

    NSLog("\(function) (\(file.lastPathComponent):\(line)): \(message)")

}
```

When you call Log, the debugging console will show the names of the class and the method that the line is in, as well as the filename and line number of the logging statement. The following command:

```
Log("Yes")
```

will produce this on the console:

```
currentCard (CardSlot.swift:31): Hello
```

Discussion

The compiler provides several "magic" variables that change based on where they're used in your code.

For example, the __LINE__ variable always contains the current line number in the file that's currently being compiled, and the __FILE__ variable contains the full path to the source code file that's being compiled. The __FUNCTION__ variable contains the name of the current function.

 When __LINE__, __FILE__, and __FUNCTION__ are used as the default values for parameters in a function, the line number, file, and function that that function was called *from* are used, instead of the line number and file at which the called function is defined.

In the solution given in this recipe, we've done a little bit of extra coding to make the logs easier to read. We mentioned that the __FILE__ variable contains the full path to the file that's being compiled, but that's often way too long—most of the time, you just want the filename. To get just the filename, you can call lastPathComponent method, which returns the last part of the path.

11.8 Creating Breakpoints That Use Speech

Problem

You want to receive audio notifications when something happens in your game.

Solution

Add a spoken breakpoint that doesn't stop the game:

1. Add a breakpoint where you want a notification to happen.
2. Right-click the breakpoint, and choose Edit Breakpoint. The Edit Breakpoint dialog box will appear.
3. Turn on "Automatically continue after evaluating actions."
4. Click Add Action.
5. Change the action type from Debugger Command to Log Message.
6. Type the text you want to speak.
7. Click Speak Message.

When the breakpoint is hit, Xcode will speak the log message.

Discussion

Using spoken breakpoints is a really useful way to get notifications on what the game's doing without having to switch away from the game. Breakpoints are spoken by your computer, not by the device, which means that they won't interfere with your game's audio (don't forget to unmute your computer's speakers).

You can also configure a breakpoint to play a short sound, by setting the Action Type to Sound and picking a sound from the list of available options. Short sounds, like "Bell", "Frog", and "Sosumi" tend to be more useful when the breakpoint is likely to be hit frequently.

Index

A
A* algorithm, 251-256
actions
    defined, 48
    nodes and, 174-176
active applications, 12
address (see street address)
AirPlay, 277
ambient light object, 228
anchor point, defined, 168
animation
    animating a popping effect on a view, 64-66
    moving images with Core Animation, 61
    sprite, 185
    UI dynamics for animated views, 59
    with SceneKit, 229
application music player, 122
ARKit
    displaying augmented reality with, 295-300
    hit-testing the AR scene, 300
arrays, filtering with closures, 24
artificial intelligence
    determining if an object can see another
        object, 258
    enhancing game design with, 270
    finding the next best move for a puzzle
        game, 257
    identifying objects in images, 265-270
    importing a Core ML model, 265
    tagging parts of speech with NSLinguistic-
        Tagger, 260
asset catalog, 56
assets
    loading during gameplay, 24
    loading levels quickly, 308
    managing a collection of, 143-145
attachment, views and, 60
attitude, 91
audio (see sound)
augmented reality
    displaying with ARKit, 295-300
    hit-testing the AR scene, 300
AVAudioPlayer
    cross-fading between tracks, 117-119
    playing sound with, 111-114
    working with multiple players, 115-116
AVAudioRecorder, 114
AVFoundation, 262-264
axis input, 276

B
background music, 127
background, applications in, 12
behavior
    calculating a path for an object to take,
        251-256
    determining if an object can see another
        object, 258
    making an object decide on a target, 248
    making an object flee when it's in trouble,
        247
    making an object intercept a moving target,
        246
    making an object know where to take cover,
        250
    making an object move toward a position,
        243-245
    making things follow a path, 245

pathfinding on a grid, 256
vector math in Swift, 241-243
beta testing, 303
Bézier curves, 182
Bézier paths, 181
blend modes, 179
body (physics concept), 198
breakpoints, 318
brute-force algorithm, 258
build process, Fastlane and, 303
button input, 276
buttons
    action methods and, 48
    pop animation for, 64-66
    segues and, 49-52
    slicing images for, 58
    storyboards and, 36-42
    view controllers and, 46

C

cameras
    controlling with SceneKit, 227
    using AVFoundation to access, 262-264
cars, creating, 221
closures
    as parameter, 19
    filtering an array with, 24
    power of, 18
    working with, 17-19
    writing a method that calls, 19
CloudKit
    adding records to database, 150
    deleting database records, 155
    querying records to a CloudKit database,
        151-155
    setup, 149
COLLADA files, 234
collider, 198
collider shapes, 201
collision scene, walls for, 205
collisions
    adding to views, 60
    defined, 199
    detecting, 209
color
    blend modes, 179
    for scenes, 167
    shape nodes and, 178
    views and, 67

compass heading, 92-93
component-based game architecture
    basics, 4-9
    GameplayKit and, 7
compressed textures, 312-314
constraint objects, 233
constraints, for positioning of views, 53-56
containers, 135
controllers (see game controllers)
coordinate systems, 158
Core Animation
    animating views with, 65
    moving images with, 61
Core ML
    identifying objects in images, 265-270
    importing machine learning model, 265
Core Motion framework, 90
crash, tracking down, 311
cross-fading, 117-119
currency, in-game, 147

D

data storage, 131-156
    adding records to CloudKit database, 150
    CloudKit setup, 149
    deleting CloudKit database records, 155
    files vs. databases, 142
    implementing best strategy for, 147
    in-game currency, 147
    local storage, 133
    managing a collection of assets, 143-145
    querying records to a CloudKit database,
        151-155
    storing information in NSUserDefaults,
        145-147
    storing structured information, 131-133
    using iCloud key-value store, 139-141
    using iCloud to save games, 134-139
databases
    CloudKit (see CloudKit)
    for data storage, 142
Date objects, 16
debugging
    adding unit tests to a game, 26-28
    creating breakpoints that use speech, 318
    logging effectively, 317
    low-memory issues, 309-311
    SKView and, 165
    tracking down a crash, 311

degrees, radians and, 161
delta time, 9-10
density, 204
dependencies, operations and, 23
direction, compass heading for, 92-93
directional lights, 229
dot product, 162
dragging
    images, 76-78
    physics objects, 218-221
dragging and dropping, 283-290
dynamic bodies, 200

E

edge chain, 206
edge collider, 199, 206
edge loop, 206
exceptions
    crashes and, 311
    fixing, 312
exit segues, 52
explosion offset, 216
explosions, 215-217
extended game controller, 271
external screens, 273
    designing effective graphics for, 281-283
    designing for larger screens, 282
    displaying augmented reality with ARKit,
        295-300
    displaying content via AirPlay, 277
    iPad screen, 282
    iPhone screen, 281
    recording the screen with ReplayKit,
        292-294
    using, 278-280

F

Fastlane, 303
feedback
    impact, 291
    tactile, 290
fill color, 178
filtering arrays with closures, 24
fire (visual effect), 183
fixed joints, 213
font families, 170
fonts
    custom, 171
    determining availability of, 170

force
    applying to an object, 213
    defined, 198
foreground, applications in, 12
frame rate
    delta time and, 10
    improving, 305-308
friction, defined, 198

G

gambler's fallacy, 31
game controllers, 271
    detecting, 273-275
    getting input from, 275
    haptic feedback with UIFeedbackGenerator,
        290
    profiles, 271
GameplayKit
    for component-based architecture, 7
    pathfinding on a grid, 256
Gaussian distributions, 30
generics, 7
geocoding, 103
gesture recognizers
    custom, 82-86
    defined, 76
gestures
    custom, 82-86
    pinching, 81-82
    receiving touches in custom areas of a view,
        86
    rotation, 78-80
    shakes, 87
    tap, 75
GPS coordinates, 103
Grand Central Dispatch (GCD), 22
graphics
    2D (see 2D graphics)
    for external screens, 281-283
gravities (unit of measurement), 218
gravity (force)
    adding to views, 60
    customizing for scene, 207
    defined, 207
    using device orientation to control, 217
grid, pathfinding on a, 256
group, defined, 175

H

haptic feedback, 290
hit-testing
    AR scene, 300
    SceneKit scene, 236

I

iCloud, 131
    (see also CloudKit)
    key-value store, 139-141
    saving games in, 134-139
iCloud containers, 135
image effects, sprites and, 180
images
    adding to menus, 56
    dragging around the screen, 76-78
    identifying contents of, 265-270
    moving with Core Animation, 61
    rotating an image view, 63-64
    slicing for use in buttons, 58
    texture sprites and, 176
impact feedback, 291
in-game resources, storing, 147
Inceptionv3 model, 266-270
inheritance-based game architecture, 2-4
input, 73-109
    accessing user's location, 93-97
    calculating user's speed, 97
    compass heading, 92-93
    custom gestures, 82-86
    device tilt, 88-91
    dragging an image, 76-78
    effective utilization to improve game design, 109
    game controller, 275
    looking up GPS coordinates for street address, 103
    looking up street address from user's location, 104
    magnet detection, 107
    notification of user's change in location, 99-103
    pinching gestures, 81-82
    pinpointing user's proximity to landmarks, 98
    rotation gestures, 78-80
    shaking, 87
    tap gestures, 75
    tilt, 88-91
    touches in custom areas of a view, 86
    touching a view, 74
    using device as steering wheel, 105-107
inverse kinematics (IK) constraints, 234
iOS Simulator, testing external screens with, 280
iPad screen, designing for, 282
iPhone
    designing for screen, 281
    haptic feedback with UIFeedbackGenerator, 290

J

joints
    connecting physics objects with, 212
    defined, 199

K

key-value store, iCloud, 139-141

L

labels, moving, 174-176
layout of game, 1-34
    adding unit tests to, 26-28
    as two-dimensional grid, 28
    calculating time elapsed since game start, 16
    closures, 17-19
    component-based architecture, 4-7
    delta time calculation, 9-10
    detecting when user enters/exits game, 11-13
    determining best approach for, 1
    filtering an array with closures, 24
    inheritance-based architecture, 2-4
    loading new assets during gameplay, 24
    making operations depend on each other, 23
    operation queues, 20
    pausing, 15
    performing a task in the future, 22
    randomization for, 30-31
    state machine for, 31-34
    updating based on timer, 13
    writing a method that calls a closure, 19
levels, loading, 308
lights, creating with SceneKit, 228
limit joints, 213
linguistic tagging, 260

loading time, compressed textures and, 312-314
location
    justifying your access to user location information, 94
    looking up GPS coordinates for street address, 103
    looking up street address from user's location, 104
    notification of user's change in, 99-103
    of user, 93-97
    pinpointing user's proximity to landmarks, 98
logging, 317
look-at constraints, 234
low-memory issues, 309-311

M

machine learning, 265
    (see also artificial intelligence)
    identifying objects in images, 265-270
    importing a Core ML model, 265
magnetometers, 93, 108
magnets, detecting, 107
magnitude, of vector, 159
main queue, 21
mass
    defined, 198
    of objects, 204
materials, SceneKit, 231
matrix/matrices, 163
memory, using compressed textures to save, 312-314
memory-pressure issues, 309-311
memory-pressure terminations, 311
menus
    adding images to, 56
    animating a popping effect on a view, 64-66
    creating view controllers, 42-49
    effective design, 71
    overlaying on top of game content, 70
    slicing images for use in buttons, 58
Metal (SceneKit rendering engine), 239
modes, blend, 179
motion sickness, 194
movement behavior (see behavior)
moving target, intercepting, 246
music
    allowing the user to select, 125-127
    controlling playback, 124

cooperating with other applications' audio, 127
getting song information, 121-123

N

nibs, 70
nodes, defined, 168
noise, visual, 194
normal mapping, 232
NSUserDefaults, storing information in, 145-147

O

omni light, 228
operation queues, 20
operations
    dependencies and, 23
    running on the main queue, 21
origin, defined, 158
orthographic camera, 228
orthographic projection transform matrix, 164
outlets, defined, 48

P

parallax scrolling, 187-194
parameter, closures as, 19
particle effects, 183
particle systems, 238
path (object), 178
paths
    Bézier, 181
    calculating, 251-256
    making objects follow, 245
    on a grid, 256
pausing
    of physics simulation, 208
    parts of game while other parts continue to run, 15
performance optimization
    improving frame rate, 305-308
    logging effectively, 317
    low-memory issues, 309-311
    making levels load quickly, 308
    working with compressed textures, 312-314
    working with watchpoints, 316
Perlin noise, 195
perspective camera, 228
perspective projection transform matrix, 164

perspective, parallax scrolling and, 187-194
physics, 197-222
　　adding physical behavior to 3D objects, 235
　　adding thrusters to objects, 214
　　adding to sprites, 199
　　adding to views, 59
　　controlling time in, 208
　　creating explosions, 215-217
　　creating static and dynamic objects, 200
　　creating vehicles, 221
　　defining collider shapes, 201
　　detecting collisions, 209
　　dragging physics objects around, 218-221
　　finding objects, 210
　　gravity, 207
　　keeping objects from rotating, 208
　　review of terms/definitions, 197-199
　　setting velocities, 203
　　using device orientation to control gravity,
　　　217
　　using UI dynamics to make animated views,
　　　59
　　walls for collision scene, 205
　　working with forces, 213
　　working with joints, 212
　　working with mass/size/density, 204
pin joints, 212
pinch gesture, 81-82
pitch, 89
playback, audio
　　controlling, 124
　　with AVAudioPlayer, 111-114
point light, 228
pop animation, 64-66
presentation context, 42
puzzle game, finding next best move in, 257

Q

Quartz Core framework, 65
querying CloudKit database records, 151-155
queues, 20
　　operation queues, 20
　　running operations on main queue, 21

R

radians, 161
randomization, 30-31
recording
　　AVAudioRecorder, 114

ReplayKit, 292-294
　　screen, 292-294
reference frame, 92
reflections, 236
release process, Fastlane for, 303
ReplayKit, 292-294
resources (see assets)
reverse geocoding, 105
roll, 89
rotation (device)
　　detecting, 78-80
　　using device orientation to control gravity,
　　　217
rotation (image), 63-64
rotation (objects)
　　constraining, 233
　　preventing, 208
　　vectors, 161
rotation (view), 68-69

S

scaling
　　scenes, 167
　　vectors, 162
SceneKit, 225-239
　　adding reflective floor to scene, 236
　　animating objects, 229
　　constraining objects, 233
　　creating a scene with, 226
　　creating lights, 228
　　customizing materials, 231
　　hit-testing, 236
　　loading a preprepared scene from a file, 237
　　loading COLLADA files, 234
　　Metal rendering engine, 239
　　normal mapping, 232
　　particle systems, 238
　　rendering 3D text, 230
　　setting up game for, 225
　　showing a 3D object, 226
　　texturizing objects, 232
　　using 3D physics, 235
　　working with cameras, 227
scenes
　　creating with SceneKit, 226
　　creating with SpriteKit, 165-167
　　finding physics objects in, 210
　　hit-testing, 236
　　moving sprites and labels around, 174-176

transitioning between, 172-173
screen-shaking effect, 184-185
screens
    external (see external screens)
    segues for moving between, 49-52
    updating based on redrawing of, 14
security, user location information and, 94
segues
    defined, 42
    for moving between screens, 49-52
    triggering, 52
sequence, defined, 175
shake gesture, 87
shaking screen effect, 184-185
shape nodes, 178
show segue, 42
shuffled distributions, 30
simulation sickness, 194
slicing images, 58
slider joints, 213
smoke effect, 183
songs, getting information on, 121-123
    (see also music)
sound, 111-130
    allowing the user to select music, 125-127
    controlling music playback, 124
    cooperating with other applications' audio, 127
    creating breakpoints that use speech, 318
    cross-fading between tracks, 117-119
    detecting when currently playing track changes, 123
    getting information on songs, 121-123
    making optimal use of, 129
    playing with AVAudioPlayer, 111-114
    recording with AVAudioRecorder, 114
    synthesizing speech, 119
    working with multiple audio players, 115-116
speech
    creating breakpoints that use, 318
    synthesizing, 119
    tagging parts of speech with NSLinguistic-Tagger, 260
speed, user's, 97
spot lights, 229
sprite
    adding a texture sprite, 176
    adding physics to, 199

animating, 185
displaying in SpriteKit scene, 168
displaying text in SpriteKit scene, 169
moving around a scene, 174-176
using image effects to change the way that sprites are drawn, 180
SpriteKit, 157, 164-195
    adding a text sprite, 169
    adding a texture sprite, 176
    adding physics to sprite, 199
    adding thrusters to objects, 214
    animating a sprite, 185
    applying force to object, 213
    controlling gravity, 207
    controlling time in physics simulation, 208
    creating explosions, 215-217
    creating images using noise, 194
    creating smoke, fire, and other particle effects, 183
    creating static and dynamic objects, 200
    creating texture atlases, 177
    creating vehicles, 221
    custom fonts for, 171
    defining collider shapes, 201
    detecting collisions, 209
    determining available fonts, 170
    displaying a sprite, 168
    dragging physics objects around, 218-221
    finding physics objects in scene, 210
    keeping objects from rotating, 208
    moving sprites and labels around a scene, 174-176
    parallax scrolling, 187-194
    physics simulation (see physics)
    scene creation, 165-167
    screen-shaking effect, 184-185
    setting velocities, 203
    transitioning between scenes, 172-173
    using Bézier paths, 181
    using blending modes, 179
    using device orientation to control gravity, 217
    using image effects to change the way that sprites are drawn, 180
    using shape nodes, 178
    view creation, 164
    walls for collision scene, 205
    working with joints, 212
    working with mass/size/density, 204

standard game controller, 271
state machine, 31-34
state, changes to, 1
static bodies, 200
steering an object toward a point, 249
steering wheel, using device as, 105-107
storage of data (see data storage)
storyboards
    defined, 35
    working with, 36-42
street address
    GPS coordinates for, 103
    looking up from user's location, 104
stroke color, 178
system music player, 122

T

tactile feedback, 290
tap gesture recognizers, 76, 300
tap gestures, 75
Taptic Engine, 290
target
    determing, 248
    intercepting, 246
    steering toward, 249
TestFlight, 303
text
    custom fonts for, 171
    determining available fonts, 170
    displaying in SpriteKit scene, 169
    rendering 3D text with SceneKit, 230
texture atlases, 177
texture sprite, 176
texture streaming, 309
textures
    compressed, 312-314
    low-memory issues and, 309
    normal mapping for, 232
    texturizing objects, 232
theming, UIAppearance for, 66
three-dimensional scenes/objects/text (see Sce-
    neKit)
thrusters, 214
tilt, detecting, 88-91
time
    calculating time elapsed since game start, 16
    controlling in physics simulation, 208
Timer, updating based on, 13
tint color, 67

torque, 214
touch, 73
    (see also input)
    detecting, 74
    receiving in custom areas of a view, 86
    states of, 74
touchscreen, 73
transform constraints, 234
transform property, 63
transitioning between scenes, 172-173
translation (of vectors), 160
translation (pan gesture recognizer value), 78
Turi Create, 270
turn-based game, finding the next best move in,
    257
two-dimensional graphics, 157-195
    (see also SpriteKit)
    coordinate systems, 158
    math basics, 158-164
    matrices, 163
    vectors, 158-163
two-dimensional grid, representing game lay-
    out as, 28

U

UI dynamics, 59
UIAppearance, 66
UIFeedbackGenerator, 290
UIKit, 35
    (see also views)
    physics engine, 61
UIView
    overlaying on top of game content, 70
    rotating in 3D, 68-69
unit tests, 26-28
updating
    based on screen redrawing, 14
    based on timer, 13
user(s)
    accessing location of, 93-97
    detection when entering/exiting game,
        11-13
    input from (see input)
    music selection by, 125-127
    notification of change in location, 99-103
    pinpointing proximity to landmarks, 98
    treating device as steering wheel, 105-107
UserDefaults, 145-147

V

value changed handlers, 276
variables
  closures and, 17-19
  watchpoints and, 316
vectors, 158-163
  adding, 160
  basics, 158
  defined, 158
  dot product, 162
  lengths, 159
  rotating, 161
  scaling, 162
  shape nodes, 178
  translating, 160
  vector math in Swift, 241-243
vehicles, creating, 221
velocity
  defined, 158, 198
  setting/changing, 203
view controllers
  creating, 42-49
  defined, 41
  UIKit and, 35
views, 35-71
  adding images to project, 56
  animating a popping effect on, 64-66
  constraints for laying out, 53-56
  creating view controllers, 42-49
  creating with SpriteKit, 164
  detecting when user touches, 74
  effective design of, 71
  moving images with Core Animation, 61
  overlaying menus on top of game content,
    70

receiving touches in custom areas of, 86
rotating a UIView in 3D, 68-69
rotating an image view, 63-64
segues, 49-52
storyboards and, 36-42
theming UI elements with UIAppearance,
    66
UI dynamics to animate, 59
using AVFoundation to access camera,
    262-264
vision, 258
Vision framework, 265-270
visual noise, 194

W

walls, for collision scene, 205
watchpoints, 316
weak references, 19
weight, 204
weighted random distributions, 30
world (physics concept), 198

X

x coordinate, defined, 158

Y

y coordinate, defined, 158
yaw, 89

Z

z-axis, 158
zero point, 92

About the Authors

Jon Manning is an independent game developer, and writer. He's written a whole bunch of books for O'Reilly Media about iOS development and game development, and has a PhD about jerks on the internet. He's currently working on Button Squid, a top-down puzzler, and on the BAFTA- and IGF Seumas McNally Grand Prize–winning adventure game Night in the Woods, which includes his interactive dialogue system, Yarn Spinner. He can be found on Twitter at @desplesda.

Paris Buttfield-Addison is a producer, programmer, and writer. He formerly worked as mobile product manager for Meebo (acquired by Google), has a degree in medieval history, a PhD in Computing, and writes technical books on mobile and game development for O'Reilly Media. He can be found on Twitter @parisba and online at *http:// paris.id.au*.

Jon Manning and Paris Buttfield-Addison are both the cofounders of Secret Lab, an independent game development studio based in Hobart, Tasmania, Australia. Through Secret Lab, they've worked on award-winning apps of all sorts, ranging from iPad games for children, to instant messaging clients, to math games about frogs. Together they've written numerous books on game development, iOS software development, and Mac software development. Secret Lab can be found online (*http:// www.secretlab.com.au*) and on Twitter at @thesecretlab.

Colophon

The animal on the cover of *iOS Swift Game Development Cookbook* is a queen triggerfish (*Balistes vetula*), so named for the two interlocking spines it can raise under threat, to firmly ensconce itself in the crevice of a reef or prevent a would-be predator from swallowing it whole. Queen triggerfish inhabit coral and rocky reefs in the Atlantic Ocean at depths of approximately 10 to 100 feet, though they have been known to seek sand- or seagrass-covered sea floors 900 feet below the surface.

Though found as often in schools as alone, queen triggerfish maintain a reputation as an aggressive fish. They fiercely defend the eggs they lay in nests on the ocean floor and use strong jaws and teeth to eat the crustaceans and other invertebrates that make up the bulk of their diet. Queen triggerfish create their nests by moving their fins quickly to direct a current of air into the sea floor. They also use this technique to avoid the longer spines on top of a sea urchin by blowing it onto its back to reach the tender meat underneath.

The queen triggerfish's appetite for invertebrates, as well as its penchant for confrontation, make it an unsuitable addition to reef aquariums. If it is placed in an aquarium, it is ideal to use a tank holding at least 500 gallons, or the queen triggerfish will attack other fish. It is also known for redecorating aquariums by picking up pieces of coral and moving them elsewhere.

The mood of the triggerfish is not, for all of its aggression, static. Its changing moods can be seen in the varying shade of yellow that mixes with blues and greens, which helps it blend in with its surroundings when it is stressed.

Many of the animals on O'Reilly covers are endangered; all of them are important to the world. To learn more about how you can help, go to *animals.oreilly.com*.

The cover fonts are URW Typewriter and Guardian Sans. The text font is Adobe Minion Pro; the heading font is Adobe Myriad Condensed; and the code font is Dalton Maag's Ubuntu Mono.

Learn from experts.
Find the answers you need.

Sign up for a **10-day free trial** to get **unlimited access** to all of the content on Safari, including Learning Paths, interactive tutorials, and curated playlists that draw from thousands of ebooks and training videos on a wide range of topics, including data, design, DevOps, management, business—and much more.

Start your free trial at:
oreilly.com/safari

CPSIA information can be obtained
at www.ICGtesting.com
Printed in the USA
BVHW08s0147051018
529238BV00013B/63/P